EAST YORKSHIRE AND YORK

HERITAGE SHELL GUIDES

EAST YORKSHIRE AND YORK

Susan & David Neave

Susan Neave
David Neave

First published in 2022 by Heritage Shell Guide Trust,
16 Mecklenburgh Square, London, WC1N 2AD

www.heritageshellguidetrustuk.org

British Library Cataloguing in Publication data.
A catalogue record for this book is available from the British Library

ISBN 978-1-7397907-0-7

Designed by: Paul Arnot
Book and print production by: alenkaoblakprint
Printed by: GPS Group

Frontispiece: West front of York Minster from Precentor's Court

FSC
www.fsc.org
MIX
Paper | Supporting responsible forestry
FSC® C118234

Contents

Foreword & Acknowledgements

Almost sixty years ago a proposal for a Shell Guide to East Yorkshire was put to John Betjeman by the York architect George Pace. The suggestion was not taken up until after John Piper had succeeded as editor of the series in 1968. Piper admired Pace's architectural work, and both were engaged at that time on the King George VI Memorial Chapel at St George's Chapel, Windsor. Pace soon began work on an East Yorkshire Shell Guide, with much help from his assistant John Hutchinson, an enthusiastic and able architectural historian. Publication was proposed for autumn 1973, but work commitments and ill health unfortunately prevented completion before Pace's untimely death in 1975.

Having collected and admired the Shell Guides for as long as we can remember, we were delighted when Peter Burton, author of a similar guide to North Yorkshire, first suggested that we 'do' East Yorkshire, an area we have been exploring, researching, writing and lecturing on for over fifty years. The contract to write the guide, to include the City of York, was received in April 2020, and so gave us an ideal distraction through the long months of the coronavirus crisis. Discussions on the book occupied us on daily walks on Beverley's great common pasture of Westwood that lies on our doorstep. 'Lockdown' presented its challenges, with churches and country houses closed and the periodic restrictions to fieldwork and photography. The emphasis in the entries is on historic architecture, reflecting our personal interests. To fit with the series East Yorkshire is defined as the present East Riding Unitary Authority, the boundaries of which are different from the historic East Riding, to which we nevertheless make reference. All the towns and most villages are covered, and we apologise to any community that has been left out. York includes the surrounding villages from each of the old ridings that now make up the City of York. The buildings of York, Hull and Beverley are described via walks, for which maps are provided.

The photographs are chiefly in colour, with the occasional black and white image echoing the charm of the earlier Shell Guides. We are greatly indebted to David Hockney, who has introduced the world to the delights of the landscape of the Yorkshire Wolds, for generously allowing us to reproduce three of his splendid paintings of East Yorkshire, and to Mark Hearld for creating a picture especially for this work, as a tribute to his mentor, John Hutchinson. We have also included some of the lively line drawings by the late Eugene Fisk. The majority of the photographs were taken by the authors, or are from their collection. Picture credits are listed later in the volume but amongst those who provided photographs we thank especially Rita Wood and Gordon Plumb.

Thanks are due also to Paul Arnot who designed the book and to Bill Glossop who took on the challenge of overseeing its publication for the Heritage Shell Guide Trust.

Susan and David Neave

opposite: Lighthouse at Spurn Point

Introduction

This guide is an introduction to the towns, villages and buildings of three distinct unitary authorities, as established in 1996: the East Riding of Yorkshire, the City of Kingston upon Hull and the City of York, the last comprising the historic city and some 30 surrounding villages formerly in the three historic ridings. It is a book about the familiar, York, and the little known, East Yorkshire. There can be few people who are not aware of York's remarkable heritage, for it is the country's best-preserved historic city, illustrating many aspects of medieval and Georgian life through its buildings and wealth of interpretative attractions. Yet East Yorkshire often gets little or no coverage in books on England's largest county, which for many means the Dales, the Moors, the coast, and the great former industrial towns and cities of the historic West Riding.

The present East Riding is bordered by water on three sides – on the west by the River Derwent, on the south by the River Ouse and Humber estuary, and on the east by the North Sea. Even the southwestern extension around Goole and Snaith is bordered to the north by the River Aire and chiefly by drainage ditches to the south. In many ways East Yorkshire can be considered an island, both physically and culturally, but it is by no means insular. The great Humber estuary enables easy access to Continental Europe, from where came a succession of migrants and new lifestyles and practices that added to the area's distinctiveness. As J.B. Priestley wrote, 'it is not really in Yorkshire, but by itself, somewhere in the remote east where England is nearly turning into Holland or Denmark.' The East Riding differs markedly from the North and West Ridings; the 'gulf' between them was considered 'apparent and profound' by J.E. Morris, author of the *Little Guide*, published in 1906. As Morris noted, East Yorkshire belongs 'in the spirit of its landscape, far more to the South [of England] than to the North'. There are three natural regions: the Wolds, the Vale of York and the Plain of Holderness.

opposite: Bempton Cliffs

The Wolds sweep in a wide arc of chalk uplands curving round from the Humber estuary, near Hessle, to the coast at Flamborough Head. Their highest point is near Garrowby Hill at 808 ft (246 m), with the cliffs at Bempton and Flamborough reaching 400 ft (122 m). Rolling chalkland dips gently to the east, with a steep escarpment on the western edge allowing panoramic views over the Vale of York. From just north of Market Weighton southwards, the foothills are of Jurassic limestone. The most exciting feature of the Wolds is the great network of steep-sided dry valleys created by fast-flowing streams that emerged out of melting glaciers at the end of the Ice Age. There are no streams now except the seasonal Gypsey Race, which enters the present East Riding at Wold Newton, its most northerly parish, before passing through Burton Fleming and Rudston to reach the sea at Bridlington. It is a land of straight roads with broad verges, large hedged fields, isolated farmsteads protected by shelter belts, and the occasional plantation, with small, nucleated villages and numerous deserted settlements.

Looking from the Wolds westwards across to the Vale of York

The open farmland gives wide vistas and big skies, a landscape created by Parliamentary enclosure in the late and 18th and early 19th centuries, which did away with the 'medieval' open fields, sheepwalks and extensive commercial rabbit warrens that had once covered the area. It is a landscape that has changed little for two hundred years, and has been introduced to the world by the paintings and drawings of David Hockney.

To the west of the Wolds is the extensive Vale of York, an understated low-lying landscape, drained – or rather watered – by the rivers Ouse (images of a flooded York are all too familiar) and Derwent. The latter frequently overflows on to the bordering low-lying farmland. Much of the Vale is covered by sands, gravels and clays left by a glacier, and lies below 30 ft (9 m). The high points are Church Hill at Holme-on-Spalding Moor, at 150 ft (46 m), and the York and Escrick moraines, ridges crossing the Vale that provide routeways and sites for villages, such as Newton-on-Derwent and Wheldrake, and the city of York.

The Vale, low-lying between higher ground to the east and west, was the obvious route between

the South (London) and the North (Scotland and the Borders), better than the more restricted corridor to the west of the Pennines, hence the Great North Road (A1) and the main railway line. Both enhanced York's role as a regional capital and, at times, England's second city. The Vale was once an area of extensive ill-drained commons, most notably Wallingfen and the adjoining Holme Moor covering some 12,000 acres (4,856 ha). In the 1770s this area was enclosed and drained by the digging of the Market Weighton Canal. Between the Ouse and Derwent, to the south and east of York, extending into half a dozen parishes, was Tilmire Common, a great source of peat, which was in demand as fuel for the city. Knavesmire and the other 'strays' are the remnants of York's common lands. Drainage and enclosure transformed much of the Vale in the 18th and 19th centuries, but Allerthorpe Common and the nature reserves of Wheldrake Ings and Askham Bog preserve something of its original 'unimproved' character and the challenges that faced the local farming communities. The southern part of the Vale is sometimes referred to as the Humberhead Levels, including the land along the Ouse and Humber, to the south of the M62, which is rather remote with quite a special feel. This area of former saltmarsh is echoed to the south of the Ouse by the Marshland parishes between Goole and the River Trent. To the south and west of Goole the drainage of the extensive fenland, another source of peat, was begun by Cornelius Vermuyden in the 17th century with the cutting of the Dutch River. It is now an area of vast, fertile fields.

'Behind Hull is the plain of Holderness, lonelier and lonelier, and after that the birds and lights of Spurn Head, and then the sea' (Philip Larkin in *A Rumoured City*, 1982). Holderness, between the Wolds and the North Sea, has its own distinctive character: low-lying, intensively farmed, a gently undulating landscape of boulder clay and gravel, not flat except along the Humber, where Sunk Island and Cherry Cob Sands have been reclaimed from the estuary. In the 'mersshy contree called holdernesse' (Chaucer in the 14th-century 'Summoner's Tale') there were once some 70 glacial lakes or meres, of which only Hornsea Mere, Yorkshire's largest lake, remains. The slight elevations, often rising to 50 ft (15 m) or more, provided the better-drained sites for the numerous villages and hamlets, linked by winding roads with many corners. In contrast to the Wolds, this is an area of numerous townships within large parishes, the isolated farmsteads with medieval origins often representing what would have been the chief house of a small manorial estate.

Soft clay cliffs line the Holderness coast from south of Bridlington to Kilnsea. Except where they are now protected by a variety of defences, the cliffs are eroded by the sea at the average rate of 6 ft (1.8 m) a year. Estimates of the extent of the erosion since the Roman period vary from 1½ to 2½ miles (2.4–4 km), and some twenty settlements have been lost to the sea since the early Middle Ages. Access to the splendid, broad sand and pebble beach is limited to a handful of locations. The coast ends with Spurn Point, a gravel spit created by the

Stone Creek between Sunk Island and Cherry Cob Sands, with Humber estuary in background

Spurn Point looking north

sea that has undergone a cycle of destruction and redeposition over the centuries, and at present its future is uncertain. The broad valley of the River Hull occupies the western part of the Plain of Holderness. Fed by a series of small streams coming from the eastern edge of the Wolds, the river commences near Driffield and follows a sinuous path, flanked by what were once extensive wetlands, to the Humber estuary. The southernmost section of the river served as the harbour for the port of Hull.

Geology largely determines what building materials are available locally, which in turn influenced the character of the built environment before the 19th century. East Yorkshire lacks good building stone. The main buildings of medieval York, including the Minster, St Mary's Abbey and the walls, and larger churches elsewhere in East Yorkshire, are built of white magnesian limestone brought from quarries near Tadcaster, North Yorkshire, 9 miles (14.5 km) southwest of York. The best native stone, but rarely of a quality for detailed carving or an ashlar finish, is the oolitic limestone from the narrow Jurassic belt on the west side of the southern Wolds. It was used for churches, including the earliest parts of Beverley Minster, and for housing in nearby villages, such as Newbald and South Cave. The plentiful chalk from the Wolds was also used for building, but it weathers badly except towards the northwest, where it is much harder. This is well illustrated by the surprisingly good condition of the 350-year-old chalk lighthouse at Flamborough. Many of the medieval churches and older farmsteads and cottages of Holderness are constructed of 'cobbles', rounded boulders from the glacial clay and gathered from the beach. Building with this distinctive and hard-wearing material was quite a skill.

Now for timber. York has more surviving timber-framed buildings than any other English city, but there are only a handful in Beverley, and scattered examples, both cruck- and box-frame, elsewhere in East Yorkshire. The York area always had more woodland than the rest of East Yorkshire, which has long been one of the most treeless areas in England. To the north of the city was the Forest of Galtres, and to the southeast the Ouse and Derwent Forest, both initially Royal hunting grounds, more open than woodland as we know it, but an important source of timber. Domesday Book records woodland to the south and southwest of Beverley, but there was little in Holderness and it was virtually non-existent on the Wolds.

East Yorkshire may not have been well supplied with wood or stone for building, but there was plenty of clay. This was used both for the walls of mud houses, common in Holderness and the Hull Valley before the 19th century, and for making bricks and tiles. Brickyards had been established in Hull and Beverley by the beginning of the 14th century (the earliest recorded in Britain since the Roman period), and it was at this time that brick was used for the transepts and choir of Hull Minster (Holy Trinity) and for the nave vaulting of Beverley Minster. Brick was also being manufactured at York by the mid-14th century, when it was used for the undercroft of the Merchant Adventurers' Hall. The earliest and grandest of East Yorkshire's country

Hull Minster from the southeast, showing medieval brickwork

houses, Burton Constable and Burton Agnes, two of the finest Elizabethan/Jacobean houses in Britain, are built of brick. By the mid-17th century it was being used for manor houses and grander town houses, in the early 18th century for farmhouses, and universally by the late 18th century.

Hull's early use and manufacture of brick undoubtedly result from its important trading links with the Low Countries and the Baltic, where this material had been in use since the mid-12th century. The brick walls and gateways of Hull, surrounded by water-filled ditches and the rivers Hull and Humber, had something of a Dutch feel that was remarked on by visitors. The painter Rembrandt, who is reputed to have been in Hull for a short time in 1661–62, would have felt at home there. The Dutch were responsible in the mid- to late 17th century for draining the Hull Valley and Humberhead Levels, and for digging the Dutch River that runs into the River Ouse at Goole. Some of their descendants still live in the region. It was from the Low Countries that pantiles first came into the area, with imports to Hull and Bridlington recorded by the 1660s. From the 1720s these began to be manufactured locally, gradually replacing thatch as the universal roofing material of East Yorkshire. But Dutch influence on local domestic architecture is not confined to building materials. Cowick Hall, built around 1670, is clearly influenced by Dutch Classicism, the hipped roof, pedimented façade and giant pilasters echoing the Mauritshuis at The Hague. Less refined but also showing Low Countries influence are the handful of so-called Artisan-Mannerist buildings, exhibiting a free use of Classical details. The finest is Wilberforce House in Hull, built *c.*1660 for a merchant who visited and

Northwest corner of courtyard, Burton Constable Hall

St Lawrence, Sigglesthorne, built of cobble, limestone & brick

traded with Holland, by the bricklayer-architect William Catlyn. Some have shaped or curved so-called Dutch gables, including the small manor houses at Arram, Hornsea and Knedlington, and in York the Treasurer's House, Ingram's Hospital and the over-restored Dutch House on Ogleforth. Much more common are tumbled gables, the name taken from the triangular wedges of bricks that give a smooth and more durable edge, another feature introduced from the Netherlands. These are to be found throughout the region, but more commonly east of the Derwent.

Proximity to the Continent has always played a part in determining the distinctiveness of East Yorkshire, with the coast and Humber estuary receiving waves of invaders and migrant groups since prehistoric times. Although more has been learned in recent years of the prehistory

Treasurer's House, York

Wilberforce House, Hull

of Holderness and the Vale of York, it is from the Wolds – one of the richest archaeological areas in Britain – that we have learned most of the region's early history. Much has been revealed by aerial photography, and among the earliest of the few features easily visible above ground are the large Neolithic round barrow Willy Howe, in Thwing parish, and the great standing stone, or monolith, at Rudston. From the succeeding Bronze Age there are numerous round barrows (burial mounds), many ploughed out, and the linear earthworks that crisscross the Wolds, of which Huggate Dykes is the most impressive.

It was in the Iron Age, under the Parisi, a tribe with cultural links to northern France, that the East Riding was most markedly distinct from the rest of Britain. Here is the greatest concentration of square barrow cemeteries and high-status chariot burials. Only a couple of the more than 25 known chariot burials are outside East Yorkshire. A 'preference for certain types of brooches, querns and pottery and the concentration of artefacts related to Vulcan' continued to make the area subtly distinctive into the Roman period, in the opinion of the archaeologist Peter Halkon, despite its having much in common with the rest of the province. York (Eboracum), as capital of the northern province and the focus of a network of Roman roads, gave the area particular significance, and this partly explains why East Yorkshire has more identified villas than the rest of northern Britain. Virtually nothing of the Roman fortress and civilian town at York remains above ground, and nothing at Brough (Petuaria) on the Humber or of the minor town at Stamford Bridge (Derventio). In the rather obscure time after the Romans, East Yorkshire retained its distinct identity, emerging as the Anglo-Saxon kingdom of Deira, which coincided with territory of the Parisi. Goodmanham, where a pagan temple was destroyed after Paulinus had converted King Edwin to Christianity in AD 627, is thought to have been near a royal seat. Driffield may have also been the site of a royal palace, as it was the burial place in 705 of King Aldfrith of Northumbria, a kingdom formed with the merging of Deira and Bernicia. More than half the settlement names in the historic East Riding recorded in Domesday Book are Anglian in origin, for example those ending in *ing*, *ingham*, *ham*, *ton* and *ington*, and more than a third Scandinavian, most commonly the endings *by* and *thorpe*. Excavations in York have revealed much new information on the Anglo-Scandinavian period, now displayed in the Jorvik Viking Centre and Yorkshire Museum. A dozen East Yorkshire churches have fragments of Anglo-Saxon sculpture, most importantly the cross shaft at Nunburnholme. As regards buildings, only the lower part of the tower of St Mary Bishophill Junior is probably Anglo-Saxon, although York had at least a dozen churches pre-Conquest.

Other than churches and timber-framed houses, medieval standing buildings are rare in the area. Little remains of the fifteen monasteries except the ruins of the church and abbot's lodgings of St Mary's Abbey, York, the nave of Bridlington Priory and the prior's lodgings at Watton. Similarly, of the medieval palaces or manor houses of the archbishops of York, only part of that at Bishopthorpe remains. Those at Beverley, Bishop Burton and Bishop Wilton have long gone, the last represented by substantial earthworks at the east end of the village. A little more survives of the Bishop of Durham's manor house at Howden, and at Burton Agnes there is a rare Norman example encased in later brick. Early castles are represented by the great mound at Skipsea, and at York by Clifford's Tower and Baile Hill. Of the so-called Burstwick Castle, an occasional residence of kings Edward I, II and III, there is nothing but earthworks of a moat. There is much more of Wressle Castle, once a favoured home of the Percy family, Earls of Northumberland, where the impressive ruin stands alongside the River Derwent. All that remains of the other grand Percy residence, at Leconfield, is a moated site west of the village.

Architecturally, medieval churches are the greatest glories of York and East Yorkshire. They range in scale from York Minster, the largest cathedral in northern Europe, to Skirlaugh, a modest village church. The finest parish church is undoubtedly Beverley Minster, a rival to York, an architectural masterpiece and more manageable

opposite: West front of Beverley Minster

in scale. Beverley also has the splendid St Mary's; no other town in Britain has two such great medieval parish churches, and there are plenty more throughout the East Riding. These include large town churches at Hedon and Hull, funded by merchants; Bridlington Priory, comprising the nave of a vast monastic church; Howden Minster, supported by the bishops of Durham; and the sublime church at Patrington, built by the archbishops of York. There is a fine series of village churches ranging from Norman at Newbald, through Early English at Skelton and Decorated at Bainton, to St Augustine's, Skirlaugh, described by Pevsner as 'a perfect piece of Perp[endicular] architecture'. Many churches have Norman features including doorways and chancel and tower arches, but most intriguing are the distinctive carved drum-shaped fonts, particularly those on the Wolds. The parish churches in York are not outstanding architecturally, but they boast a tremendous collection of medieval stained glass and superb 17th- and 18th-century woodwork.

The region's Georgian churches are modest but have their charms, especially the Gothick touches at Boynton and the simple Italian style of Goxhill. In contrast, East Yorkshire has some of the best rural Victorian churches in Britain. South Dalton, with its soaring spire, is possibly the best known, a work by J.L. Pearson for Lord Hotham, whose agent had recently commissioned the same architect to design the little gem at nearby Scorborough.

Pearson was employed by Sir Tatton Sykes I to restore the churches at Bishop Wilton, Garton-on-the-Wolds and Kirkburn in the later 1850s. His son Sir Tatton II furnished these three churches lavishly, especially Garton, and restored, furnished, built or rebuilt a further fourteen churches in the historic East Riding, of which half lie within the present unitary authority area, all exhibiting superb craftsmanship in wood, iron and stained glass. G.E. Street was the principal architect but Sledmere, the greatest of the 'Sykes' churches, was designed by Temple Moore, who, like Pearson, effectively began his distinguished career in East Yorkshire. Church building after the Second World War, a consequence of bomb

St Mary, South Dalton
opposite: St Patrick, Patrington

damage and the growth of local-authority estates, saw rival architects Francis Johnson and George Pace producing markedly different but outstanding churches in town and country.

Despite lavish spending on Anglican churches, the residents of the area were mainly Nonconformist in the Victorian period. This was the most Methodist region in England, after Cornwall, and almost every village had a chapel; many had two, Wesleyan and Primitive. Of the few Georgian chapels still in use, those at Newport (Methodist) and Cottingham (Congregational) are the best. York has an unusual 1690s Presbyterian chapel (now Unitarian) in St Saviourgate, a street with an impressive Victorian Methodist chapel.

There are other good Victorian chapels at Beverley, Market Weighton, Pocklington and Snaith, with imposing façades but altered interiors; more eccentric is Burlington Methodist chapel

Norman fonts: Kirkburn (top); Bessingby (middle); Nafferton (bottom)

at Bridlington, with a touch of the Orient in its turrets. Roman Catholicism is represented by two charming barn-like churches at Marton and Hedon, the more stylish Bar Convent chapel, York, a great Italian chapel at Everingham and the stunning St Charles Borromeo, Hull. The High Victorian Gothic St Wilfrid's, York, once the pro-cathedral of the former Roman Catholic diocese of Beverley, has a tower apparently built as a challenge to the nearby Minster.

The present character of the rural landscape and the fabric of the villages owe much to the actions of landowners in the 18th and 19th centuries. In the 1870s a dozen great landowners owned 30 per cent of the 700,000 acres (283,280 ha) of the historic East Riding. A surprising number of these landed estates, although now usually smaller in extent, have remained in the hands of the same family or direct descendants for over 250 years. Parts of the estate of the Hotham family now based at South Dalton have been in the family since the 13th century; the Bethells have held Rise since the late 16th century; and the Sykes have had Sledmere since the mid-18th century.

Of country houses the two finest, Burton Constable and Burton Agnes, both open to the public, have already been mentioned. Everingham Hall and Houghton Hall – ideal, smallish, mid-Georgian – are not open; the first is by the celebrated John Carr, the other by his lesser-known rival Thomas Atkinson, two architects responsible for some of the best Georgian houses and public buildings covered by this volume. Other houses regularly open are the delightful Regency Wassand Hall, in its fine setting next to Hornsea Mere, the early 18th-century Sewerby Hall, now presented as an Edwardian country house, and the splendid Sledmere House. The last, largely of the 1780s, was gutted by fire and reconstructed sympathetically at the beginning of the First World War by Walter Brierley, who also designed Goddards (*National Trust*) at Dringhouses, York, a charming Arts and Crafts house.

The library at Sledmere House, arguably the region's finest room, looks across extensive parkland, laid out following the removal of the

The library at Sledmere House

village, with advice from the landscape gardeners Lancelot 'Capability' Brown and Thomas White, both of whom provided plans for improving the setting of other local houses. Earlier in date is the park at Londesborough (on the Yorkshire Wolds Way), of great significance because it illustrates the transition from the formal to more natural landscaping. This was undertaken by Lord Burlington, possibly with advice from his protégé the Bridlington-born William Kent, the man who 'leaped the fence, and saw that all nature was a garden' (Horace Walpole). Another way of improving the setting of a country house was to create a picturesque estate village such as at Bishop Burton, Warter and West Ella.

In the winter months the gentry families gravitated to York, the great social centre of the north, a role Beverley fulfilled for the East Riding. Many of the fine Georgian town houses built by them or by prosperous tradesmen, physicians and attorneys survive. Fairfax House, York, illustrates superbly their lavish lifestyle. In Hull the grander houses, including Maister House, were built by the wealthy merchants trading with Scandinavia and the Baltic. The smaller market towns also have plenty of Georgian houses, albeit on a lesser scale. Not to be missed is the 'Old Town' at Bridlington, with its great array of late 17th- and 18th-century houses and Regency shop fronts.

The rebuilding of the region's towns and villages owed much to agricultural prosperity and improved communication, via turnpike roads and waterways. The latter included the building of locks that can be seen on the rivers Derwent, Foss and Ouse and at the junction of the Beverley Beck and River Hull, the digging of the canals serving Driffield, Market Weighton and Pocklington, and that from Knottingley to Goole that led to the foundation of the last as a new inland port. There is something to see of all these, and a walk along the side of Pocklington Canal with its locks and attractive bridges, or a boat trip from Melbourne, can be recommended. The so-called Industrial Revolution has left little mark upon East Yorkshire, for, as Henry Strickland wrote in 1812, the area 'may indeed be looked upon as almost purely agricultural, perhaps there is not another in the kingdom of equal extent more completely of that description ... The surface of this Riding is little calculated for manufactures of any kind, having neither coal, nor wood for charcoal within itself, nor any rapid streams for working machinery.' There were, however, once many mills in the countryside, both water and wind. Of the latter only two with sails remain, Skidby and Holgate, York. The port of Hull benefited greatly by the late 18th- and 19th-century industrial growth in the West Riding and throughout the Midlands, its hinterland having expanded by improved navigation. Many of the raw materials required by the industries were imported through Hull, and the products exported. To cope with this great increase in trade the medieval walls around the Old Town were replaced with a circle of docks, which are still there in some form. Hull then expanded rapidly, overtaking York as the most populous settlement in the region.

Pocklington Canal near Melbourne

York was transformed after 1840 following the arrival of the railways, which became the city's major employer along with the confectionery firms Rowntree's and Terry's. At Hull too the opening of the railway, which coincided with the arrival of the fishing fleets, broadened trade. New industries emerged, many linked to imports, especially oilseed crushing, paint manufacture and flour milling. Of the new firms Reckitt's, originally a starch manufacturer, is probably the best known. Although the splendid railway stations and their later additions survive at York and Hull, the trade and industries they helped to stimulate have left few physical remains apart from warehouses and other dock buildings, and remnants of the factories and mills. It is through the surviving terraced and courtyard housing, schools, pubs, churches and chapels, comfortable middle-class suburbs, and magnificent public buildings, especially in Hull, that the Victorian and Edwardian growth and prosperity of these cities is demonstrated. Both places benefited from the philanthropy of wealthy industrialists, most notably in providing greatly improved working-class housing at New Earswick and Hull Garden Village.

Hull is now promoted as Yorkshire's Maritime City, and it is the maritime nature of East Yorkshire as a whole, bounded on three sides by water, that underlines and contributes to its distinctiveness. The docks of Hull and Goole have their attractions, but it is the compact early 19th-century harbour at Bridlington, with its stone quays and fishing and pleasure boats, that has the greatest charm. The long seafront, wide sandy beach and views

above: Hull's waterfront from the Humber | *below:* Bridlington harbour

across the bay to Flamborough Head help to make the resort, which first welcomed visitors for sea bathing in the mid-18th century, East Yorkshire's main tourist destination.

Elsewhere access to the beach along the Holderness coast is limited, except at the minor resorts of Hornsea and Withernsea. The wide estuary of the Humber, long a barrier, became much more appreciated when the magnificent Humber Bridge was opened in 1981, the hoped-for catalyst for the economic recovery of the region. Regeneration has been slow but the future now seems promising. Looking east from the bridge across the city the view is now dominated by what has come to symbolise Hull's planned future as a leading 'green energy' centre: the giant towers of the offshore wind turbines under construction.

In 2017 Hull, or more correctly Kingston upon Hull, became the UK City of Culture, an accolade that brought many outsiders to the area for the first time. Sometimes dismissed as a decayed Northern fishing port with nothing worth going to the end of the line to see, the city was finally put on the map (quite literally in the case of the BBC weather map) and grasped this golden opportunity to show off its historic and cultural significance. We hope this book will encourage even more people to explore the many buildings of interest not only there and in York, one of Europe's most important historic cities, but throughout East Yorkshire.

North Landing, Flamborough | *opposite:* The Humber Bridge

East Riding of Yorkshire

Gazetteer
East Riding of Yorkshire

Adlingfleet On the west side of the Trent, near where the river meets the Ouse to form the great Humber estuary. Small marshland village, once a port, with impressive All Saints' church, rebuilt in the 13th century, the chancel shortened by the Georgians. Light and spacious interior, with some good monuments including a memorable one with life-size figure to Mary Ramsden, d. 1745. It was intended for St Catharine's College, Cambridge, to which she left her fortune. To the south the recently restored remnant of a former rectory, also mid-13th century. The reset doorway, like the south door of the church, is Norman. Blacktoft Sands, an important RSPB wetland nature reserve, is in the parish. [E3]

Airmyn Once a small port on the River Aire, near its junction with the Ouse, it was established by St Mary's Abbey, York, by the 13th century. After decline it revived in the later 17th century, but trade was hit by the opening of the Selby Canal in 1778 and the Knottingley–Goole Canal in 1826. The older houses are, in part, on only one side of the road, looking across to the grassy tree-lined riverbank. Plenty of front doors with distinctive round-arched panels showing it was once an estate village. At the corner the pretty little school of 1834, with a bellcote and simple Y-tracery windows, is overshadowed by the remarkable tall Gothic clock tower. It was erected in the 1860s to commemorate the landowner, the Earl of Beverley, becoming Duke of Northumberland. The duke's Smithson ancestors built Airmyn Hall in the early 18th century and also provided the small red-brick St David's church in 1676, both much altered in the later 19th century. In the parish the steel swing bridge over the Ouse at Boothferry, opened 1929, was largely replaced in 1976 by the long, elegant Ouse Bridge on the M62. [E2]

opposite: East Riding of Yorkshire delineated

Aldbrough From the late 18th century this former market village attracted visitors for sea bathing. A large hotel was built by the sea in 1840, and a chalybeate spring discovered, but lack of a railway hampered development. Holiday bungalows and shacks were later built on the eroding cliffs, since replaced by caravans. The church of St Bartholomew, of cobble, was largely rebuilt in 1870–71, but there are two 11th-century windows in the north wall of the chancel. These may survive from the church that Ulf built as recorded by an Anglo-Scandinavian inscription on a sundial on the south aisle wall. The long, narrow nave probably follows the plan of this early church. The lower part of the tower is of *c.*1200, and the north chapel 14th century. The latter contains two late 14th-century tomb-chests with effigies of a knight and lady. [D7]

Allerthorpe The main village street where the earlier houses are is flanked by wide grass verges. Allerthorpe Hall, opposite the Plough Inn, dates from around 1805. Older and more characterful is The Gables, with hall and cross wings. It was probably built towards the end of the 17th century, although one wing is later and a thorough restoration took place in the 1880s. St Botolph's church stands well at the end of the village, its distinctive west end with polygonal bell-turret facing down the street. It was designed by the Atkinsons of York and built in 1876. Near the entrance is a memorial stone to Thomas Cooke, one of the greatest telescope makers, born in the village in 1807, and later of York. His father was a shoemaker. Allerthorpe Common, a small area of protected heathland, is noted for its adder population. [C3]

Anlaby A suburban village much favoured as a country residence by Hull merchants and professionals in the late 18th and early 19th century. Of the seven large mansions they built, only Anlaby House survives. On higher ground to the west is Tranby Croft (Hull Collegiate School), a large three-storey Italianate cream brick mansion with a 72-ft-high (22 m) corner tower and equally showy stable block. Built 1874–76 and enlarged 1889, for Arthur Wilson, a Hull shipping magnate. The Prince of Wales was staying here in 1890 when a charge of cheating at cards, against another guest, led to the infamous 'Tranby Croft Scandal'. Wilson and his wife are commemorated by wall tablets in a late 17th-century style in St Peter's church, rebuilt 1885. Brick, with pretty bell-turret and small spire. Around the corner in Church Street, the simple, small brick building with hipped pantile roof was built as a Wesleyan chapel in 1809. East of the village centre, Anlaby Hall, although altered, retains something of its 17th-century character. [D5]

Atwick A 'plague' village, the only one in the area, with the first of more than two dozen deaths recorded in December 1665. The village was 'shut up', presumably like Eyam in Derbyshire, to prevent the plague from spreading. Irregular village green, crossed by roads, with the remains of a medieval cross. At the northeast corner, behind a low brick and cobble wall, is Atwick Hall, a large early 19th-century farmhouse. St Lawrence's church, rebuilt 1876, is a long way west of the village centre. Red brick with a steep tiled roof and prominent gabled north tower. The unconventional design by H.Roumieu Gough was a bold choice for such a rural setting. Cliff Road, east of the village, leads to a caravan site perched close to the crumbling mud cliffs, below which is a sandy beach. Several 'pillboxes' from the Second World War survive along this part of the coast. [C6]

Aughton A track west of the village leads to All Saints' church in its lonely setting full of atmosphere, overlooking the often-flooded Derwent Ings. On one side of this track the earthworks of a motte-and-bailey castle, on the other Aughton Hall, a late 18th-century house built on the moated site of the manor house of the Aske family. It was Robert Aske of Aughton, a lawyer, who in 1536 led the rebellion known as the Pilgrimage of Grace. He was executed the following year. His brother Christopher rebuilt the church tower, on which is an enigmatic inscription thought to refer to the uprising. More frivolous is the carving on the tower of a newt, also known as an asker, or aske. Plenty of Norman work inside, including a rather good chancel arch. There is a brass to earlier members of the Aske family. [D2]

Bainton Off the busy main road, to the east, is one of the finest village churches in the East Riding. All of a piece, St Andrew's was largely

Newt or aske carved on tower, All Saints, Aughton

St Helen, Barmby Marsh

rebuilt in the 1330s–40s by the rector William de Brocklesby, possibly following destruction by the invading Scottish army in 1322. The impressive west tower once had a spire that was damaged by the 'Great Wind' in 1715 and finally removed in the 1860s. Wonderful reticulated (net-like) tracery fills the large windows that light the chancel and the spacious nave with its elegant four-bay arcade. In the south aisle is the remarkably complete crocketed ogee canopy over a military figure, said to be Sir John de Mauley, rector, who fought at Bannockburn, and died 1331. Other monuments include an early 15th-century brass to a priest, and good mid-Georgian wall tablets to the Grimstons of Neswick, a deserted hamlet in the parish.

By the roundabout north of the village is the former New Inn (now Wolds Village – restaurant, B&B and craft shops), built *c.*1779. It was the location of the magistrates' fortnightly petty sessions for the Bainton Beacon division in the early 19th century. [B4]

Barmby Marsh At the end of the road from Howden, near the junction of the rivers Ouse and Derwent, with the vast Drax Power Station to the southwest. The High Street is lined with a good series of Georgian farmhouses, reflecting that it was an open village of small freeholders where the medieval open fields were not enclosed until the 1850s. The charming small church of St Helen, acquired by the Friends of Friendless Churches after being made redundant, has some medieval masonry in the nave and restored 15th-century windows. The pretty brick tower with ogee cap is of 1773, the chancel 1870. [D2]

Barmby Moor The village lies north of the Beverley–York road, turnpiked in the 1760s, where the elegant bow-fronted Barmby Moor House, a former coaching inn, *c.*1780, was a favoured stopping place. St Catherine's church, medieval tower with spire, nave and chancel of 1850–52. The chancel is paved with Minton tiles, donated by the vicar's brother-in-law Herbert Minton, head of the Stoke pottery firm. There are also Royal Arms in Minton tiles and late Victorian wall paintings by J.W. Knowles of York, quite rightly better known for his stained glass. Hidden away on a moated site to the southeast of the church is the intriguing mid- to late 17th-century Manor House. In 1862 eleven-year-old Alice Donkin was photographed climbing out of a first-floor window by Lewis Carroll, who was visiting his brother Wilfred, assistant to Edward Donkin, land agent, tenant of the house. [C3]

Barmston At the west end of the village is the medieval church of All Saints, a pleasing mixture of stone and cobble typical of Holderness. The earliest parts are Norman, as is the drum-shaped font, boldly decorated with a lozenge pattern. Alabaster tomb-chest with the figure of a knight, probably William Monceaux, d. 1446. Later monuments commemorate members of the Boynton family who lived at Barmston before they moved to Burton Agnes Hall. Near the church, on a moated site, are the remains of their 17th-century manor house, brick with stone quoins, mullioned windows and two great chimney stacks. On Sands Lane, which leads east towards the sea, a modest whitewashed brick building, now two cottages, has a plaque indicating that it was built by Sir Griffith Boynton in 1726 as almshouses. In 2000 a Millennium Stone was placed at the western end of the village to record the distance from the sea, which comes ever closer as the coastline is eroded. [B6]

Beeford A long village street of 18th- and 19th-century houses, running west from the Bridlington road. To the north, in a large churchyard, stands the fine largely 15th-century St Leonard's church with an impressive west tower. The chancel, with two 13th-century lancet windows, is partly built of cobbles, as is the nave. The north arcade and aisle were added in the mid-19th century. There is a pretty charity board and two medieval memorials – an early 14th-century figure of a priest, and a brass to a rector who died 1472.

The Cottage, Bridlington Road, is single-storey with mud walls, possibly 18th century, a great rarity. Just to the east of the junction a pair of whalebones flank the entrance to Crow Grange, a Georgian-style farmhouse of 1849. [B6]

Bempton Coastal village best known for the RSPB reserve with visitor centre at Bempton Cliffs. The dramatic 400-ft (122-m) white chalk cliffs are breeding grounds for numerous seabirds, chiefly gannets, kittiwakes, guillemots and the much-loved puffins. It was Revd Henry Barnes-Lawrence, incumbent at nearby Bridlington Priory, who established the Association for the Protection of Seabirds in the 1860s, resulting in legislation that made it illegal to shoot them. Nevertheless, the practice of 'climming', whereby men and women were lowered down the cliffs on ropes to collect eggs, carried on at Bempton and elsewhere until the mid-20th century. In the village to the south some of the more rustic buildings are constructed of chalk, with the traditional brick-coloured pantile roofs. The random mix of pale and electric-blue glazed pantiles on the 1930s White Horse is certainly not traditional, and at best might be described as eye-catching. St Michael's church has a strange 14th-century top to its tower, octagonal but with uneven sides, and a brick chancel of 1829. The chancel screen with slender columns may also be of the latter date.

Barely a field separates the village from the shrunken settlement of ***Buckton***, and a mile (1.5 km) or so beyond there, in splendid isolation, stands Buckton Hall, just visible from the main road. If the traditional building date of around 1745 is correct, the style is decidedly old-fashioned. What makes the house stand out is not so much the Baroque features, such as the rusticated door surround with heavy stone quoins, as the choice of chalkstone for the façade. A serious fire in 1919 destroyed the interior. [A6]

Buckton Hall

Bentley A handful of cottages and farmhouses, and a former school-cum-chapel built in 1855. To the northeast, on the east side of the A164, is the stump of one of the medieval crosses that marked the sanctuary limits of Beverley Minster. [D5]

Bessingby A small village on the outskirts of Bridlington. The older houses include Hall Farm with its dark-blue glazed pantiles, a feature more commonly found in East Anglia. The porch is dated 1805, which is probably when the stone-mullioned windows that help to give the brick and chalk cottage its quaint appearance were introduced. Various outbuildings including a rectangular dovecote with 1670 datestone, now a house. The church of St Magnus is an accomplished Temple Moore work of 1894. Central tower with recessed spire and projecting stair-turret, and sloping roofs that extend over the aisles. Inside, a large but squat Norman font, the decoration chiefly geometric but including a pair of Romanesque lions, mirror images of each other. The sculptor seems to have chosen cats as his model. Between the village and main road is the parkland of Bessingby Hall, a neat yellow-brick villa designed by Thomas Cundy senior, in 1807. The entrance front has a semicircular porch topped with a balustrade. [A6]

Beswick A Hotham family estate village, now bypassed, but well worth turning off the main road to see the hall and church. Beswick Hall (*private*) with its irregular façade, part two-storey with large mullion and transom windows, and part three-storey with hung-sash windows, has clearly undergone substantial changes but remains a delightful building. Of red brick with an elaborate diaper pattern of dark headers, it was built *c.*1600–10 for the Daniel family, one of whom was the eccentric Royalist poet George Daniel. Other occupiers include the celebrated 18th-century hunting squire William Draper and his son-in-law Hugh Bethell, a close friend of the poet Alexander

Pope. The hall was altered in the 1830s, when it was divided into the present two farmhouses. Opposite is the neat, well-kept St Margaret's church of 1871, designed by Fowler of Louth to replace a mean thatched building. [C5]

Beverley One of England's finest if lesser-known towns, Beverley never fails to impress. It is best approached from the north, via North Bar Without, a wide and lovely street leading to the one surviving medieval gateway, or from the west. The latter brings one over Westwood, the most visually rewarding of the town's vast common pastures, with a splendid view of the great west front of Beverley Minster. Aglow in the setting sun this must have been a wondrous and uplifting sight for the medieval pilgrims who came to visit the shrine of St John of Beverley in the church, or for fugitives seeking sanctuary there.

Beverley has not one but two outstanding medieval churches, the Minster to the south and St Mary's to the north, but it is at the former that any tour must start, for this is where the town grew up. The town was the tenth most populous English settlement outside London in the later 14th century, noted for its cloth trade and manufacture, but its fortunes had declined by the 16th century, when the Minster lost its collegiate status, a further blow. The layout of the medieval town survives, but many of the best buildings are from the Georgian period, when Beverley became the social and administrative centre for the East Riding of Yorkshire. It still houses the headquarters of the East Riding unitary authority, and remains a popular residential town.

Around the town there are many sculptures, some set into the pavements, representing the medieval guilds and crafts (*trail leaflet available*). [C5]

Beverley Minster from the south | *opposite:* Beverley Minster from Westwood

Beverley Minster: A monastery established by Bishop John of York at 'Inderawuda', where he was buried in 721, was later re-founded as a college of secular canons, Beverley Minster. Bishop John was canonised as St John of Beverley in 1037, and his tomb in the Minster became a place of pilgrimage. The church was rebuilt from *c.*1220 onwards, starting at the east end. Apart from the great east window, glazed in the early 15th century, externally practically everything as far as the west walls of the transepts is Early English with the usual tall lancet windows. Then comes the rebuilding of the nave, begun *c.*1310 but halted by the Black Death in 1349. Here the work is in the Decorated style, evident in the window tracery. In contrast to the local Newbald oolitic limestone used for the east end, an attractive creamy-white magnesian limestone imported from the Tadcaster area (North Yorkshire) was chosen for this and later work. Building resumed towards the end of the 14th century, and to this phase belong the majestic west front with graceful twin towers, in the now fashionable Perpendicular style, and the imposing north porch.

In 1548 the college of canons was dissolved and the Minster became simply a parish church. This explains the mysterious double staircase in the north choir aisle that now leads nowhere, for it once gave access to an octagonal chapter house, demolished at that time. Major restoration work took place in the early 18th century under the supervision of Nicholas Hawksmoor, although it was William Thornton of York who devised a great wooden frame that prevented the collapse of the north transept front. Much has been published on the history and architecture of this great church, and space permits only a few of the highlights to be mentioned.

Visitors enter the Minster via the north porch, and this provides an opportunity to admire the

Beverley Minster
above: Chapter House staircase
below: Carved capital, nave, south aisle arcade
opposite: Looking west along the nave

Beverley Minster
above left: Font and cover
above right: Athelstan and St John of Beverley
opposite: North front of Percy Tomb

breathtaking view down the ***nave***, with its clusters of slender pillars and rib-vaulted roof. Ahead is the 18th-century organ with brightly coloured pipes and elaborate late Victorian screen, carved by James Elwell of Beverley (see Walk 3), and then comes the ***choir***. The floor here is from the early 18th-century restoration, cleverly designed to give a three-dimensional cube effect. The early 16th-century choir stalls have 68 misericords, the scenes including a sow playing the bagpipes accompanied by dancing piglets. The crowning glory of the choir is the sumptuous reredos of stone and Purbeck marble, similar in date to one of the Minster's greatest treasures, the adjacent Percy Tomb, with its exquisitely decorated stone canopy, probably of the 1330s.

The reredos divides the choir from the ***retrochoir***, where there is an excellent series of monuments to the Warton family, notably that to Sir Michael Warton, one of the Minster's main benefactors, 1732 by Scheemakers. At the west end of the church is the 12th-century font, made of Frosterley marble, a gigantic piece with magnificent early 18th-century font cover by William Thornton, 1720, whose firm was also responsible for the elaborate west door.

Elsewhere in the church look for the simple 7th-century stone frith stool, 17th-century painting of King Athelstan and St John of Beverley, and wonderful carvings, including many of medieval musicians with their instruments, along the nave aisles.

Beverley

1. St John (R.C.)
2. North Bar
3. St Mary's church
4. Norwood House
5. Methodist/URC Church
6. Guildhall
7. County Hall
8. Lairgate Hall
9. Treasure House
10. Theatre
11. Minster
12. Friary
13. Railway Station
14. East Riding College

Walk 1

The southern part of the town

The walk begins at the north porch of the Minster. Ahead is ***Highgate***, the southern part of the 'Alta Via' or High Street that ran through the medieval town. The plots on the east side originally extended to Eastgate and were infill on the town's first marketplace. Until the mid-18th century Highgate was full of shops, some let to London wholesale merchants who came to the great Ascensiontide Fair, giving rise to the alternative name Londoners' Street. When the fair and nearby weekly market came to an end, shops were abandoned and houses built. At right angles to the street, replacing the wing of a larger building, is No. 38, an attractive five-bay brick house of the 1740s. The building contract specified 'Holland' tiles, in other words pantiles. It was later the Bluecoat School. On the opposite side the largest and smartest of the Georgian houses, No. 25/25A, where Brigadier-General Oliver de Lancey, an American loyalist refugee, once lived. The Monks Walk, which should have kept its old name (George and Dragon), also looks mid-18th century, but the brick façade with central passage hides Beverley's best timber-framed building. No. 2, on the west side, was a childhood home of Mary Wollstonecraft, author of *A Vindication of the Rights of Woman* (1792).

Wednesday Market, the apex of the once vast market place, has a pleasing mixture of buildings dating from the 17th century onwards. It was more enclosed until the railway reached Beverley in 1846. Railway Street, lined with austere three-storey terraces roofed with slate, almost certainly brought by rail from Wales, was constructed soon afterwards. It provides the link to G.T. Andrews' elegant station with seven-bay façade with portico and wings. From Wednesday Market head back towards the Minster via ***Eastgate***, where Nos 26–28 have unusually delicate doorcases, an example of Georgian recycling. They were constructed from the internal fittings of Hotham House, a grand but short-lived Palladian villa that once stood on the opposite side of the road. Designed by Colen Campbell, it was built 1716–20 for Sir Charles Hotham but demolished after about 50 years. In the 20th century a factory making shock absorbers was built here. As the site expanded, the ***Old Friary*** on Friar's Lane, off Eastgate, came perilously close to demolition but was saved after a protracted campaign by local residents. This fascinating building – the remnant of a medieval Dominican friary, altered in brick and decorated inside with wall paintings post-Reformation, when it became a private house – is now a Youth Hostel. The surrounding factory has gone and an imaginative housing development fills the area between Eastgate and the railway line. A brick gateway into the grounds had already been saved during road widening in the 1960s by moving it across the road. It was placed in the wall surrounding a house built

Beck porter, Beckside, on the Medieval Guilds & Crafts trail

as the Minster vicarage in 1704, although the grey-brick façade dates from the early 19th century.

Near the Minster Eastgate becomes ***Flemingate***, from the medieval Flemish merchants who traded in Beverley. First comes the Sun Inn. Although Beverley was described by John Leland in the 16th century as 'well builded of wood', it is one of only a handful of buildings with exposed timber framing. Beyond the railway line looms the Flemingate Centre, a shopping and leisure complex developed in the early 21st century on the site of the town's largest tannery, which in turn covered part of the extensive Dominican friary site. Worth going this far to see the unusual and striking view of the east end of the Minster.

(For those feeling energetic, Flemingate leads to ***Beckside***, named from the canalised watercourse that feeds into the River Hull. A small port developed here in the Middle Ages, and it was not until the late 20th century that houses overlooking the water in the manner of a Dutch town replaced warehouses and mills. On Figham Road, nearby, the imposing stone gateway with pilasters in front of modern Mill View Court is a remnant of the town's gasworks of 1824. A short distance north of the head of the

The Old Friary, Beverley

Beverley Beck looking west

beck, on Holme Church Lane, stands the church of St Nicholas, 1879–80, its medieval predecessor that served this part of the town having been demolished in the 17th century.)

Back at the Minster, turn left into ***Minster Yard South***. Here the 1980s low-level housing-association development was controversial but is unobtrusive. Hall Garth, a protected open space, is where the archbishops of York, lords of Beverley, had their manor house. On the right is St John Street, where the row of rendered cottages (Nos 8–11) was originally one house constructed at the very beginning of the 18th century. It was built on the foundations of a communal medieval residence of the Minster clergy, the delightfully named House of the Seven Parsons or *Berefellari*. From Minster Yard South continue along ***Keldgate***, an interesting street with several large houses dating from the 1690s onwards, most built by the owners of tanyards or other small industries that once dominated this area. On the north side are the splendid Ann Routh's almshouses, the original block with blank arcades built 1749 to a design by James Moyser. Pediment with elaborate cartouche decorated with horn of plenty overflowing with produce.

Continuing west, No. 54 has a well-preserved late 17th-century interior, and has managed to keep its flat or 'English' roof tiles, now rare in a town where pantiles had become the norm by the mid-18th century. Opposite is Keldgate House (No. 51), with somewhat large brick addition of *c.* 1740 designed as a music room. Turn right into ***Lairgate***, where a piece of Gothic church masonry perches on the porch of a small Regency villa, Holborn House. Return to the Minster via ***Minster Moorgate***, which has another almshouse, Warton's Hospital, built 1689 as a single-storey block, and some of the town's best-preserved smaller Georgian terraced houses, many with horizontal sliding-sash windows.

Walk 2

The central area, beginning at St Mary's church

St Mary's Church: 'There is another church called St Mary's that is very good and large, I thought that had been the Minster at first entrance of the town' (Celia Fiennes, 1697). This is a mistake that many visitors make, for St Mary's, at the north end of the town, is one of the finest parish churches in the country. Established by the mid-12th century, but mostly rebuilt from the late 13th century onwards, this was the church of the townspeople and benefited from merchant wealth. It is cruciform, with a central tower and aisled nave and chancel. The west front with lantern turrets dates from *c.*1400, and is reminiscent of that of King's College Chapel, Cambridge. In 1520 the tower collapsed during a service, killing some of the parishioners. (Ironically, the death toll would have been higher had many not chosen to attend a bear-baiting instead.) The tower and nave were rebuilt almost immediately.

St Mary's is full of splendid things. The early 14th-century ribbed vaulting in ***St Michael's chapel*** is superb. (Look nearby for carving of the Pilgrim Rabbit that may or may not have been the model for Lewis Carroll's white rabbit.) Equally impressive is the restored ***chancel ceiling*** depicting the kings of England, originally painted in the mid-15th century. So too are the carved roof bosses, over 600 in total, many on the nave ceiling that was part of the 1520s restoration. They depict jesters, mythical beasts, Adam and Eve, etc., brightly coloured and gilded. Among those who contributed to the rebuilding after the tower fell was the northern

St Mary, Beverley, from the southwest

guild of minstrels, and a delightful carving of a group of them, complete with instruments, adorns a pier. The ***15th-century choir stalls*** have many misericords with images such as St George slaying the dragon and a knight attacking a wild boar. In the Priest's Room, reached by a winding stone staircase, is a wealth of miscellaneous objects including a rare maiden's garland, a decorated wooden frame carried at the funeral of Elizabeth Ellinor, who died in 1680. The grandest of the monuments are three of more or less the same design to members of the Warton family who died between 1700 and 1714. (See also *Beverley Minster.*) Numerous floor slabs, many commemorating the minor gentry, professionals and tradesmen who dominated the Georgian town. A modest wall

Minstrels' pillar, St Mary, Beverley

plaque in memory of Samuel Butler is inscribed with a Shakespearian quotation: 'A poor Player, that struts and frets his hour upon the Stage, and then is heard no more.' Butler was actor-manager of the Richmond theatre circuit and died in 1812 at Beverley, where his company was performing.

Walk 2 begins at the west end of St Mary's. Turn left into ***Hengate***, a narrow, gently curving street spoiled only by traffic. It is hard to imagine that in the 1960s there were plans to demolish Georgian houses here for road widening. The south side is dominated by the White Horse Inn, where the curved brick front conceals timber framing. Popularly known as Nellies after a former landlady, it still has Victorian fixtures and fittings including gaslights. The most distinctive of the 18th-century houses opposite, with stone quoins and hipped roof, is No. 7, built 1707. Beyond the junction, in Norwood, is Norwood House, now offices, an exceptionally fine house built around 1765 for an attorney, and almost certainly designed by Thomas Atkinson of York. Handsome five-bay south front, the ground floor faced with stone, the rest of orange-red brick. Pediment with circular window with surrounding cartouche.

Back on Hengate, turn left opposite St Mary's into ***Ladygate***, which takes you to the junction with Sow Hill Road, which was pushed through in the 1960s giving access to Sow Hill, the north end of ***Saturday Market***. The marketplace here was established in the 12th century, as the focus of the town that had grown up around the Minster shifted north. Ladygate continues beyond the junction, and originally formed the east side of the marketplace before blocks of infill turned it into a backstreet. The most remarkable survival, Nos 19–21, can be seen in the distance on the left. Its long Georgian brick façade with tall cart entrance conceals a timber-framed building with crown-post roof dated to 1330. Turn right into Sow Hill, where a pair of cream telephone boxes, unique to the Hull area, stand at the end of the Dings, a row of mid-18th-century buildings, including No. 23 Saturday Market with figure of a White Swan above, denoting a former inn. No. 18, once the Holderness Gun and Cycle Stores, retains a Cyclists' Touring Club sign. Opposite is the rather fine ***Market Cross***, which is not a cross but an open shelter with eight columns with lantern-topped cupola roof. Erected 1714 and affectionately but quite incorrectly known locally as the bandstand.

Saturday Market, vibrant when filled with stalls on market day, has examples of many styles of architecture. The west side was originally the Merchants' Row but was mostly rebuilt from the 18th century onwards, and some of the most imposing buildings are Victorian banks and shops. Where Saturday Market opens into a square at the south end, most prominent is the former Corn Exchange, dated 1886, ornate façade with stepped gable and terracotta panel with town arms. Now a department store, but for many years a cinema. On the east side No. 28, tall and narrow with a good shop front with shutters, was built in the 1760s, but the width is probably that of a medieval burgage plot. The King's Head, which once offered stabling for 60 horses, is near ***Dyer Lane,*** which leads to [Old] Walkergate. The Walker Beck, now

Norwood House, Beverley
opposite: St Mary, Beverley: chancel ceiling

culverted, runs alongside the street, which takes its name from the fullers who 'walked' cloth here in the Middle Ages. (The parallel road, New Walkergate, was made *c.*1980, part of an inner ring road that took traffic away from the town centre.)

Turn left along ***Walkergate*** to Tymperon House, an early–mid-18th-century former almshouse, with distinctive blank arches and heavy brick eaves cornice. Opposite stands Walkergate House, late 18th century, the flat tiles suggesting it was the work of local builder/architect William Middleton, who had a penchant for reusing these old-fashioned tiles. The plaque identifies it as the home of William Crosskill, whose iron foundry manufacturing agricultural machinery was the town's largest enterprise in the mid-19th century. The plaque should actually be on No.17, an interesting but much-altered house, late 17th century in origin, briefly known by the same name. Now right along Walkergate beyond Dyer Lane end, passing Nos 90–92, built in the 18th century as a short-lived theatre. On the same side a passageway by the Methodist schoolrooms leads to Toll Gavel Methodist Church, an imposing late Victorian chapel with a good interior.

Market Cross, Saturday Market, Beverley

At the end of Walkergate comes Butcher Row. Instead of following this street to reach Wednesday Market (see Walk 1), turn right into Toll Gavel, where No. 65 with steeply pitched roof was built *c.*1705. Before turning left into Cross Street, look ahead to No. 44 Toll Gavel, which has an early 19th-century shop front with snakes coiled around the doorway columns. They symbolise Asclepius, god of medicine, signifying that this was the premises of a chemist and druggist.

Off Cross Street, laid out *c.*1827, are Register Square and the ***Guildhall*** (*open to public Wednesdays and Fridays*), with a great Greek portico added in the 1830s. Its origins lie in a merchant's house purchased for use as a guildhall in 1500, and in the magnificent 1760s courtroom with fine plasterwork some of the medieval timber framing can still be seen. The west side of Cross Street is mainly filled by ***County Hall***, 1890, accomplished Flemish Renaissance, with a charming Regency house opposite. Ahead is the overlarge and bland modern Magistrates' Court, beyond which is the former Baptist chapel, 1910, Art Nouveau Gothic, successfully converted to the ***East Riding Theatre***. Turn right from Cross Street into Champney Road, where the ***Treasure House*** on the left is made up of the 1906 Queen Anne-style library and excellent art gallery, and an extension opened in 2007 housing the county archives, exhibition area, cafe, Tourist Information Centre, etc. The oval tower provides rooftop views. In the grounds of County Hall, opposite, is one of the turrets from St Mary's church removed at the mid-19th-century restoration.

At the end of Champney Road look across to ***Lairgate Hall***, now offices. This important house, once with extensive grounds, was built *c.*1755 for Thomas Pennyman with additions *c.*1770, for Sir James Pennyman, probably by John Carr. Fine interior, including a room with hand-painted Chinese wallpaper. Turn right into ***Lairgate***, where the best buildings include Nos 72–74, a semi-detached three-storey pair with pretty fanlights, built at the end of the 18th century. Turn left into ***Newbegin***, where some of the town's most interesting houses are to be found. On the south side the 18th-century façade of No. 5 hides substantial timber framing, the remains of a 15th-century merchant's house. No. 3, completely rebuilt *c.* 1750, was originally part of the same property. No. 9 was built *c.* 1700. On the opposite side is a series of good houses beginning with Nos 6–8, which date from around 1780, then No. 10, 'lately erected' in 1746 but subsequently heightened and refronted. The most rewarding house is undoubtedly Nos 14–16, set back in large grounds, built *c.* 1689 for Charles Warton. Five bays, three storeys with dormers, and hipped flat-tiled roof. At the end of the street, where one of the town gates stood, is Newbegin Bar House, 1746. At this point turn right into St Mary's Terrace, built on the line of the town ditch, then right again into Wood Lane, where there are early–mid-Victorian houses towards the east end with wide entrances that originally gave access to workshops behind. The lane begins to feel medieval as it narrows almost to footpath width before opening out on to North Bar Within, with welcome views of St Mary's, North Bar and the Market Cross.

Beverley Guildhall: Courtroom

Walk 3

Around and beyond North Bar

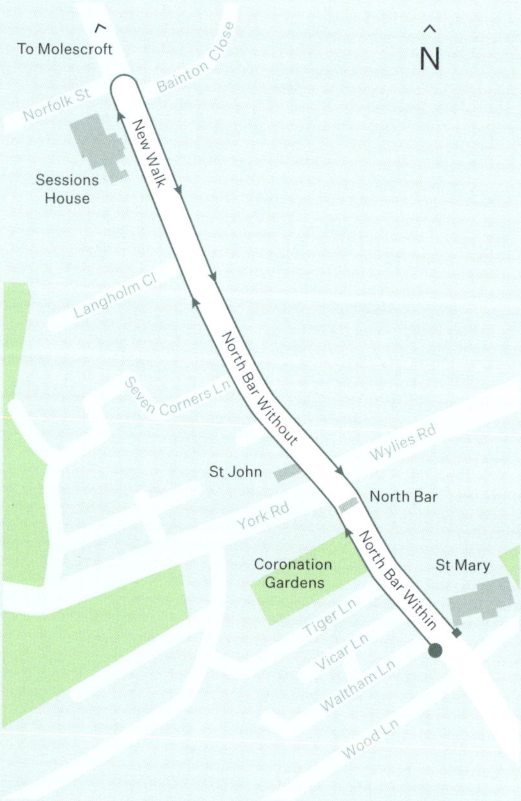

Begin on the west side of ***North Bar Within*** (opposite St Mary's), one of the most interesting streets in the town with an eclectic range of architectural styles. The handsome Beverley Arms hotel, 1794–96, benefited from a 21st-century renovation that included the welcome removal of a 1960s mini skyscraper behind. In complete contrast is Nos 37–39 (Pizza Express), a three-storey Italianate building by Cuthbert Brodrick of Leeds Town Hall fame, built 1861 as a pair of houses although in style more commercial. Then a long block, Nos 41–47, now divided into shops. This began life in 1740 as the Tiger Inn, a rival to the Beverley Arms as one of the East Riding's principal meeting places. ***St Mary's Court***, timber-framed, is a remarkable survival given that in the early 20th century the centre part was broken through when it was converted to a car showroom and workshop by the motor engineer Gordon Armstrong, inventor of the shock absorber. (Set into the pavement in front are two Anglo-American Oil Co. manhole covers, a relic from the days when there were petrol pumps here.) The timbers have been dated to the 1330s, a time when Beverley was at the height of its medieval prosperity. On the cast-iron gates and gate piers into the tranquil ***Coronation Gardens***, a former burial ground for St Mary's, the sharp-eyed might spot the name of the local maker, William Crosskill (see Walk 2, *Walkergate House*), and the date, 1829. Next is a handsome 18th-century terrace on land once associated with the Warton family's 17th-century mansion, Bar House. What survives of the great house dates mainly from a rebuild of 1866, when the belvedere giving views over Westwood common was added to the roof. The resited gate pillars from the old house can be seen on York Road.

Beverley was once surrounded by a ditch and gates or bars, of which ***North Bar***, 1409–10, is the only one remaining, and the earliest English gate in brick. Both Beverley and Hull had medieval brickworks. It has a room above the arch accessed from Bar House, and on the north side the arms and squirrel crest of the Wartons. Go through the bar into North Bar Without, crossing York Road (the way to the racecourse), where on the south side, at the beginning of Westwood, Willow Row has some pretty double-fronted houses, 1850s but in late Regency style.

On ***North Bar Without*** the west side begins with the Jacobethan Rose and Crown, followed by St John's Roman Catholic church, 1898, with quirky asymmetrical turret. After that comes a harmonious mixture of 18th- and 19th-century houses in a variety of styles. No. 29, set back, was built by a woollen draper in the 1740s but later heightened to three storeys; the grounds once extended to Westwood. Seven Corners Lane

Beverley Arms, North Bar Within

Oak House, North Bar Without

North Bar, Beverley

provides a glimpse of the charming first-floor bow windows at the back of Nos 33–37, a late 18th-century terrace. There are a couple more Georgian houses before two excellent examples of late Victorian mock timber framing. No. 45, Oak House, 1880, was commissioned by James Elwell, whose local woodcarving firm was responsible for the interior. No. 47, Pinewood, 1894, was designed by Elwell and has a carved panel depicting a scene from *The Cricket on the Hearth* (1845) by Charles Dickens.

A little further on, North Bar Without becomes ***New Walk***, named for the tree-lined promenade on the east side laid out 1780. Houses came much later. Towards the end of New Walk work began in 1805 on the ***Sessions House*** with massive portico, a figure of Justice topping

Sessions House and pissoir, New Walk, Beverley

the pediment, scales in hand. In the grounds an unusual and rather pretty cast-iron 'pissoir', presumably for the relief of some of those attending the court. Round the corner on Norfolk Street, the houses on the left, Nos 5–13, including the three-storey Octagon House, were converted in 1880 from the early 19th-century ***House of Correction***. The historic town boundary is just south of Gallows Lane but the road continues to ***Molescroft***, a residential suburb with a few early houses, an inn and a late 19th-century mission church left from the original hamlet.

Return via the east side of New Walk, which still has its trees and Victorian postbox. Here the most imposing houses, Nos 2–10, are *c.*1870 by the local architect William Hawe in a French Classical style. Soon after comes No. 62 North Bar Without (Ash Close), undoubtedly the finest house in the street, built *c.*1732 of brick with Westmorland slate roof, round-arched doorway, and courtyard in front. No. 56, with impressive Georgian doorcase featuring a shell motif, is also set back. Other houses of note between here and North Bar include No. 48, 1730s, with good-

Figure of Justice, Sessions House, Beverley

Elwell's woodcarving on No. 4 North Bar Without, Beverley

quality brickwork. Wylies Road (until *c.* 1960 a narrow lane) must be crossed to reach Nos 4–8, James Elwell's woodcarving business premises, remodelled by him in 1890. Mock half-timbering with a riot of carvings including shields, figures and mythical beasts, some painted in jolly colours. A red devil crouches on the projecting corner turret, and there are carved panels, one inscribed 'The Political Cheap Jack', based on a cartoon from Punch. Elwell's son Fred, a well-known painter, lived for many years at Bar House with his wife, Mary, also an artist. They are well represented in ***Beverley's art gallery (Treasure House)***, and all around the town you will see reproductions of their paintings displayed.

Go through the bar back to ***North Bar Within***, where ***St Mary's Manor***, an elegant Regency villa (now apartments) once set in extensive grounds, dominates the east side. Interior remodelled around 1828, when the house was still quite new, the grand staircase of this date featuring a wrought-iron landing balustrade that was once part of the altar rails of Beverley Minster. Pretty cast-iron Gothic pump in the street nearby. [C5]

Victorian Gothic pump, North Bar Within, Beverley

Coates Bridge and lock on Pocklington Canal, Bielby

Bewholme Striking former vicarage made particularly distinctive by its slate roof with overhanging eaves and long flying brackets, a feature sometimes found in northern France. Designed by William Burges in 1859, but his plans for a church were not executed. Instead the modest mission church of 1900 dedicated to St John the Baptist was built, brick with bargeboards and a bell-turret, rather more Scandinavian in character. Both are a great contrast to the former Primitive Methodist chapel of 1839, a neat cube of brick and pantile with round-arched windows, originally single-storey. More than a mile (1.5 km) south of the village, off Bewholme Lane, is Arram Hall, a small 17th-century manor house with shaped gables. [C6]

Bielby St Giles' church rebuilt in 1792 incorporating remnants from its Norman predecessor. The design is simple, just a rectangular stone block with a small slate-hung bell-turret. For many years the exterior was covered with rendering, but this has been removed, revealing the blocked 13th-century north arcade. Contemporary pulpit and box pews and fragment of medieval wall painting. Former Wesleyan chapel dated 1837 with a good sundial made by a local man, John Smith. On Mill Lane, which runs north towards Bielby Beck, a three-storey watermill built in 1855 has been converted to a house. Further north the picturesque Coates Bridge and lock on the Pocklington Canal. [C3]

Bilton Almost but not quite part of Hull. Once a small estate village of the Dawnays, Viscounts Downe, who paid for the rebuilding of St Peter's church in 1852. Simple design of combined nave and chancel with double bellcote. Remnants of estate housing including two terraces and, on Lime Tree Lane, The Cottage, which just might be by William Butterfield. A mile (1.5 km) east is the hamlet of ***Wyton***, popular with Hull merchants. The earliest of their country villas, all on the north side, is Wyton Abbey, *c.*1765, hidden from view. The entrance is opposite a former Methodist chapel with delightful 1840s lettering. Wyton Lodge, grey brick with hipped roof, 1836, can just been glimpsed beyond the contemporary roadside lodge. Next comes the late 18th-century Red House, red brick as the name suggests (it was formerly Wyton Villa), and finally up a long drive is Wyton Hall, *c.* 1765, rendered. [D6]

Bishop Burton 'Bishop Burton gave me the most entrancing glimpse of a pond, old walls and red roofs. Within a second, I had settled there and was done with the world: the bookish hermit of Bishop Burton.' So wrote J.B. Priestley, during his journey round England in the 1930s. Except for the Altisidora pub, named after a racehorse that won the St Leger, the whitewashed cottages, some with rustic porches and mock-timbered gables, and Georgian brick farmhouses of this pretty village sensibly stand mostly back from the busy road around two large greens, each with a pond. All Saints' church, prominently sited above the larger pond on the south side, has an unusual 13th-century tower with doorways to the north and south. The nave was rebuilt in the 1820s 'in strict accordance with the original building', and the chancel in 1865. Some good stained glass by C.E. Kempe and Clayton & Bell. A half-timbered lodge of 1888 guards the entrance to Bishop Burton College, opened in 1954. The site, surrounded by the ditch and bank of the medieval deer park of the archbishops of York, is that of a Jacobean house and its Victorian replacement, the latter built for the Watt family, Liverpool merchants and owners of slave plantations in Jamaica. The astronomer William Donkin (1814–69) and the entomologist William Spence (1782–1860) were born in the village. [C4]

Bishop Wilton A most appealing village sited along the sides of a valley cut into the lower slopes of the Wolds. A stream runs down the centre, between grassy banks, with an attractive mixture of 18th- and 19th-century houses on either side. At the east end are the prominent earthworks of the medieval manor house of the archbishops of York. On the north side St Edith's church, with a 15th-century tower and spire and a richly carved Norman south doorway with animal faces and human figures. Restored by J.L. Pearson, 1859, the sumptuous interior was transformed by G.E. Street and Temple Moore for Sir Tatton Sykes. The roof of nave, aisles and tower ceiling were prettily painted by Clayton & Bell, who also did the excellent stained glass. Striking brass and iron chancel screen and, most original of all, the black and white mosaic floor with pattern of birds, 1902, a copy of a floor in the Vatican. [B3]

Blacktoft Strung out along the north bank of the Ouse. Early Victorian church, Holy Trinity, built with fine ashlar. It retains a Gothic west gallery on cast-iron pillars, some painted glass, and numbered box pews, a reminder that rent was once paid for the privilege of sitting here. [E3]

Little Green, Bishop Burton

Carving on south doorway, St Edith, Bishop Wilton

Boynton A village of whitewashed chalkstone cottages. From the main road a lane leads south to St Andrew's church, which, except for the Perpendicular stone tower, was rebuilt in brick in 1768, probably to the designs of John Carr. A charming Georgian Gothick interior with the Strickland family pew over the west end. Unusually the sanctuary, framed by pairs of columns, is in the centre of the building, with the east end reserved for the family's mortuary chapel. Two colourful 1670s memorials, but a refined Classical work by Rysbrack is the finest of the monuments. The 20th-century lectern is in the form of a turkey, the Stricklands' crest, but there is no truth in the story that the family's founder, William Strickland, was the first to bring turkeys to Britain. He did build the splendid Boynton Hall (*private*) in parkland south of the church. A stone-built core of *c.*1550 was greatly extended to the north and south in red brick with dark diapering *c.*1580–1600, resulting in an H-shaped house. It was 'modernised' around 1730 for Sir William Strickland, 4th baronet, a Lord of the Treasury and Secretary of War, with advice from Lord Burlington. In the 1760s-70s the north front was completed when John Carr added the octagonal library in the centre. In the grounds a delightful small brick banqueting house of *c.* 1600. [A6]

Boynton Hall
opposite: Brantinghamthorpe Hall

Brandesburton The shaft of the village cross stands on Cross Hill, the scene of markets and fairs up to the mid-19th century. Nearby, flanking the road up to the church, are the Regency Old Rectory and the admirable village school built in 1843 by the Lord Mayor and Corporation of London, who as Trustees of Emanuel Hospital were Lords of the Manor for over 300 hundred years. St Mary's church, of cobble and medieval brick, has some Norman features but the wide nave, chancel and possibly the tower are 13th century, the clerestory 14th century. Brass to 14th-century rector, now headless, as is the brass to Sir John de St Quintin, d.1397. His wife, Lora, beside him survives intact. West of the village is Brandesburton Hall (now apartments) a late 18th-century house. Largely rebuilt in the late 19th–early 20th century, it was the home of Colonel Harrison, an explorer, best known for bringing to England a group of Pygmies from the Congo in 1905. [C6]

Brantingham A tranquil place nestling at the foot of Brantingham Dale. All Saints' church, standing alone on Dale Road, was largely rebuilt in 1872, but the dark-orange pantiled roof is later and contrasts well with the mellow limestone walls. Good stained glass by C.E. Kempe and Christopher Whall. The oldest cottages in the village are constructed from similar materials to the church, including one on Spout Hill that has a 1713 datestone with set square and compasses suggesting it belonged to a stonemason. Limestone was quarried at Brantingham from the Middle Ages onwards, and it was during quarrying in 1941 that the site of a Roman villa was discovered, a mosaic from which is now in the Hull and East Riding Museum (see *Hull*).

Several large houses, including Brantingham Hall, tall, thin and elegant, of brick rather than stone. It was built in the 1760s for a Hull merchant. Hidden in parkland some distance from the village is Brantinghamthorpe Hall. A house on the site was greatly extended and altered from the late 1860s onwards for Christopher Sykes, who wanted to make his new home somewhere grand enough to entertain the Prince of Wales,

Funfair in winter, Esplanade, Bridlington

a regular visitor. At the same time cottages belonging to the Brantinghamthorpe estate were made more picturesque by adding rustic porches and other embellishments. Opposite the drive to the mansion is the prominent war memorial constructed in 1922 using fragments rescued from Hull's demolished Victorian town hall. Other features from the same source, such as urns and plaques with crowns, can be spotted around the village. [D4]

Bridlington There are two Bridlingtons, the delightful Old Town and, a mile (1.5 km) away, the Quay, the seaside resort with its wonderful sandy beaches and glorious views across the bay to Flamborough Head. Most holidaymakers never visit the Old Town, a place full of surprises, including the Priory Church, one of the greatest parish churches in Yorkshire, in both scale and architectural importance. The priory was founded *c.* 1113 for Augustinian canons, and when a former prior, John of Thwing, was canonised in 1401 his shrine attracted many pilgrims, including kings Henry IV and V. On its dissolution in 1537 most of the priory buildings were demolished, leaving only a gatehouse (the Bayle) and the nave of the church, the present building. But what an impressive nave, 185 ft (56 m) long, 13th century except the greater part of the west end, which was rebuilt in the 15th century, possibly after the fall of the southwest tower. Its present distinctive uneven appearance can be blamed on Sir George Gilbert Scott, who in the 1870s added the top stages to the

Bridlington Priory viewed across the allotments

towers, making the southwest tower taller with its parapet and pinnacles. Between the towers is a great Perpendicular window, with below a fine doorway with crocketed ogee canopy. The porch on the north side has the most elaborate carved capitals; along the south wall a line of corbels mark the position of the cloister roof, and bases of piers the vaulted undercroft of the prior's lodgings. Supporting the east end are large buttresses that enclose two west pillars of the demolished great central tower. The interior impresses with arcades of tall, broad pillars; the three westernmost on the south side, 15th century, have panelled sides. The three easternmost bays of the nine-bay aisled nave now form the chancel. Sections of the sumptuously carved mid-12th-century cloister arcade have been re-erected at the west end of the north aisle. The circular black Frosterley marble font is 14th century, the elaborate clergy stalls and south aisle screens 20th century by Robert 'Mouseman' Thompson. The best glass is in the north aisle and south chapel windows by Burlison & Grylls. Of the many monuments, the earliest and most intriguing is a large 12th-century slab of Tournai marble with flat relief carvings of a lion, two dragons, a fox and goose and a Byzantine-style church. Equally entertaining is the nautical ledger slab to the merchant William Bower, d.1671, with mermaids, anchors, etc.

Across the green is the Bayle, the priory gatehouse, possibly built by the mid-12th century, with major changes, including the addition of a third floor, after permission was given to crenellate (fortify) the priory in 1388.

Bridlington Priory, 12th-century Tournai marble grave slab

It later housed the grammar school and has been a museum since 1928, with excellent displays on priory and town (*open weekdays*).

The ***Old Town***, as it is now known, developed at the gates of the Priory along High Street and its extension, Westgate, lined with a great range of buildings from the 17th to the mid-19th century, forming one of the most enjoyable streets in the region. Exceptional number of Regency bow windows. On the north side the charming Craven House, with a front of 1806, but as with other houses on the street the interior reveals late 17th-century origins. Home and later offices of the celebrated 20th-century Classical architect Francis Johnson. No. 22, a large mid-19th-century house, and No. 29 opposite were the homes of medical men, the latter the childhood home of Humphry Sandwith, the 'hero' of Kars. The best house by far is No. 43, The Toft. Built in 1673 by the wealthy merchant William Hudson, its façade is of the 1840s, but the interior is a riot of late 17th-century Artisan-Mannerist woodwork. Swags and drops of fruit, flowers and leaves decorate chimneypieces and doorcases, and the fine oak staircase once ended inside a glazed turret from which Hudson could view his ships in the harbour. Next door, No. 45, with fine bow windows, is of national significance as the childhood home of the great William Kent, architect and landscape designer. A stone at the rear has the initials of Kent's parents (his father was a joiner) and date 1693. It was refronted in the 18th century. For a time it was owned by Lewis Carroll's brother. Nos 42–48 are all charmingly bow-fronted, and three are built partly of reused priory stone. Bestworth House (Nos 51–53), *c.*1712, has an unusual seven-bay façade with full-height pilasters. The Manor House (No. 64), built by a surgeon in 1785, is now the offices of the Lords Feoffees of the Manor of Bridlington, the successor to the townspeople who bought the manor in 1636. Off to the north is Market Place, a broad street lined with Georgian houses. Plenty of good doorcases. Westgate, the continuation of High Street, begins with the remarkably intact Hebblethwaite House, built in 1681 by a merchant, Thomas Wilson, son-in-law of the builder of The Toft (above). Restrained Artisan-Mannerist brick façade and a wonderful restored coved eaves cornice richly decorated with acanthus leaves. Next the Old Star Inn, 17th century in origin, then three houses that were the homes of Georgian attorneys: West End House, No. 29, built *c.*1720, altered *c.*1760, front stuccoed *c.*1870; Westgate Lodge, built *c.*1828; and finally the Avenue, an imposing three-storey five-bay house with pilasters flanking the central bay and at the corners, dated 1714 on the rainwater heads. Back to the east end of High Street, where St John Street runs south becoming Quay Road leading down to the resort and harbour, with a few

High Street, Bridlington

Belle Vue Terrace, Bridlington

buildings to note on the way. Most striking are the rather exotic Burlington Methodist Chapel, 1884; the former Roxy cinema, 1912, elaborate Baroque façade of painted stone with faience decoration; and the showy Town Hall, 1932, in a Neo-William and Mary style, with domed cupola and grand marble staircase. Then the railway station, rebuilt 1912, originally located here in 1846, midway between the Old Town and the Quay in an attempt to satisfy both communities, and Christ Church, 1841, an early work by George Gilbert Scott.

Now ***Bridlington Quay***, the resort, has been reached. There has almost certainly been a harbour here, where the Gypsey Race – the small river that runs through the northern Wolds – reaches the sea, since the Roman period. In the 17th century it was a flourishing port, importing timber from the Baltic and coal from Sunderland, and exporting corn, malt and West Riding cloth. It was in decline by the 1730s, but sea bathing was just becoming fashionable so Bridlington developed instead as a resort, favoured by those who preferred somewhere more peaceful and less hilly than Scarborough. The gentry of East Yorkshire, the merchants of Hull and many from further afield flocked to 'Burlington Key' in the late 18th and early 19th century. (Both town and port were alternatively called Burlington from the 12th century until the mid-19th century. The title Earl of Burlington was chosen by Richard Boyle, Earl of Cork, at the request of Queen Henrietta Maria, who had landed here in the Civil War, when he was granted an English Peerage in 1665.)

The first bathing machines arrived in 1765, and lodging houses and inns were built. The Brunswick Hotel, Manor Street, of the 1790s, is one of the few that remain of this period, largely unaltered externally. The Promenade, running north, parallel to the sea, was laid out in 1771. Little of interest here, although there is the odd original bow front and pedimented doorcase and the delightful Belle Vue Terrace, a row of two-bay three-storey brick houses, with round-arched doorways and radiating fanlights, set back with gardens in front.

Bridlington Harbour

The harbour, one of the attractions of the resort, suffered greatly from storm damage and coastal erosion until the mid-19th century. The stone-built North Pier, begun in 1816, reached its present extent, some 730 ft (223 m), in 1866. Here Charlotte Brontë, on a visit in 1839, observed the 'absurdity' of the packed evening parade when 'people had to march round and round in regular file to secure any movement whatever'. The South Pier, built in the 1840s, is 1,500 ft (457 m) long. The Harbour Heritage Museum (*open Easter to end of October*) is worth a visit. A sea wall was built northwards from the harbour from the mid-1860s onwards, and Royal Princes Parade constructed behind. Here is the Floral Pavilion, 1904, much altered but retaining its original cast-iron structure, and there are all the usual seaside delights – amusement arcades, a funfair, boat trips, ice creams, candy floss, fish and chips and hungry seagulls. The surviving mid–late Victorian terraces of substantial three- and four-storey houses, inland from the parade and along the seafront further north, were built to accommodate the increasing number of visitors following the coming of the railway. These included, in August 1881, Friedrich Engels and his wife, who stayed at No. 1 Sea View, Promenade. At the far end of the seafront is the large Expanse Hotel, built 1937 in a rather ill-informed International Modern Style.

South of the harbour the excellent seafront promenade stretches for over half a mile (800 m). The scene is dominated by the Spa, East Yorkshire's chief entertainment and conference venue, the third building on the site. A cast-iron and glass construction of 1896 was replaced 30 years later by an angular Art Deco concrete building. This was destroyed by fire in 1932 and the present Spa built later that year, the work taking just 52 days! It was refurbished and redeveloped with additions in 2006–08, and the splendid Spa Theatre with its charming Edwardian interior was restored.

T.E. Lawrence ('of Arabia') lodged at the nearby Ozone Hotel (now the Royal Yorkshire Yacht Club) in the 1930s, when serving with an RAF

The Spa and Spa Theatre, Bridlington

David Hockney, 'Bridlington Rooftops, October, November, December', 2005 © David Hockney

Marine Craft Unit. Away from the seafront smart suburban sub-Arts and Crafts villas, with half-timbered and tile-hung gables, rendered façades, stone mullions, leaded lights and Art Nouveau glass, line Cardigan Road. On South Cliff are three large Norwegian timber chalets of 1897–98. It was nearby, with a view of the sea, that David Hockney made his home for eight years from 2005. Woldgate, a country lane that runs west from the town, was the focus of many of his paintings, drawings and films. [A6]

Broomfleet The church of St Mary the Virgin is entered through the north tower with its steep pyramidal tiled roof mimicking a short spire. By J.L. Pearson, 1861, as is the adjacent former vicarage with tall stacks and decorative brickwork. Of the village houses the most interesting is Pigeoncote Farm, early–mid-18th century, with iron tie plates in the form of IR for John Roebuck, the letters I and J being interchangeable. Built as the manor house; the present name refers to the oversized pigeon loft that came later. A mile (1.5 km) southwest a lock and sluice built 1773 on the Market Weighton Canal where it feeds into the Humber. [D3]

Brough Roman *Petuaria*, a fort and civilian town with theatre and ferry crossing over the Humber. It then faded into insignificance until the railway came in 1840. Thereafter suburban villas for

Hull families were built, the grandest along Cave Road, and its popularity with commuters seems undiminished as more and more new estates are built. Brough aerodrome, used for testing seaplanes on the estuary during the First World War, became an important centre of aircraft manufacture. In 2008 the Art Deco flying club and control tower were converted into a business centre. [E4]

Bubwith Sited on the River Derwent, crossed here by a stone bridge, erected in 1793 when the road from Market Weighton to Selby was turnpiked. The village then became a minor trading and industrial centre with a wharf, two breweries and a weekly corn market in the mid-19th century. Some good late Georgian houses, including Mulberry House, Chain Bar Farm and Lindum House, the last with pretty Regency bow windows. Close to the river is All Saints' church with a handsome early 15th-century tower built following a bequest by Nicholas Bubwith, Bishop of Bath and Wells, to his birthplace. At the same time the 13th-century nave arcade was extended by one bay. The chancel arch is Norman, and above on the east wall of the nave are two blocked openings of the same period. The clerestory is 15th century, as is the five-light east window. [D2]

Bugthorpe An estate village of the Lords Halifax, much prettier than the name suggests. Neat brick and pantile houses, many of which overlook a spacious green. St Andrew's church stands at the southwestern end of it, and is quite large, with the chancel longer and more prominent than the nave. Inside it has the curious distinction of having two chancel arches, the earlier of which is Norman and has interesting carvings. The ceilings are painted sky blue, and above the altar is a striking and colourful canopy, blue and red with gold suns, installed by Lord Halifax in 1937. Good monuments of the 17th and 18th centuries to the Watkinson and Payler families. [B3]

Burnby St Giles' church, a small but rewarding building with a convincing Norman-style west

Mulberry House, Bubwith (drawing by Eugene Fisk)

door and bellcote, the work of a rector in the 1840s. It once had a Norman north aisle and north chapel, and the blocked arcades of these remain. On the south side is a most unusual tall, narrow window of *c.* 1200, and in the chancel, rebuilt 1583, a three-seat sedilia or stone seat said to have come from Warter Priory. Burnby House was built in 1840 by a jockey, Simeon Templeman, who rode three Derby winners. [C3]

Burstwick An important centre in the Middle Ages, first as the administrative base of the Lords of Holderness after they left Skipsea, then as a royal manor where three kings, Edward I, II and III, stayed, and where Robert the Bruce's queen was imprisoned in 1306–08. All that remains of the 'castle' is a moated site near the 18th-century farm known as South Park, named after one of the two medieval deer parks. All Saints' church, although much restored, is essentially medieval. Part cobble, with limestone used in the 15th century for the north aisle, chancel and part of the tower. The Royal Arms of Charles I that hangs inside was painted by John Catlyn, the Royalist vicar, and placed in the church in 1676. The reverse is a painting of the execution of the monarch, most unexpected and slightly disturbing. Burstwick expanded rapidly in the second half of the 20th century, and many of the earlier buildings are much altered. An exception is The Cottage on Hariff Lane, one and a half storeys, a well-preserved example of the modest brick and pantile vernacular housing common in the region from the early–mid-18th century. [D7]

Burton Agnes The view from the southeast across the front of the Elizabethan-Jacobean hall to the Norman manor house and medieval parish church is the most enthralling in East Yorkshire. Manor House (*English Heritage, open*) built *c.* 1170–80, is a rare survival, with a wonderful vaulted stone undercroft and, at the rear, a donkey wheel used to draw water from the well. Burton Agnes Hall (*open*) quite rightly figures in Simon Jenkins' top ten English country houses. A favourite of many people, not just because of its architecture and fine

Burton Agnes Hall

St Martin, Burton Agnes
opposite: Undercroft, Manor House, Burton Agnes

interior, but also for its modern art collection, paintings and sculpture, and wonderful walled garden. The house, built 1601–10 by Sir Henry Griffith, was almost certainly designed by Robert Smythson. A grand gatehouse with four octagonal turrets leads to a topiary-lined avenue that runs up to the delightful south front of the hall. Symmetrical, with a pattern of semicircular bows and square bays, of a pleasing brick with stone mullions, quoins and balustrades. The glories of the interior are the Great Hall, with its sumptuous and rather eccentric screen and chimneypiece, the great oak staircase and the splendid Long Gallery.

St Martin's church, reached along a dark avenue of ancient yews, is basically Norman, as shown by the north arcade of the nave and the chancel arch. The south arcade is 13th century, the tower and clerestory late 15th century. The chancel was rebuilt in the 1840s by the rector, Robert Isaac Wilberforce, who included a carved head of his father, William Wilberforce, the emancipator. The box pews, pulpit and monumental family pew are of *c.* 1730. The north chapel has a great array of monuments from the early 14th to the late 18th century. The most striking are the alabaster effigies of Sir Walter Griffith, d. 1481, and his wife, and the rather macabre monument to Sir Henry Griffith, d. 1654, and his two wives, who are represented by three black coffins, set above

Angel from monument to Sir Henry Griffith (d. 1654) and two wives, St Martin, Burton Agnes

a relief of skulls and bones. In the village near the large pond a pretty Gothick Methodist chapel of 1837, now a house. [B6]

Burton Constable Burton Constable Hall (*open*), the grandest country house in East Yorkshire, stands majestically alone in a wide expanse of parkland. The grounds on the west side are much as landscaped by 'Capability' Brown in the 1770s, with a large lake crossed by a five-arched bridge and a pretty pedimented pavilion at the north end.

The house is brick-built with some diaper patterning. The north tower has medieval origins, as does the north wing, but the great east front, south tower and south wing were added after Sir John Constable was granted the Lordship of Holderness in 1560. The southern half of the west front is of the early 17th century, the rest

Burton Constable Hall

The Orangery at Burton Constable

completed *c.*1770 for William Constable, who had great interest in the arts and sciences. He spent lavishly on the transformation of the interior. The impressive Great Hall of the Elizabethan house was given its present appearance in the 1760s by the architect Timothy Lightoler, who was also responsible for the Neoclassical dining room and large staircase hall that leads up to the long gallery. Among other rooms of note are the ballroom designed by James Wyatt and the ornately furnished Chinese room. In the grounds a charming orangery of 1788 and a massive red-brick stable block of *c.*1768 with a large early 19th-century indoor riding school.

At ***Marton*** 1½ miles (2.5 km) north it is a surprise to come across a Roman Catholic church and cemetery in such an isolated rural setting. Built in 1789, the church of the Most Holy Sacrament was paid for by William Constable, whose family and many of his servants and tenants were Catholic. The low-key design, a simple brick rectangle with arched windows and adjoining presbytery, reflected the need for discretion before Catholic emancipation. [D6]

Burton Fleming A village through which flows the intermittent stream called the Gypsey Race, from the Old English *gypsia* – 'to spring suddenly into life'. Plenty of 18th- and 19th-century farmhouses and cottages in a mixture of brick and chalk. Manor House on Front Street looks late 19th century with its rendered façade, but at the back are remnants of the house where Queen Henrietta Maria is thought to have spent a night in 1643. Her visit is recorded in the parish register. North Burton Hall, a stuccoed Regency house, is more imposing, seven bays with a pretty cast-iron balcony over the porch. St Cuthbert's church is medieval, including the chunky stone tower, but much restoration in cobble and especially brick, with 'churchwarden Gothick' windows inserted in the early 19th century. Several 18th-century fittings including a charity board with especially good lettering. Showy Victorian Methodist chapel with polychromatic brickwork. [A5]

Burton Pidsea Medieval cobble and stone church (St Peter's) with aisles and handsome tower. In the first half of the 19th century several large houses with grounds were built within the village, giving it a distinctive character. Most belonged to wealthy farmers, but Graysgarth House on Back Lane, a gracious grey-brick villa, was built for a medical man. The south front has full-height bow windows. On New Road the brick and cobble wall boldly dated 1843 belongs to another of the villas, The Paddocks. The owner bred racehorses, including one after which the village inn, The Nancy, is named. [D7]

Carnaby Small village with some chalkstone buildings. The church, dedicated to St John the Baptist, is on an elevated site to the north. Medieval stonework, including the tower, but brick was used for the early 18th-century chancel and for the clerestory added in 1830, not a good choice. The fittings include a fine drum-shaped Norman font with lozenges and chip-carved stars. In open farmland some distance north of the church stands Carnaby Temple, a two-storey octagonal brick folly topped with a lantern. The locals called it the Pepperpot. It was built *c.* 1770, as a lookout with views of Bridlington Bay, by Sir George Strickland of Boynton Hall. [A6]

Catton There are two villages, High and Low Catton. All Saints' church is at the latter. Norman, originally cruciform, of which the north transept survives. The north aisle with round pillars and pointed arches is 13th century, the south aisle a little later. The windows in the south aisle are 15th century, as is the top of the tower. The chancel, largely rebuilt in 1866, has a much higher roof than the nave, giving the church an odd appearance externally. Lots of good stained glass, the best the glorious east window of 1866 by Morris & Co. to designs of Burne-Jones. The churchyard has three excellent cast-iron Victorian lamp posts. [B2]

Catwick A 'doubly thankful' village, where all those who served in both the First and Second World Wars returned. The forge on Main Street, successfully converted to a house, is where the local blacksmith nailed a lucky horseshoe on the doorpost and added a coin below for each of those who enlisted. Tucked away on the back street is St Michael's church, mainly cobble with stone dressings, with a solid brick and slate rectory next door. Both were rebuilt in the 1860s, although old materials were used for the church, and the tower is medieval. On the north wall of the chancel is a small Norman sculpture, a figure with arms crossed. [C6]

Cherry Burton At the east end trees and parkland make for a rewarding entrance to the village. Cherry Burton House, *c.* 1830, lies on the north side of what becomes the long village street, and is hidden from view. In a more open setting on the south side is Cherry Burton Hall, remodelled in the mid-19th century. St Michael's church is

Carnaby Temple

close by, also mid-19th century though in a late 13th-century style. Excellent east window, one of seven by C.E. Kempe, 1898 onwards. Further along Main Street a small pond, plenty of greenery, and mellow brick farmhouses and cottages, a contrast to the extensive area of modern estate housing built from the 1960s onwards. [C4]

Cottingham A large one-time market village, now a town in character that proudly keeps its independence from Hull, although much of what was the eastern half of the parish lies within that city's present boundary. Cottingham was a chosen place of residence for the port's merchant and professional classes by the 18th century. Here they built 'genteel country houses with gardens and pleasure grounds, laid out in the modern taste'. A number survive, including, of the 1780s, Newgate

House and Eastgate House on Newgate Street, and, on its continuation Thwaite Street, Tudor House, refronted *c.* 1830, and Green Wickets. Thwaite Hall, built 1805, altered and enlarged, fortunately retains its extensive landscaped grounds. Much earlier is Southwood Hall (*private*), off Southwood Road on the west side, an outstanding mid-17th-century red-brick house with Artisan-Mannerist details. Five bays with a central three-storey porch, the entrance flanked by pilasters. Splendid interior with original staircase, pedimented doorcases and bolection-moulded panelling.

Further west the Regency castellated Cottingham Castle, built by the banker and first Methodist MP Thomas Thompson, has long gone. The present Castle Hill hospital is on the site, but Thompson's prospect tower of 1825, with Gothick windows, still stands, close to the A164. Thompson also promoted a scheme on the east side of Cottingham, Paupers' Gardens (named New Village by 1830), twenty smallholdings for poor families. On Middledyke and Endyke Lanes a couple of the modest cottages built on the plots survived little altered until recently.

St Mary's Cottingham is one of the great medieval churches of the East Riding. The tall 15th-century crossing tower with corner stair-turret dominates the building, of which the earliest features are 13th century. The nave is early 14th century and the chancel was built in the 1370s by the rector Nicholas of Louth (de Luda), who is depicted on a monumental brass. Another brass has figures of John Smith, d.1504, and his wife, and there are lots of memorials to the merchant families of the parish. At the back a series with obelisks and urns to the Burton family of Hotham Hall and Hull Bank House (Haworth Hall), the latter a fine mid-Georgian house by the river at the far eastern extent of the original parish. Much Victorian stained glass by Capronnier of Brussels. It seems so alien here, for, as Pevsner noted, English glass at that time was so much 'truer to the medium'. On Hallgate two contrasting Nonconformist chapels, the elegant grey-brick Zion URC, 1819, with its original galleried interior, and the showier Italianate Methodist, 1879.

To the northwest The Lawns, built as innovative student accommodation in the 1960s for Hull University by Gillespie, Kidd & Coia. Six staggered blocks of buff brick that fit well into the landscape. [D5]

Cowick Cowick Hall, now the headquarters of the chemicals company Croda International, was built *c.* 1670 for Sir John Dawnay, 1st Viscount Downe. However, the handsome nine-bay front with giant pilasters, in honey-coloured stone, owes much to a mid-18th-century remodelling by James Paine, who probably designed the two lodges. In the mid-19th century the Dawnays commissioned the austere brick parish church, Holy Trinity. William Butterfield's design features an unusually thin west tower, thought to be modelled on St Mary's, Lindisfarne. Adjacent school and former vicarage, opposite, also by Butterfield. On Spa Well Lane at ***West Cowick*** an interesting former brewery complex. The house nearby was an inn. [E2]

Cowlam Access to the small church, St Mary's – restored and partly rebuilt in 1852 – is through a farmyard. Worth visiting if only to see the tub-shaped Norman font, which is a delight. Arcades with crude figure carvings that include Adam and Eve either side of an apple tree, around which is coiled the crafty serpent. The strangest scene is the pair of wrestlers, perhaps symbolising the struggle between body and soul, or good and evil. Immediately east is the site of Cowlam village, finally depopulated towards the end of the 17th century. A surprise, therefore, to come across the large former rectory southwest of the church. It was built in 1883, when some 60 people lived in the parish, most of them hired farm servants and probably from Methodist families. This isolated spot must have seemed a far cry from civilisation to the Cambridge-educated rector who took up residence in the parish that year. [A4]

Dunnington (near Bewholme) The charm of the tiny late Victorian church of St Nicholas, alone at the south end of the village, is its simplicity.

Nave, chancel and bellcote, all of red brick, more or less the same colour as the roof tiles. It stands well in the flat Holderness landscape. [B6]

Easington At the southeast corner of Holderness, the last settlement of any size before one reaches the Spurn peninsula. The poet Robin Skelton was born at the old schoolhouse. Medieval church of All Saints built mainly of multicoloured local cobbles, although stone was used in the late 14th century for the tower and clerestory. The well-lit interior has some interesting features, including a rare free-standing 12th-century piscina (basin), graffiti of a ship, 17th-century monument and a carving on the tower arch of the 'Easington imp'. South of Rectory Farm, close by the church, is an impressive aisled timber-framed tithe barn with thatched roof, possibly post-medieval, a unique survival in the East Riding. On Seaside Road a mid-19th-century house with lookout tower has in the garden a pillar constructed of medieval masonry.

It is another world on the coast with the great network of pipes, containers and towers of two North Sea gas terminals, one named after the village, the other after Dimlington, one of several settlements in the area long since lost to the sea. [E8]

East Cottingwith Unfussy Georgian brick church, St Mary's, with slender tower giving it a Continental touch. Contemporary hexagonal pulpit. At the end of Church Lane the village hall was built in 1788 as a Quaker meeting house. The irregular village has some well-built houses, including Sycamore House on Main Street where complementary soft pink and orange brick colours highlight the refined Flemish bond façade. The earliest is probably the rendered brick house on the east side of the church, *c.*1700, formerly the Ship Inn. The nautical name reflects

Tithe Barn, Easington | *opposite:* St Mary, Cottingham

Medieval glass, St Michael, Eastrington

the proximity of the River Derwent, which is joined by the Pocklington Canal east of the village. The lock here dates from 1815. [C2]

Eastrington Historically the largest village in Howdenshire, now outpaced by its former township, Gilberdyke. The large medieval St Michael's church is described by Pevsner as 'one of the trickiest churches in the Riding' for the architectural historian. There are many clues to its Norman origin, including the pilasters flanking the east window and the curious carved panel of paired animals in the porch. Internally, the north and south arcades are of the 14th century, and there are many features of the 15th century, including the tower. Most unusual are the three timber arches inserted on the north side of the chancel, when it was rebuilt, as an inscription records, after it 'fel' in 1632. In the north chapel is a mid-15th-century tomb-chest with the defaced alabaster figures of Sir John Portington, Justice of the Common Bench, and his wife. The family came from ***Portington***, a mile (1.5 km) northeast, where stands their E-shaped brick manor house of *c.*1670. [D3]

Ellerker A neat village with a stream running through it. The larger houses include Ellerker Hall set back from Main Street. At the edge of the unusually large green is Sebastopol Cottage with its strange castellated wall with blank Gothic arches, put up in 1857 to commemorate the siege of Sebastopol in the Crimean War. Tucked away up Church Lane is St Ann's chapel of ease, built 1843–44, noteworthy chiefly as the first church designed by J.L. Pearson (architect of Truro Cathedral). [D4]

Ellerton At the western extremity of the village stands the redundant parish church, St Mary's. An accomplished early work by J.L. Pearson, 1848, with an unusual but charming bellcote. Its medieval predecessor was associated with a small Gilbertine priory. Pearson's church was saved thanks to the efforts of Ellerton Church Preservation Trust, set up in 1995, which commissioned several stained-glass windows from Ann Sotheran, Helen Whittaker and Andrew Anderson reflecting the church's history and its wonderful atmospheric setting overlooking the Derwent Ings. Also redundant is the unspoilt Wesleyan chapel, 1811, with charming Gothick windows and box pews. The most characterful village building is the single-storey Boot and Shoe inn, once thatched. [C2]

Elloughton Soon after the nave and chancel fell down in 1843, J.L. Pearson was engaged as architect for the rebuilding of St Mary's church, another of his earliest commissions. The sturdy early 16th-century tower was kept. In the surrounding streets are some of the older village houses, built of local limestone. After the railway reached neighbouring Brough in 1840, Elloughton became a popular place of residence for Hull families. The most memorable of the larger 19th-century houses is Castle House on Sands Lane, built in 1886 in the style of a mock castle. [D4]

Elstronwick A small Holderness settlement with church (St Lawrence's) rebuilt in 1875 using a mixture of cobbles and cut cobblestone. Elstronwick Hall began as a modest Georgian house, to which a

opposite: St Mary, Ellerton, from across the Ings

large block was added in the late 19th century. The view from Front Lane is of the south façade created at that time, essentially a Victorian villa with entrance portico. More interesting but hidden from view is Danthorpe Hall, a mile (1.5 km) or so east of the village, which has some Artisan-Mannerist features such as moulded brick pediments dating from the 17th century. On Mill Lane, northeast of Elstronwick, just in ***Lelley*** township, is a derelict brick windmill with tall chimney alongside added after it was converted to steam. [D7]

Etton A classic East Riding village, with a satisfying mixture of brick and pantile farmhouses and cottages of the 18th and 19th centuries. Plenty of original windows, including some with horizontal or 'Yorkshire' sliding sashes. The houses with distinctive blue doors belong to the estate of the Lords Hotham of South Dalton. Almost everything is on Main Street, including St Mary's church – largely Neo-Norman but with enough that is genuine Norman to make it interesting. The tower arch of four orders is especially fine. Several pieces of medieval sculpture, including a figure of St Peter with an oversized key, from the demolished church at Holme-on-the-Wolds (see *South Dalton*). A modern wall plaque records the birth at Etton in 1584 of Revd John Lowthorp, one of the early migrants to New England who left his homeland to escape religious persecution. Etton was also the birthplace, in 1797, of Thomas Carling, founder of Carling's brewery in Canada. Low Hall, at the east end of village, is little more than the service wing of a large, late 17th-century house with a three-storey tower added to the west. High Hall, mid-Victorian with shaped gables, is tucked away up Chantry Lane. [C4]

Everingham A former estate village of the Constables, a prominent Roman Catholic family, as evidenced by the monumental Catholic church that rather overshadows the delightful brick Everingham Hall. The hall (*private*) was built 1757–64 to designs of John Carr. Substantially enlarged in the 1840s but in 1963 it was reduced to its original size, and the interior sympathetically restored by Francis Johnson for the Duke of Norfolk.

The Catholic church of St Mary & St Everilda (*private, but occasionally open*), so unexpected in the East Riding countryside, was built to the designs of an Italian, Agostino Giorgioli, 1836–39. The rather plain stuccoed Italianate exterior gives way to a lavish Baroque interior lined with giant Corinthian columns and niches with statues of the Apostles. A great contrast to the simple interior of the Anglican parish church, St Everilda's, which (except for its medieval stone tower) was rebuilt in brick in 1763. Splendid Royal Arms of 1773, and pulpit and other fittings of 1842. [C3]

Everingham Hall and Roman Catholic church | *opposite:* Derelict mill, Lelley, near Elstronwick

Fangfoss Triangular village green and a church (St Martin's) rebuilt in 1850 making excellent use of masonry from its Norman predecessor. South doorway with beakhead ornament, and corbel table with a good array of carved heads. A private drive leads to Fangfoss Hall, built in 1766, its simple but elegant design attributed to John Carr of York. A mile (1.5 km) or so west of the village, on the road to Wilberfoss, is a neat mid-19th-century railway station and master's house built 1847 for the York & North Midland Railway. No trains have passed this way since 1965. [B3]

Fimber A parish rich in prehistoric sites, as befits the birthplace (in 1825) of the celebrated archaeologist John R. Mortimer. Village sited round a green, with a large pond. At the west end, on a Bronze Age barrow, a small Victorian 'Sykes' church, St Mary's, designed by G.E. Street in a 13th-century style. Usual excellent craftsmanship inside, including windows by Clayton & Bell. Near Fimber crossroads the Yorkshire Wolds Railway has relaid a very short stretch of the former Malton to Driffield line. [B4]

Flamborough The dramatic coastal scenery of Flamborough Head has long attracted visitors. The large village, with its terraces of 19th-century brick fishermen's cottages and older chalk buildings, is some distance inland. At the south end stands the limestone and cobble church, St Oswald's, externally largely Victorian but with medieval work inside, including a Norman chancel arch. The chief glory is the splendid early 16th-century rood screen, perhaps rescued from Bridlington Priory. Near the altar is the tomb of Sir Marmaduke Constable, a veteran of Flodden Field, which has a lengthy brass inscription in verse recounting his distinguished military career. Having survived the battlefield, his death in 1520 is said to have resulted from swallowing a frog. In a field northwest of the church are earthworks surrounding the remains of a medieval square chalk tower with traces of a vaulted undercroft, all that survives of Flamborough 'castle', the Constable family's fortified manor house.

The western boundary of Flamborough parish is Dane's Dyke, an ancient and massive defensive earthwork some 2½ miles (4 km) long stretching from coast to coast, cutting off the Flamborough headland. The date of construction is uncertain but might have been during the 7th or 8th century. The southern section lies within a nature reserve. On the other three sides of the parish the boundary is the sea. The stunning chalk cliffs of Flamborough Head, in places battered into strange formations by the force of the waves, are home to thousands of seabirds. There are caves, too, once useful places to store smuggled goods. The tip of the headland is some 2 miles (3 km) east of Flamborough village, and is reached via Lighthouse Road. In fact there are two lighthouses, the more unusual an octagonal chalk tower built in 1674 as a private venture. The 'new' lighthouse, of white-painted brick, dates from 1806. At the foot of the chalk cliffs is Selwick's Bay, one of the sheltered coves where access to the foreshore is possible. It was off Flamborough Head that a great naval battle took place in 1779 (see *Sewerby*).

Throughout its history, fishing has been important at Flamborough, reaching a peak in the early 20th century. The traditional flat-bottomed boats, called cobles, were kept either at South Landing (probably the medieval harbour), where the Yorkshire Wildlife Trust Living Seas Centre is now located, or at the more picturesque North Landing. Some fishing still takes place, and there are boat trips in the summer to see the numerous seabirds that breed on the cliffs. [A7]

Fordon The hamlet lies in a chalk valley on the Wolds. Just a few houses and the simple but sweet little church of St James, its stone walls patched with brick and roof covered with pantiles. The earliest parts of the church, including the south doorway, are Norman, but the 1768 datestone hints at a Georgian restoration, when the two Gothic pointed windows must have been inserted. More restoration in 1876, when the brick vestry and bellcote were added. [A5]

opposite: Flamborough Head and Georgian lighthouse

Old lighthouse, Flamborough

Foston-on-the-Wolds Despite its name, the straggling village is not on the Wolds. Towards the north end is the medieval St Andrew's church with roughcast nave and chancel. The stone tower has battlements, also a feature of the clerestory. At the south end Mill Lane leads to an interesting cluster of houses near Foston Beck, where a brewery and watermill once stood. Goods were transported via the beck, which feeds into the River Hull. Northeast of the village is the hamlet of ***Gembling***, which has a 14-acre (5.7-ha) green, a rarity in East Yorkshire. This great expanse of common land was used to rear large flocks of geese. [B6]

Fraisthorpe Manor Farm on Main Street dates from the 17th century and has Artisan-Mannerist brickwork, including triangular pediments in the gables. Just along the road signed to the beach is the little parish church of St Edmund, rebuilt in 1893, a simple building with undivided nave and chancel, mainly of cobblestone. It commemorates the good works of Mary Simpson, a clergyman's daughter who provided evening classes for local farm servants. The road continues east for more than a mile (1.5 km) to Auburn Farm, which has an interesting courtyard of farm buildings, and nearby is parking for the popular sandy beach. Auburn village lies mostly under the sea, and according to local folklore a distinctive sound made by the waves washing over the ruins gave rise to the strange saying 'Auburn Dolly is sobering'. A Normal font from the church here, demolished in 1731, is at Wragby (West Yorkshire). [B6]

Fridaythorpe At some 575 ft (175 m), this is the highest village on the Wolds. Just off the large green is St Mary's church with its squat Norman tower, made showy by its elaborate black and white clock face by F.C. Eden. This was added in 1903 as part of the restoration of the church by C.H. Fowler for Sir Tatton Sykes, when the north aisle was added, opening up a blocked 13th-century arcade. A delightfully patterned Norman doorway of three orders leads to the charmingly modest interior with simple Norman chancel arch, good stained glass and elaborate carved reredos. What is the meaning of the curious inscription 'this 713 found hear' carved on a pillar? [B3]

Grimston Garth, Garton-in-Holderness

Full Sutton The oldest part, with houses facing a large green, is at the east end of Moor Lane. On the opposite side of the road, hidden from view and reached by a footpath, is St Mary's church, 1840s using old masonry. In 1987 a high-security prison, HMP Full Sutton, was opened on a former RAF base to the south of the village. [B2]

Garton-in-Holderness Distant from the small village, on the Grimston road, is the well cared for St Michael's church, cobble-built as are many in Holderness. Probably 13th century with late 14th-century south arcade and 15th-century windows to south aisle. Also of the 15th century is the font, a screen and the head of a churchyard cross. Grimston Garth (*private*), an enchanting Gothick confection by John Carr, was built close to the sea in the 1780s as a summer retreat for Thomas Grimston of Kilnwick. It consists of a central hexagon within an equilateral triangle with a round tower at each corner. Two service wings to the rear, in the same style, added *c.*1810. Inside on the ground floor a hexagonal dining room, with ornate Gothick detail and great display of heraldry, and a drawing room above of the same shape. A large gatehouse of 1812 guards the entrance to the grounds from the west. [D7]

Garton-on-the-Wolds Garton is best approached from the south, with the church of St Michael and All Angels in an open setting on the edge of the

St Michael and All Angels, Garton-on-the-Wolds

village. An exceptional Norman building with a bold west tower that looks as if it was planned for defence or as a place of refuge. The interior, a great surprise, is one of the most remarkable in any village church. Sir Tatton Sykes, 5th baronet, had every inch of the walls and roofs of the nave and chancel painted in 1873–76 by Clayton & Bell, who also produced the fine series of stained-glass windows. The walls of the nave are covered with stories from the Old Testament; in the chancel they are from the New Testament and the roofs are brightly decorated with floral designs. On the summit of Garton Hill, on the road to Sledmere, is the Sykes Monument, 120 ft (37 m) high, a major landmark in the Yorkshire Wolds. Built in 1865 as a memorial to Sir Tatton Sykes, 4th baronet, who is shown in relief on horseback. [B5]

Goodmanham All Saints' church, on a large mound in the centre of this quiet, secluded village, is probably a successor to a 'heathen' temple destroyed by the high priest Coifi following the conversion to Christianity of King Edwin by Paulinus in 627. The church is largely Norman, including the substantial squat tower, south doorway, chancel arch and north arcade. The chancel is 13th century, the top of the tower and windows on south side of nave 15th century. Carefully restored in the 1890s by Temple Moore, whose work is commemorated in a chancel window. Ornate font of *c.*1530, decorated all over. Opposite is the former Methodist chapel of 1828, the pointed Gothic windows introduced when Francis Johnson incorporated it into the charming All Hallows Cottage in 1964. Behind, hidden away in fine treed grounds, is Hall Garth, a splendid Regency villa by Charles Mountain junior of Hull, built as the rectory. [C4]

Goole England's most inland port, 50 miles (80 km) from the North Sea, is a far more interesting town for the visitor than might be expected. Until 1826 it was little more than a scattering of farmhouses and cottages at the point where the 17th-century Dutch River entered the River Ouse. Following the opening by the Aire and Calder Navigation Company of the Knottingley to Goole Canal, it was transformed into a thriving coal-exporting port. As well as building two docks by 1826, the company had begun laying out a new town based on a plan by Doncaster architects Woodhead & Hurst. Only a third of what had been proposed was built, triangular in shape, with a grid of streets and brick and slate buildings in a uniform style with rounded corners as a distinctive feature. It is a great pity that most of this Georgian planned town was demolished in stages from the late 1960s, leaving only Aire Street, originally the main commercial street, and sections of three lesser streets. Most of the surviving buildings are listed but appear uncared for, except for the grand Lowther Hotel, which has been well restored. The seven-bay, three-storey hotel, built in 1824, was the first permanent building to be completed in the new town. On the first floor the walls of three rooms are covered with murals, some depicting scenes in the port, for which payment was made to a Mr Bromley in 1834. To the north the Royal Hotel has the typical rounded corner, and further down Adam Street the long building with five full-height round-headed blind arches was built as the Literary and Scientific Institute in 1841. It is inscribed 'Public Rooms', and the words 'Theatre Royal', which it became in 1872, can also just be discerned.

Lowther Hotel, Aire Street, Goole

Mural of the docks and warehouses, Lowther Hotel, Goole

Nearby in Cross Street is a two-storey 'lock-up' with slit windows. Also of the early days of the new town is the Anglican Church of St John the Evangelist, a large cruciform building of 1843–48 designed by Hurst & Moffatt of Doncaster for the Aire and Calder Navigation. Rather plain, with large Perpendicular windows; the finest feature is the tall central tower and spire with supporting buttresses. The spire along with the slender brick water tower of 1883 and its slightly taller circular concrete replacement of 1927 dominate the Goole skyline.

The late Victorian–Edwardian era was Goole's heyday, as reflected by the grander buildings in the town centre. These include the Italianate former York City and County Bank (now Wetherspoons), 1880; the police station and former courthouse, 1888, in Queen Anne style; the red-brick Renaissance-style Bank Chambers (now East Riding Council offices), 1892 (the last two by local architect H.B. Thorpe); and the Market Hall of 1896, also with a Renaissance touch. On Boothferry Road the handsome Goole Academy (originally Grammar School), 1909, by Willink & Thicknesse of Liverpool. Goole Museum, above the town's library, has a good display relating to the history of the town and port, and a large collection of paintings by the Goole marine artist Reuben Chappell (1870–1940).

Between 1826 and 1912 nine docks, all interconnected, were constructed along with four locks providing access from the River Ouse. The docks are still very much in use, but can be partly explored via a public footpath that begins just south of the Lowther Hotel. It runs along the right-hand side of the Lowther Swing Bridge with, on the left, the Ouse Dock (originally Steam Boat Dock) and Ouse Lock of 1838, and the longer Victoria Lock, 1888. The path then goes down the side of Ship Dock, 1826, before crossing over the end of Ocean Lock to the south side of Barge Dock, 1826. From here go via Bridge Street to the north

side of the Dutch River, where on South Dock, 1910, is the last remaining 'boat hoist', with its distinctive pepper-pot turret. Cleverly designed to transfer coal directly to ships from canal barge compartment boats known as 'Tom Puddings'.

Alongside is a small lighthouse, originally sited at Trent Falls at the junction of the rivers Trent and Ouse, and a restored mid–late 19th-century hydraulic accumulator tower. Return to the town north along Bridge Street, noting on Railway Dock, 1848, a rare coal wagon hoist built in 1906. [E2]

Goxhill Simple late Georgian church, St Giles', with only a house and farmyard nearby. The stuccoed tower is capped by a pyramidal slate roof that overhangs the eaves, as do the roofs of nave and chancel, giving it an Italianate touch. Oil lamps still light the interior. Some early fittings including a Norman font rescued from the adjacent farmyard, an ornate piscina (basin), a 14th-century canopied monument and a ledger stone to Marmaduke Constable of Wassand, who was buried here in 1690. [C6]

Former maltings, Skerne Road, Great Driffield (drawing by Eugene Fisk)
opposite: Boat hoist and lighthouse, South Dock, Goole

River Head, Great Driffield

Great Driffield The commercial and shopping centre of the Wolds. A good place to start is at All Saints' church, Middle Street North, with its imposing 15th-century tower, 110 ft (34 m) high. The nave is of the early 12th century, with round pillars and arches, and small round-headed windows in the clerestory. The windows of the aisles are of the mid-14th century and those of the chancel 15th century. Restored by George Gilbert Scott junior, 1880, with later additions to the north by his former pupil Temple Moore, who had married the vicar's niece. For the vicar Moore enlarged Beechwood, at the south end of the town, in Queen Anne style, and at the north end, for a Hull merchant, he transformed Highfield from a modest villa into a half-timbered mansion. Near the latter is Moot Hill, the remnant of the motte of an early 13th-century royal castle, and North End Park, the site of the medieval manor house. The stream that runs along the eastern edge of the park continues south through the town, determining the plan of one main street, Middle Street, running north–south, and two parallel lesser streets, Eastgate and Westgate. In the Market Place (the centre section of Middle Street) the chief inn, the Bell, with mid-19th-century stuccoed façade and Doric porch, and nearby the accomplished Neo-Georgian former bank, 1927. No. 41, with striking French Classical stone façade, built for a wholesale grocer in 1865, was designed by William Hawe, the town's most accomplished Victorian architect. Further south is the more restrained Classical façade of No. 51 Market Place, 1856, by Cuthbert Brodrick, who was also responsible for the Gothic school on Cross Hill.

The stream continues to River Head, tucked away at the southern end of the town, a most delightful spot. Here at the head of the Driffield Navigation, opened 1770, is a fine series of late 18th- and early 19th-century warehouses and two mid-19th-century cranes. The opening of the navigation transformed an agricultural village, and centre of hunting and trout fishing for the gentry, into a bustling town trading and processing the produce of the new, improved farms of the region. Just north of River Head is the railway station on the Hull–Bridlington line, opened 1846, which gave a boost to the town's trade and eventually led to the demise of the navigation. Near the station Victorian villas were built on Beverley Road, St John Street and Lockwood Street, the last laid out in the 1870s with semi-detached houses of a 'superior class'. Here the archaeologist and corn merchant John R. Mortimer built a museum (now Masonic Hall) in 1878 to house his finds from the many burial mounds he excavated on the Yorkshire Wolds. On the edge of the town is Driffield showground, the setting for the annual agricultural show, the East Riding's most important farming event, first held 1854. [B5]

Great Givendale A little church (St Ethelburga's) in an idyllic setting on the western edge of the Wolds, overlooking a series of lakes in the valley below. It was rebuilt in 1849 incorporating earlier material. Externally just one range with bell-turret, but inside an impressive Norman arch with zigzag decoration separates the nave and chancel. The churchyard is the burial place of John Singleton, d. 1793, who purchased the Givendale estate after making his fortune as a professional jockey. The 40-mile (64-km) Chalkland Way, a circular walk, passes close by. [B3]

Great Hatfield Small village with splendid medieval cross shaft that has decorative carving on three sides and the figure of a bishop or saint on the fourth. The stepped base has lions on each face. [C6]

Grindale A neat stone church dedicated to St Nicholas, built 1874, a contrast to the brick and chalk buildings that make up this little village. Two early fonts, one a plain Norman tub, the other a crude weathered bowl reputedly from the deserted village of Argam, a mile (1.5 km) or so west, where the church had gone by the early 17th century. [A6]

Halsham Seat of the Constable family before they moved to Burton Constable. At the west end of the scattered settlement earthworks mark the site of their manor house. These lie north of the medieval church of All Saints, in which there is a fine alabaster effigy of a knight, probably Sir John Constable, who died in 1451. Elaborate piscina (basin) and triple sedilia or stone seat, and pulpit dated 1634. In 1802 the bones of members of the Constable family buried in the church were moved to the elegant mausoleum by Thomas Atkinson, which stands across the road, at the end of a yew-lined walk. It took ten years to build this domed Classical temple, but the result was worth the wait. Next to the church is an interesting brick house with crow-stepped gable, built in the 1580s as a grammar school with almshouse below. [D7]

Constable family mausoleum, Halsham

Former grammar school and almshouse, Halsham

Harpham The church is not to be missed. Dedicated to St John of Beverley, who was reputedly born in the village, it has Norman origins but was largely rebuilt in the 14th century, when tower and north chapel were added. The interior is packed with delight. The fittings are Georgian, including west gallery, pulpit, box pews and a large collection of 18th-century painted glass by William Peckitt of York. All but one of the windows commemorate the St Quintin family, who with their descendants have owned much of Harpham since the early 13th century. In the north chapel their numerous memorials include, under a crocketed ogee canopy, a mid-14th-century alabaster tomb-chest with the incised figures of William St Quintin and his wife, and two 15th-century brasses, one the finest in the East Riding. Good wall tablets, and in the chancel a stylish monument to Charlotte St Quintin, d.1762, by Joseph Wilton. St John's Well, east of the village, is decorated on the Tuesday nearest to the saint's feast day (7 May), and a procession takes place from the church. [B6]

Harswell A tiny place alongside the modest River Foulness. Manor House Farm reputedly stands on the site of its medieval predecessor, and alongside it is St Peter's church, rebuilt in 1871. It was designed by Fowler of Louth, who reused the south doorway from the little medieval church that it replaced. Inside a painted roof and an elaborate stone reredos. The latter is in memory of Sir Charles Slingsby of Scriven near Knaresborough, 'a liberal landlord' who accidentally drowned with five others during a hunt in 1869. [C3]

Hayton On the old Roman road (A1079) linking Brough (Petuaria) and York, at a strategic point where the Vale of York and the Wolds meet. Just south is the site of a small Roman fort. St Martin's church with ungainly west tower, the top stage overhanging the rest. Could this really have been deliberate? Good Norman work inside, including many mask-like faces, both animal and human. Nave and chancel have excellent king-post roofs, probably late 16th century. Unfenced churchyard, more like a village green apart from

St Augustine, Hedon from the southeast

Roman Catholic church, Baxtergate, Hedon

the gravestones. Next door is the former rectory, rebuilt in 1858 by the Pocklington architect Thomas Grant. [C3]

Hedon A planned new town established by the Count of Aumale in the early 12th century as a port for Holderness. With access to the Humber, it flourished for a time, having a mint in the 1150s and a royal charter *c.*1170. Competition from Hull, and the silting up of the haven, brought decline, but the town continued to serve the local area as a trading and minor social centre. In the Middle Ages there were three churches, but only one has survived, the magnificent St Augustine's, which dominates the townscape. One of the largest and grandest churches in Yorkshire, the chief reminder of Hedon's early importance. Of the early 13th to early 14th century, except the great Perpendicular crossing tower of *c.*1430. The impressive transepts owe much to G.E. Street's restoration 1868–77. Good interior detail and fine 14th-century font, Elizabethan and early Hanoverian Royal Arms, and plenty of Victorian and later stained glass. To the north of the church is Market Hill, an open green, original site of the market and fairs. On the west side Ivy House, late 18th century, has a remarkable collection in its grounds of architectural fragments from local churches. They were collected by local lawyer James Iveson, who in 1828 placed in Holyrood, off Baxtergate, a tall medieval cross, said to have been erected on Spurn Head to commemorate the landing in 1399 of Henry Bolingbroke, later King Henry IV.

Plenty of good buildings throughout the town, many of them Georgian, including the delightful simple brick and pantile Roman Catholic church (St Mary & St Joseph) on Baxtergate, 1803, and the former Baptist chapel, 1801, on Magdalen Gate. The best houses are on Fletchergate: Old Hall of *c.*1700 and New Hall of the 1730s. The Market Place has on its east side a fine three-storey terrace of 1829. As a borough, with some 200 voters, Hedon returned two MPs until 1832. Henry Guy MP paid for the building of the Town Hall, St Augustine's Gate, in 1693. Impressive staircase with heavy vase-shaped balusters and a council chamber with good pedimented doorcases and furniture. Behind the Town Hall is the excellent small Hedon Museum with permanent and changing exhibitions (*open Wednesdays and Saturdays*). Half a mile (0.8 km) south, by the 18th-century haven, the Haven Arms (formerly the Borough Arms), with interesting plaque showing that it was built by the Hedon Corporation in 1825. [D6]

Hessle Now a large residential town on the edge of Hull, Hessle was until the later 18th century an agricultural village, with some shipbuilding and a ferry across the Humber. Then wealthy Hull merchants began to build country villas here, the earliest and grandest Hesslewood Hall, now a business centre. Built 1784–91 to designs by Charles Mountain senior, for Joseph Pease, the handsome five-bay white-brick house is linked by three-bay wings to pedimented pavilions. Four elegant Regency villas were built on higher ground to the west, but only two, Tranby House and Hessle Mount (both schools), remain. The opening of the Hull–Selby railway line in 1840 led to the development of housing for the middle classes on the pleasant tree-lined streets of Southfield and the Davenport Estate. In the centre, to the north of The Square, is the medieval All Saints' church, with prominent spire, chiefly 13th–15th century but greatly enlarged 1868–71, when the nave was lengthened and the aisles rebuilt. Lots of good Victorian stained glass, the best by Morris & Co., 1899, and numerous monuments, including brass engraved with full-size figure of Anthony Bannister, d.1878, promoter of Withernsea, and bronze plaque with portrait of Frederick Blunt, first Bishop of Hull, 1912.

Hessle's great attraction is the magnificent Humber Bridge, one of the great engineering and architectural triumphs of late 20th-century Britain. Built 1972–81 it was, on opening, at 4,626 ft (1,410 m), the longest single-span suspension bridge in the world. Pedestrian access is via the visitor car park and viewing area off Ferriby Road. On the Humber foreshore, below the bridge, and reached via Cliff Road, is the six-storey tower of a whiting mill associated with the vast former chalk

Humber Bridge from the west, Hessle foreshore

quarry that is now the well-wooded Humber Bridge Country Park. The snow-white quarry face has given rise to the local name Little Switzerland. [D5]

Hilston The village is just a scattering of farms and cottages, but worth the journey to see Francis Johnson's Scandinavian-inspired 1950s church. Given the rural location, it might come as something of a surprise to learn that its Victorian predecessor was destroyed by a stray bomb in 1941. The brick and pantile replacement, funded by the War Damages Commission, sits comfortably in its surroundings. Carnaby Temple (see *Carnaby*) provided the inspiration for the unusual cupola lantern on the tower. Norman stonework reused by the Victorians was salvaged from the bombsite and used to construct the arch around the south door. Johnson designed all the fittings and furnishings, including the delightful wrought-iron communion rails decorated with daisies or marguerites, a reference to St Margaret, to whom the church

St Margaret, Hilston

is dedicated. On a knoll in the flat Holderness landscape north of Hilston stands Admiral Storr's tower, an octagonal brick lookout dated 1750. It was built by Joseph Storr and named after his son Rear Admiral John Storr. [D7]

Hollym The tower of the yellow-brick church of St Nicholas dates from 1814, but the nave and chancel decorated in Victorian fashion with bands of red brick were rebuilt in 1884. The churchyard has a poignant mid-18th-century gravestone to Mary Tock, who probably died giving birth to two unnamed children, also commemorated. Crude but charming carvings of an angel's head and two faces growing out of flowers. Further east along Northside Road is an 18th-century circular pinfold, built of cobbles, where stray animals would have been impounded. [E8]

Holme-on-Spalding Moor Covering some 11,500 acres (4,650 ha), Holme is the largest parish in the East Riding. Spalding Moor was a vast expanse of often waterlogged common land, drained and enclosed in the 1770s. The medieval parish church of All Saints stands alone on the top of Church Hill, some ¾ mile (1.2 km) from the village, forming a prominent landmark in the otherwise flat Vale of York. Largely of the 13th century, with a 14th-century north chapel and lofty 15th-century tower. Lots of interest inside, including a 17th-century pulpit, Georgian west gallery and Royal Arms, and early Victorian box pews. Adjoining the large, unspoilt churchyard is a Roman Catholic burial ground. The Langdales and their successors as lords of the manor from the 1630s were Catholics, and their home, Holme Hall (*private*) can be seen from Church Hill. Built in the 1720s and enlarged in the 1750s and the 19th century, it has a Roman Catholic chapel of 1766 attached.

South of the village, on the Howden Road, is Workhouse Farm, built as the parish workhouse in 1790, with a circular lock-up. At ***Bursea***, 3 miles (nearly 5 km) southeast, a small, well-kept Anglican chapel. Red brick with blue-brick decoration, a surprisingly modest work by William Butterfield, 1872. It cost £350. [D3]

Gravestones: *above:* Hollym
below: Holme-on-Spalding Moor

Holmpton Church of St Nicholas, rebuilt in 1874, when the thick cobble walls of the medieval nave and chancel were encased in yellow and red brick, unmistakably Victorian. The churchyard has a handful of rustic early 18th-century gravestones, uncommon in East Yorkshire. Just south of the village is a former nuclear bunker, built in the 1950s at the height of the Cold War and now a visitor attraction. [E8]

Hook Situated on the eponymous hook of land in a loop on the west side of the River Ouse, just south of Goole. The medieval church, St Mary's, much restored by the Victorians, has an unusual stained-glass window in memory of Queen Victoria, portraying her in a wheelchair and wearing spectacles. One imagines she might not have been amused. Hook Hall at the north end of the village is an imposing brick house built for the Sotheron family in 1743. [E2]

Hornsea Proclaimed as 'Lakeland by the Sea' on early 20th-century railway posters, this popular residential town lies between Hornsea Mere and the North Sea. A favourite destination for visitors from Hull from the early 19th century, but even after the arrival of the railway in 1864, and the building of a short-lived pier in 1880, the town failed to develop fully as a resort. This is evident from the present rather haphazard range of buildings facing the sea, but the immediate seafront, with its well-maintained promenade and accessible and extensive sandy beach, is a great attraction. Inland the town centres on Market Place, with the Old Hall, a mid-17th-century brick manor house with shaped gables, built for the Acklam family. Nearby is the large medieval parish church of St Nicholas, on Newbegin, chiefly built of cobbles collected from the beach, as are several cottages on Southgate and elsewhere in the town. The church tower is 13th century with 14th-century nave arcades and 15th-century east end, lit by large windows throughout. Beneath the chancel is a two-roomed crypt where the early 18th-century parish clerk is reputed to have

Hornsea Mere

Railway poster by Charles W. Loten, decorator and plumber of Hornsea, c.1910

Tiles on Farrago, Wilton Road, Hornsea

kept smuggled goods. Interesting monuments, including medieval figures of a knight, lady and civilian, an alabaster tomb-chest, and one with 17th-century punning rhyme. Good early 20th-century windows by Burlison & Grylls.

Going east from the church, along Newbegin, first the vicarage, a neat late Regency villa set back from the street. Then comes Hornsea Museum, housed in an 18th-century farmhouse and two cottages. Concentrating on rural life, it is the best of the small museums in the East Riding, with much to see including an excellent display of Hornsea Pottery. (The site of the former pottery factory, 1954–2000, south of the town on Rolston Road, is now the Freeport 'outlet shopping village'.) Bettinson's Folly, down the lane opposite the museum, a circular tower of over-burnt bricks, was built in 1844 as a lookout by a Hull brewer.

Further east – past Swiss Terrace, 1840s Swiss-chalet style; Marine Villa, *c.*1810; and the 1870s Gothic URC church with prominent tower – is New Road, developed in the 1860s–1870s by the Hull timber merchant J.A. Wade, who promoted the railway. He owned the brickworks that produced the patent acorn-shaped interlocking tiles that completely cover No. 31 New Road. To the south an estate of large late Victorian houses, including, on Wilton Road, Nos 1–2, exotic rendered façades with tiled panels, and No. 6, Farrago, decorated inside and out in a most eccentric way by its builder, David R. Robinson, 1906–08. Decorative and pictorial tiles cover the walls and floors, some broken and arranged in jumbled patterns comparable to work by Gaudí. On Railway Street, off New Road, the former station, red brick with five-arched porte cochère, 1864 (closed 1964), and alongside the Alexandra Hotel, 1867. Directly west of the town, Hornsea Mere, at 467 acres (189 ha) the largest freshwater lake in Yorkshire, is reached by a track off Southgate. [C7]

Hotham An attractive village with several 18th-century limestone farmhouses and cottages along the main street. The Old Rectory, *c.* 1775, has a hipped Westmorland slate roof instead of the more usual pantiles. Next door is St Oswald's church with its unmistakably Norman west tower, broad but squat, with a zigzag frieze. Nave and rebuilt chancel with red tile roof. Early 19th-century addition to north side to house the first-floor squire's pew, complete with fireplace. Excellent series of stained-glass windows in vibrant colours designed by Douglas Strachan, 1938–45, commissioned by local landowner Thomas Clitherow. His family lived at Hotham Hall (*private*), a fine house of *c.* 1720 with pavilions added in 1772, and a splendid stable block. The west pavilion was replaced by a larger range in 1871. Near the entrance, at the south end of the village, are Victorian estate cottages and an earlier stone one with half-hipped pantile roof, once thatched. The unusual rustic veranda was added in the 19th century to make it more picturesque. Hotham Hall is surrounded by extensive parkland with a serpentine lake, a feature also found in the landscaped grounds of Hotham House (*private*) further north. [D4]

Howden 'Howden is a very pretty town, there being many fine houses in it, and a pretty church,' wrote the diarist and antiquary Abraham de la Pryme in 1685. It was a thriving market town until the early–mid-19th century, when it suffered by the rise of Goole. Decline left it in 'pleasing decay', and helped to preserve many of its Georgian buildings and its captivating townscape of winding streets and narrow alleyways. These are now appreciated, and the town is experiencing greater prosperity.

Stained glass by Douglas Strachan, St Oswald, Hotham

Howden Minster, with its majestic 135-ft-high (41 m) tower and green copper roof, is a landmark for many miles, especially from the M62. In 1086–87 the church and manor of Howden were granted to the Bishop of Durham, who shortly afterwards gave the church to Durham Priory. It was made a collegiate church, governed by a chapter of canons, in 1267, and rebuilding began: the transepts, central crossing and first bay of the nave *c.* 1270, the rest of the nave *c.* 1310, the choir completed *c.* 1320. The superb octagonal chapter house was added to the south side of the choir in the 1380s, the great tower *c.* 1430, and finally the two-storey Grammar

School on the south side of the nave *c.*1500. After the Reformation the choir was abandoned; the roof collapsed in 1696, and that of the chapter house in 1750, leaving the present dramatic ruin (*English Heritage, not open to public*). Enter the church at the splendid west end, into an impressive nave with six-bay arcade and a clerestory with inner wall passage, large geometrical-style windows throughout. Plenty of Victorian and 20th-century stained glass. Heraldic glass of the 1840s in the south aisle and also in the Saltmarshe chapel, which has a fine series of monuments to the Metham and Saltmarshe families, from the early 14th to 20th century. The earliest a knight and lady in a recess with ogee gable and effigy of a knight on a tomb-chest. Coffin lid of Frosterley marble to Walter Kirkham, Bishop of Durham, who died here in 1260. Outside along the west and north sides a series of sculptures by John Maine 2002–08 echoing the round Norman pillars in Durham Cathedral. Southeast of the church is the remnant of the Bishop of Durham's manor house. Many of the prince bishops on their journeys between London and Durham stayed here, among them Bishop Walter Skirlaw, d.1405, who rebuilt the house. What survives is the great hall, originally open to the roof with three large Perpendicular windows to full height on each side. A private house from the late 17th century, more recently an events venue. Its former grounds with moat and fishponds became the Ashes Playing Field in the 1920s.

A walk round Howden is very rewarding. Start at the Market Place, dominated by the rather ambitious Shire Hall of 1872 by Hadfield & Sons. A Low Countries town hall, with large stepped gable and corner clock tower, which once had a short spire. Follow the narrow, winding Vicar Lane through to St Helen's Square, which has an elaborate 'Art Nouveau Gothic' war memorial cross by Clement W. Jewitt, 1920. Then along Bridgegate past the large 19th-century Bowman's and Wellington hotels, formerly at their busiest during the famous September horse fair. After the fair in 1823 a young Howden stable boy, Thomas Ward, delivered a horse to Vienna for the Count of Liechtenstein. This set Ward on a path that led to him becoming a Baron of the Austrian Empire and Chief Minister of the Duchy of Parma. Continue along Bridgegate, where the tall nine-bay terrace and Bridgegate House, a fine six-bay brick and pantile town house, are of the mid–late 18th century. Then, in contrast, the large northern headquarters of the Press Association, 2003, quite a surprise. The central block, stone-faced, has a restrained 1930s Classical feel with vaguely Neo-Georgian flanking buildings of red brick. Further east, behind a high wall on Flatgate, is Howden Hall of *c.*1700.

right: Bishop of Durham's Manor House, Howden (drawing by Eugene Fisk)
opposite: Tower through east window of ruined choir, Howden Minster

Back along Bridgegate, left down Bishopgate, developed in the 1830s, and right into Hailgate, glimpsing to the left Hailgate House, 1840s, with a pedimented Greek Doric porch. Round the corner an attractive pair of grey-brick houses, built for Wesleyan Methodist ministers in 1837. Rudyard Kipling's grandfather was one of the early residents. Opposite is No. 78 Hailgate, a three-storey late 18th-century house where the novelist Nevil Shute lodged when working at Howden Airship Station, helping Barnes Wallis to build the R100. Then, on the left, Highbridge House, once a fine house of *c.* 1700; conversion to a cinema, then offices, has destroyed many of its features. The street continues south with more pleasing Georgian buildings, one with pretty bow windows, to Treeton Road. Here is Lockwood's neat Italianate police station of 1843, and nearby a Roman Catholic church, in late 13th-century style, by J.A. Hansom, 1852. Back to the town centre via Pinfold Street. [D2]

Huggate A small village high on the Wolds, with steep-sided dry valleys to the north and east, and prehistoric earthworks spread across the parish. Most amazing are the multi-ditched and banked Huggate Dykes. The early 14th-century spire of St Mary's church is quite a landmark. The church has a Norman nave and aisles with round pillars, a Norman chancel arch, and an early 15th-century clerestory. [B3]

Humbleton At the end of a shady lane, past the Gothick vicarage, stands the fine medieval church, St Peter's, light and spacious, with wide clerestoried nave. Inside, an unusual semicircular stair-turret projects into the nave and reappears high up in the tower. The pretty Church Cottage (former school and schoolhouse) next to the churchyard was built in 1830 by the Hotham family, as were the Victorian estate cottages at the south end of the village. On Fitling Road

David Hockney, 'Huggate, St. Mary's Church Spire, August 2005' © David Hockney

stands Humbleton Hall, an elegant Regency villa with broad, gently curving two-storey bow windows. [D7]

Hutton Cranswick It is made up of two settlements, Cranswick to the south with a very large village green, no doubt the site of the medieval market and fairs, and the smaller Hutton, ½ mile (0.8 km) to the north, with the parish church of St Peter. Norman in origin, as shown by the restored south doorway and beakheads over the south aisle windows, but the arcades are 13th century and the west tower 15th century. Cranswick has the buildings of a typical Victorian open village: pubs, shops, a Board school, a friendly society hall and a handsome Methodist church of 1861. Small railway station, a neat Italianate work by G.T. Andrews, 1846. [B5]

Keyingham A large Holderness village, one that grew in the 1960s–70s. On Main Street is a former meeting hall with cottages below built 1857 by the Ancient Order of Foresters friendly society. Note the elaborate plaque. Such organizations provided sickness and funeral benefits for their members before National Insurance was introduced, and their annual feast days were the great social event in village communities. Church of St Nicholas with Norman origins, to which nave aisles and tower were added in the late 13th century. Much rebuilding done after 1392, when the church was severely damaged by lightning. The broach spire added to the tower at that time was removed in 1969. Inside, an iron stand for an hourglass, once used to time the sermon, and a monument to John Angel, 1647, a member of the family who owned Spurn Head and built a lighthouse there. [E7]

Kilham More than a mile (1.5 km) in length, with the large church of All Saints on a raised site midway between the two 'ends'. Impressive south doorway with six orders of zigzag, unmistakably Norman. So too is the wide nave, although the pointed windows with Gothick glazing bars are, of course, Georgian. Fine chancel, the features all suggesting a late 13th-century date. In the churchyard a stone block with tethering ring, a grim reminder of bull-baiting. Medieval Kilham served a large rural hinterland, and kept its weekly market until the later 18th century, when trade was lost to nearby Driffield, which now had the advantage of a canal. Plenty of good houses, the most stylish of which is Hall Farm on East Street, brick with pilasters and stone dressings, helpfully dated 1716. It was built for Robert Thompson, a gentleman whose brother Jonas was Lord Mayor of York, which perhaps accounts for its sophisticated design. [A5]

Kilnsea and Spurn Aside from the caravan sites, Kilnsea is little more than a straggle of cottages, a pub and a small redundant Victorian church (St Helen's), an early work by William Burges, built to replace one washed into the sea in 1831 – the fate of much of the old village. A stone cross, apparently erected to mark the future Henry IV's landing at Spurn Head, was removed before it too was swept away, and is now in a garden at Hedon. The most unusual feature, in a field near the sea, is a concrete acoustical sound mirror, an early-warning system dating from the First World War.

The great attraction is the Spurn peninsula (now a nature reserve of national importance: ywt.co.uk), the long, curving spit of sand and shingle that reaches like a giant tongue into the Humber estuary.

First World War sound mirror, Kilnsea

Kilnwick Percy Hall | *previous:* Spurn Point, looking north from the lighthouse

At the Kilnsea end is the Yorkshire Wildlife Trust visitor centre, opened 2018, an imaginative building with flood-resilient lower floor and timber with glass panels above. From here it is about 3½ miles (5.5 km) to Spurn Point, one of the most atmospheric spots in Yorkshire. The spit has been breached on numerous occasions, and the point, with its stripy lighthouse of 1895, can now be reached only on foot or by a special 'safari' vehicle. This was the site of Ravenser Odd, a short-lived town given a royal charter in 1299 but destroyed by the sea before the end of the 14th century. The sinister wedding-cake-shaped structure in the Humber estuary is Bull Sand Fort, constructed in 1915 for defence purposes. [E8]

Kilnwick In the late 1830s the squire, Charles Grimston, 'improved the appearance of the village, by taking down the ancient thatched and stud and mud cottages, and erecting in their stead neat, brick and tile dwellings, with small gardens'. The ten semi-detached pairs then built remain, although most have been altered. At the west end, All Saints' church, largely rebuilt in 1871, retains its earlier tower. The upper two thirds are brick, possibly late 17th century. The north doorway, reset, is Norman, and the north arcade with round pillars early 13th century. Rather fine 17th-century pulpit once in Beverley Minster. Hatchments and wall tablets to members of the Grimston family, whose home, Kilnwick Hall, was demolished in 1952 except for a substantial 17th-century range. John Carr, who altered the hall, probably designed the distinctive Townend Farm with its blank-arched façade and detached pavilions. [C5]

Kilnwick Percy Driving up to the Wolds from Pockington, there is a tantalising distant view of Kilnwick Percy Hall, set in parkland, above a lake, with only a small church for company. The village disappeared in the late 16th century. The Elizabethan hall (now a Buddhist centre) was transformed in two stages in the 18th century and then greatly enlarged in the 1840s, when the gigantic Ionic portico was added. After the Second World War the rear half of the house was demolished. St Helen's church, now redundant, was rebuilt with some success in 1865 in the Norman style of its predecessor, using some original stonework. The corbels on the north and south walls, featuring animal masks and human heads, are good copies. Inside are memorials to the Anderson family, 18th-century squires, and a brass inscription that recounts the life of Thomas Wood, d.1584, who 'buylt thowse hereby to this churche'. [C3]

Kirby Underdale An estate village of the Lords Halifax of Garrowby Hall. Manor House of *c.*1700, U-shaped with hipped roof, and opposite the Old Rectory, where Connop Thirlwall wrote his celebrated *History of Greece* in the 1830s. All Saints' church, wonderfully sited on a sloping hillside above a small stream, is largely of the 12th century, restored in the 1870s by G.E. Street, who rebuilt the chancel. Rich Anglo-Catholic interior with rood beam by Temple Moore and Victorian and 20th-century stained glass by Hardman, Burlison & Grylls, Ninian Comper and F.C. Eden. Here also a flag captured at the Battle of Camperdown, 1797. Above the church is the burial ground of the Halifaxes. The early 19th-century Painsthorpe Hall, ½ mile (0.8 km) east, was an Anglican Benedictine monastery for four years up to 1906, when the monks left to found Caldey Abbey, South Wales. At the foot of Garrowby Hill, on the A166, is a distinctive black and yellow AA Box (No. 573), now listed. [B3]

Kirkburn An exceptional Norman church, St Mary's, in a large churchyard backing on to a small but deep valley through which flows the 'burn' that gave the village its name. Built *c.*1120–40 by Guisborough Priory, there are lots of original corbels on nave and chancel, and a spectacular south doorway, carved with beakheads, zigzags,

Norman capitals, south doorway, Kirkburn

spirals, beasts and other figures. Inside, a simple aisleless nave with intriguing open stone staircase to tower, and an entertaining Norman font covered with rustic carvings, including a cat and mouse. The chancel, sympathetically rebuilt by J.L. Pearson in the 1850s, was lavishly fitted out by G.E. Street for Sir Tatton Sykes in the 1870s with a richly carved and painted screen and marble reredos. The village has pairs of Sledmere estate cottages and a former school paid for by Lady Sykes, 1860. [B4]

Kirk Ella Suburban village where in the late Georgian period 'several of the wealthy merchants of Hull' had 'elegant places of residence'. The grandest to survive, Kirk Ella Hall (Hull Golf Club), late 18th century, stands in large grounds west of the village, with others along Church Lane. Opposite the church a Tudor-style former vicarage of 1839 by H.F. Lockwood. St Andrew's church, mostly early 13th century with 15th-century west tower, thoroughly restored, is packed with memorials to members of Hull's merchant gentry families. Unmissable is that to Joseph Sykes of West Ella, d. 1805, who is shown rising out of his coffin among shattered rocks, with below the figure of Commerce and bales, tools, etc. [D5]

Old Hall, Knedlington

Knedlington Just west of Howden stands Knedlington Old Hall, an exceptional 17th-century brick manor house. South front of three storeys and two broad bays, each with an elaborately shaped gable with stone coping. Stone quoins and mullioned windows throughout. Inside, some contemporary oak panelling and chimneypiece. Fine pair of 17th-century gate piers. [D2]

Langtoft Sited at the junction of four steep-sided valleys, Langtoft, with its numerous chalkstone buildings, has suffered more than once from disastrous floods. St Peter's church stands on a hillside above the village. Largely 13th century including the tower, it underwent a major, and successful, restoration by C. Hodgson Fowler for Sir Tatton Sykes in 1900–03. Excellent stained glass, by Kempe & Co. (look for the wheatsheaf and tower symbol) in the chancel and in the aisles by Burlison & Grylls. The marvellous Norman font, crudely carved with figures of Adam and Eve, the Tree of Life, and the martyrdom of saints, including St Margaret being eaten by a dragon, came from the abandoned church at the deserted village of Cottam. [A5]

Laxton Churchyard with chancel of a medieval church including good 14th-century east window. The rest was rebuilt *c.* 1770, then demolished a century later to build a new church (St Peter's), on the opposite side of the road. Stone and tile, with prominent buttresses, generously sized nave with small double bellcote. Much stained glass by Knowles of York. Of the older brick and pantile houses the most distinctive is Hall Farm, early 18th century, with pilasters either side of the central bay. The rear staircase wing is typical of this part of the riding. [E3]

Leconfield In the Middle Ages the Percys, Earls of Northumberland, had a great house here. Only the extensive moated site remains. The sites of two of the three vast deer parks associated with their 'castle' are covered by a former RAF base, which is now home to the Defence School of Transport. The Percys had their own chapel, which perhaps explains why St Catherine's church is not grander. Of many dates, the exterior is a jumble of limestone, brick and chalk. Tower and south porch (with 1684 datestone) both brick. Inside, the earliest feature is the remnant of a pre-Conquest window in the south aisle. Fragments of medieval stained glass, some of it heraldic. Set back in grounds opposite the church is the well-restored Manor House, a late 18th-century house that was derelict for many years.

St Martin's chapel at Normandy Barracks, converted from an old wooden parachute packing shed, has a good series of 1930s stained-glass windows and reredos by Martin Travers, brought here from Longmoor in Hampshire when the Defence School of Transport relocated. [C5]

Leven Of the medieval church, St Faith's, only the graveyard survives. The site is near Hall Garth, an 18th-century farmhouse on Carr Lane, a mile (1.5 km) or so west, beyond Little Leven. That church was replaced in 1845 by the present one, dedicated to the Holy Trinity, in the village centre; it has

White Cross Cottage, Leven

a font and some early fragments of sculpture, including a splendid 15th-century cross head, from its predecessor. The greatly expanded village has a couple of buildings worth mentioning. New Inn on South Street must have come soon after 1802, when the nearby 3-mile (4.8-km) Leven Canal, now disused, was cut to link with the River Hull. Canal House, built at the head of the canal around the same time, was made grander in 1967, when the projecting bay with mid-18th-century pedimented doorcase from High Street, Hull, was added. West of the village, by the roundabout on the Beverley to Hornsea Road, is the castellated White Cross Cottage. It was built *c.*1800 by the owner of Riston Grange in the adjoining parish, and is sometimes mistaken for a toll-keeper's house. All that remains of the medieval cross for which it is named is the base with replacement shaft. [C6]

Lissett Approach Lissett from the northwest, via Gransmoor Road, and be prepared for a ghostly sight, especially in the twilight. The silhouettes of seven airmen, more than life-size, suddenly come into view, eerily realistic. This is the memorial to RAF 158 Bomber Squadron, stationed here during the Second World War. The evocative steel sculpture was commissioned from the local artist Peter Naylor in association with a wind farm developed on the former airfield in 2008. Twelve turbines dominate the skyline. The scattering of buildings that make up the village include the small church of St James, heavily restored in 1876 but with a certain charm. Rendered, with some brick and cobble exposed, a red-tiled roof and double bellcote. The white-painted wooden porch, also tiled, wouldn't look out of place in an Edwardian suburb. [B6]

Little Driffield The site of Driffield's four annual fairs. There was an Anglo-Saxon church here, the reputed burial place of Aldfrith, King of Northumbria, who died 'on Driffelda' in 705, of which nothing remains except fragments of a cross. The lower part of the tower of the present church (St Mary's, formerly St Peter's) is Norman, the top part 14th century. The rest of the building was sympathetically restored by Temple Moore, who is said to have 'converted the hideous low-backed deformity into an elegant Gothic edifice'. His are the charming Jacobean-style pews. The wall tablet to Viscountess Downe, d.1812, notes 'For her character and other particulars see *The Gentleman's Magazine* May MDCCCXII', and is identical to one in York Minster. In the parish stood the historically and architecturally important Elmswell Old Hall, built by Henry Best, author of a famous 17th-century farming book, until it was tragically and ruthlessly reduced to a distressing ruin in the 21st century. [B5]

Lockington A stream runs along Front Street, which has wide grass verges on which sheep occasionally graze. From the early 18th century the main landowners here were the Hothams of South Dalton. Initially they rebuilt cottages in a local vernacular style, recycling old materials, but pattern-book designs were adopted for the pairs of houses that came in the later 19th century.

St Mary, Lockington

Steps and urns at site of Londesborough Hall

Standing at the southern edge of the village, St Mary's church is an odd-looking but fascinating building. A low nave with Norman south doorway, and a much taller chancel, 13th century (heightened in the 1890s), with south chapel added in the 14th century. The stonework is much patched with brick, which was also used to rebuild the squat tower. Delightful interior thanks to sympathetic restoration by Temple Moore. In the south chapel is a monument to Mary Moyser, who died in 1633 and is now condemned to lie eternally on her side, propped up on one elbow, her hand resting on a skull. The chapel walls are panelled and painted with 173 heraldic shields recording the ancestry and connections of the Estoft family. The small manor house called Hall Garth, built 1685, alone in fields to the south of the church, has the Estoft arms over the door. [C5]

Londesborough A 'paradise on earth' was how the Duchess of York, wife of the future James II, described Londesborough after a visit in 1665. In many ways it remains a paradise, a tranquil place, rich in history, in a delightful setting in the Wolds. All around are reminders of the three great families who made their home here:

the Cliffords, Earls of Cumberland; the Boyles, Earls of Burlington; and the Denisons, Earls of Londesborough. During the Cliffords' time in the late 16th–early 17th century it was one of the greatest households in the north of England, a leading cultural centre with frequent visits from groups of actors, musicians and dancers. The architect and great patron of the arts Richard, 3rd Earl of Burlington, spent part of every year in seclusion here, when among his regular guests was the playwright and actor David Garrick. Much later the Londesboroughs entertained Edward VII, when Prince of Wales and king, on numerous occasions, and Osbert Sitwell, grandson of the 1st Earl, has an amusing account of family visits here.

The Elizabethan house, enlarged in the late 17th century, was demolished in 1818 by the Duke of Devonshire. An open area of grassland, with four urn-topped plinths above broad steps, marks the site of the house, a moving and romantic spot. It looks across an important early 18th-century landscape (*private*), with formal and informal elements. The Wolds Way crosses the park. The present Victorian hall, Londesborough Park, part Tudor, part Scottish Baronial, lies hidden away among the trees to the east of the village. On Top Street are pairs of late Victorian estate cottages with the cipher of the Lords Londesborough, and the large Concert Room, built as a laundry for one of the visits of the Prince of Wales. The buildings on Low Street are older. At the west end are charming almshouses, built 1678, the same year as the stables at the other end of the street, part of which remain. In the centre, set back, is the Georgian former rectory, and opposite is the medieval church of All Saints. Unusually for an estate village, the church was not rebuilt, or over-restored, in the 19th century. Above the simple Norman entrance doorway an Anglo-Scandinavian cross head. Early 13th-century north aisle and tower, except the top stage, which is 15th century, as is the large window on the south side of the nave. The funeral helms and, on the north aisle wall, the rare banners, were carried at the funeral of the 1st Earl of Burlington in 1698. Nearby are nine coffin plates taken from the Burlington family vault, and in the side chapel early 17th-century monuments to Grisold, Countess of Cumberland, and her infant grandson. In the churchyard a pyramidal tomb commemorating Thomas Knowlton, the celebrated botanist, d.1781, who was estate gardener here for 55 years. [C3]

Long Riston Cobblestone church (St Margaret's) in fields at the north end, heavily restored in the 1850s. Facing each other at the opposite end of the village are two early 19th-century farmhouses of near-identical symmetrical design, Burton Cottage and Ivy House. They were probably built by the Bethells of Rise, as were several cottages here, including the brick terrace of four named School Row, dated 1871. The Tudor hoodmoulds over the doors and windows and the generous front gardens are typical features of Victorian estate housing. [C6]

Lowthorpe The former chancel of St Martin's church is roofless and in ruins. It was built in the 14th century, when the church was made collegiate, served by a rector and several chantry priests. The college was dissolved at the Reformation, and the chancel gradually fell into disrepair. It was finally abandoned in the 18th century. In the nave of the church is a most curious monument, 14th century in style, possibly commemorating Sir John Heslerton, who founded the college at Lowthorpe. Two life-size effigies side by side, one male, one female.

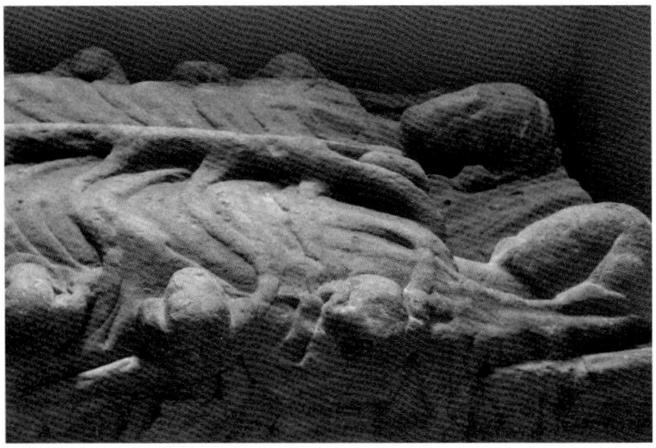

14th-century monument, St Martin, Lowthorpe
opposite: Manor House gateway, Lund

They are covered by a sheet, over which is laid a stylised tree with branches terminating in thirteen small heads. Churchyard cross to the east of the ruined chancel, said to have come from the market village of Kilham. [B5]

Lund A quintessential East Yorkshire village. In the centre a small green with old pump and stone cross, flanked by cottages, early 19th-century inn and former smithy. On the road to the west a mounting block has an iron plate giving the distances to Beverley and Malton, indicating that this is the old turnpike road. It stands in front of Ivy House, an unspoilt mid-18th-century brick and pantile farmhouse. On a slight rise north of the green is All Saints' church with its medieval tower, the only part not rebuilt by the Victorians. Inside the monuments include two late 14th-century alabaster effigies from a tomb-chest, thought to be of a husband and wife. The woman is holding her heart. Near the church is the 18th-century manor house, reputedly built using materials from its predecessor that belonged to the Remington family, whose descendants in America became well-known as manufacturers of rifles and typewriters. The entrance is on Lockington Road, through a fine 17th-century stone gateway. [C4]

Mappleton For years the soft mud cliffs of the Holderness coast have been falling into the sea at an alarming rate. Sea defences built at Mappleton in 1991, using massive granite boulders brought from Norway, have helped to protect the small village, although at a cost to the area to the south, where erosion has increased. A wide concrete pathway near the public car park provides easy access to the beach. All Saints' church, largely rebuilt in stone and cobble in 1856, has a prominent spire, a useful marker for sea vessels. [C7]

Market Weighton A compact little Georgian market town, given new life since it was bypassed, and well worth exploring. A natural trading centre, where the main road across the Wolds

from Hull and Beverley to York met the Roman road from Brough and the Humber, below the steep Arras Hill. Particularly prosperous in the late 18th and early 19th century, in part owing to the opening of a canal, with a weekly corn market and the greatest sheep fair in the north of England. In the early 1790s it was said that in the past twenty years 'a number of elegant buildings have been raised by spirited individuals and considerable improvements are daily making so that the town now begins to assume an air of neatness and convenience united.' Many late Georgian buildings survive on Market Place and High Street, the grandest being the red-brick Londesborough Arms, elegant, five bays, three storeys, a coaching inn built for the Duke of Devonshire about 1780, possibly by John Carr. At the west end, tucked away through an arched entrance to the left of the imposing Italianate Victorian Methodist church, is its humbler predecessor (the oldest Methodist chapel in the East Riding), a neat hipped-roofed building of 1786.

All Saints' church is largely hidden from view by a row of buildings on the north side of Market Place, which probably began as stalls erected on the churchyard. The church is 11th century in origin – as can be seen by a section of herringbone masonry – but mainly 13th century, with the north arcade of the nave early 14th century and the south arcade late 14th century. The top of the tower was rebuilt in brick in 1785, when the spire was removed. Inside are a fine George IV Royal Arms and numerous wall tablets, including one erected by the Venezuelan government to Market Weighton-born Sarah Andrews (1774–1847), the 'wife' of General Francisco de Miranda, Independence pioneer. Another is to the long-serving vicar Revd George Skelding, d.1819, tutor of the celebrated lesbian diarist Anne Lister 'Gentleman Jack', whose family home was on a farm in the parish for over twenty years. 'Giant' William Bradley, d.1820, the town's most famous son, has a plaque which records that he was 7 ft 9 in. (2.4 m) tall and weighed 27 stone (172 kg).

The Green, Market Weighton (drawing by Eugene Fisk)

Londesborough Arms, Market Weighton.

He is also commemorated by a large wooden statue near his home at the west end of Market Place.

Northeast from the churchyard St Helen's Square leads past Red House, a good early 19th-century farmhouse, and a former mill house with stream and millpond, to the Green, a delightful backwater. On the eastern side is the late 18th-century Manor House, and further south on Finkle Street the elegant Tryste House, dated 1791 on rainwater heads, the entrance flanked by Venetian windows. [C3]

Melbourne A village that grew after enclosure of its open fields in 1782 and the opening of the Pocklington Canal in 1818; Thornton Lock and the charming Church Bridge are in the parish. (Short canal trips are run from Melbourne on Sundays and Bank Holidays.) On the main street are some good Georgian farmhouses and two delightful early Methodist chapels: the Wesleyan, 1811, with Gothic pointed windows; and the former Primitive, 1821, with round-arched windows. Tucked away among modern housing is the unforgettable former church of St Monica. Of corrugated iron, made by the Windsor Iron Works, 1882, it looks as if it should be in the Australian outback. Now a house, it remains a great delight. [C2]

Middleton-on-the-Wolds The village grew rapidly in the second half of the 20th century. Older houses towards the centre, including one converted from a group of early 18th-century chalkstone cottages overlooking a small pond. St Andrew's church is chiefly a rebuilding of 1874, but the early 13th-century chancel survives and there is an excellent Norman font. Four early medieval grave slabs in the churchyard reputedly came from the deserted village of Kiplingcotes, its site near Kipling House Farm, at the west end of the parish. Not far away is the finishing post for the Kiplingcotes Derby, a 4-mile (6.5-km) race run annually on the third Thursday in March. The race was endowed in 1669 (not 1519, as is often stated), but there are references to horse racing here in the mid-16th century. [C4]

Millington Picturesque setting on the edge of the Wolds escarpment. The small village with 18th-century inn is a favourite stop for ramblers. Homely country church (St Margaret's), long and low, with Norman nave and slightly later chancel. A tiny brick tower was added in 1824, the base of

St Monica, Melbourne, before conversion to a house

which is visible behind the west gallery, another late Georgian addition. Excellent stained-glass window by Tom Denny, 2007. To the north of the village is one of the few remaining wooded dales in the Yorkshire Wolds, Millington Wood, a local nature reserve with a small car park. In spring the ancient ash wood is full of bluebells. [B3]

Nafferton A big village at the foot of the Yorkshire Wolds, on the Hull to Scarborough railway line. Several quite modest 18th-century brick and pantile houses have datestones with the owners' initials, a sign that this was a settlement with a number of independent freeholders. Most of the larger houses date from the 19th century, including, on Nethergate, Nether Hall of *c.*1860. It replaced a medieval manor house of which the large moat survives. On a raised site at the centre of Nafferton, where four roads meet, is the medieval church of All Saints, with tall 15th-century tower, Norman font with unusual loop and trellis design, and early 19th-century box pews. Equally prominent is the mere – really a large millpond – into which flows Nafferton Beck. The view across the great expanse of water changed dramatically when the associated watermill and maltings were demolished in the 1980s and houses built on the site. [B5]

Newbald A rectangular green, where a weekly market would have been held in the Middle Ages, is at the centre of this attractive village, where the older houses are of the locally quarried creamy limestone. The outstanding Norman church of St Nicholas lies southwest of the green. Cruciform with a central tower and transepts, it was probably built *c.*1140, when the manor and church were owned by canons of York Minster. Entered through a Romanesque doorway on the south side, above which is a seated figure of Christ, the nave is aisleless, and dimly lit by small round-headed windows. The 15th-century chancel has large Perpendicular windows. In between is the showpiece, the crossing, with its four fine Norman arches. Early 19th-century memorial to Sir Philip Monckton, d.1679, a leading royalist army officer during the English Civil Wars. [D4]

Newport An industrial settlement created in the late 1770s on the former great waterlogged common of Wallingfen, after it had been drained and enclosed. Newport was established where the Market Weighton Canal met the Cave causeway, the main route from Hull to the West Riding. Here, on digging the canal, excellent brickmaking clay was found, brickworks were built and by 1851 the population was approaching 800. Set back off the main road, in a secluded burial ground, is a rare unspoilt early Methodist chapel, 1812, a delightful two-storey brick building with pyramidal pantile roof and pointed windows with Gothic glazing bars. Inside, the original three-sided gallery survives, with its high-sided pews and rows of hat pegs. It is a great contrast to the urban-scale Anglican church, St Stephen's, built to the west of the village in 1898. Of local yellow brick, it was designed by Smith, Brodrick & Lowther of Hull, who were also responsible for the large former vicarage alongside. [D3]

St Nicholas, Newbald

Interior of Methodist chapel, Newport (drawing by Eugene Fisk)

Newton-on-Derwent A mile (1.5 km) east of the river from which it takes part of its name. Farmhouses and cottages line one long street. [C2]

North Cave A large village along three parallel streets, with a good mixture of late 18th- and 19th-century houses, many constructed from the local oolitic limestone. Also of the local stone is All Saints' church, standing prominently at the east end of the village. Described as 'new built' in 1318, it is largely late 13th–early 14th century, although the lower part of the tower is Norman, and the top 15th century. The windows in the nave and the prominent south transept have simple Y-tracery. Lots of excellent stained glass by some of the leading late Victorian and early 20th-century designers. Of particular note are the Arts and Crafts east window in the south transept by Robert Anning Bell, 1901, and the striking east window by Douglas Strachan, 1949. Two Jacobean alabaster figures to members of the Metham family who lived in the adjacent North Cave Hall, long demolished. The present Manor House, an attractive limestone and pantile farmhouse with pretty octagonal dovecote, may have been constructed from part of the hall. North Cave Wetlands nature reserve *(Yorkshire Wildlife Trust)*, northwest of the village, was created from a large sand and gravel quarry. [D4]

North Cliffe Samuel Fox from Stocksbridge, Sheffield, whose fortune came from the invention and manufacture of the modern steel-ribbed umbrella, bought the North Cliffe estate in 1861. Soon afterwards he built the handful of grey-brick estate cottages that make up the hamlet, and in 1873 he paid for the simple stone church, St John's, with tiled roof and squat bell-turret. Half a mile (0.8 km) to the west, off Sand Land, is Cliffe Lodge, built for Fox himself, a modest but interesting house in a mixture of styles. Close by is North Cliffe Wood nature reserve (*Yorkshire Wildlife Trust*), which is carpeted with bluebells in springtime. [D3]

North Dalton All Saints' church is on a raised site at the south end of the village, opposite the large pond. The earliest parts are Norman, including the splendid south doorway, with bold zigzag decoration and delightful capitals. East window with Crucifixion scene by Morris & Co., designed by Burne-Jones. The present Manor House, south of the church, is Georgian but the entrance is marked by a good pair of late 17th-century gate piers. Most of the village houses, including some unspoilt cottages, are on Main Street. At the west end a Victorian school stands on an island site opposite the former Wesleyan chapel, both now private dwellings. [B4]

North Ferriby Its name refers to a ferry that crossed the Humber to South Ferriby, North Lincolnshire. Three Bronze Age boats have been discovered here. From the late 17th century it was a favourite place for merchants from Hull to live, or spend the summer, 'free from the noise and hurry of the town'. Three of their grand Georgian mansions survive, the best Ferriby House. A plan for villas for 'families of the first respectability' after the opening of the railway in 1840 was not implemented, but from the 1890s grand houses were built on the higher ground to the north, and the sale of the main estate in 1904 released land for development within the village. All Saints' church, with its distinctive spire, designed by J.L. Pearson, dates from 1848, replacing a medieval building. First-rate monument to Capt. Luke Lillingstone, d.1713, who accompanied William III to England in 1688, and his Dutch-born wife. He in armour, kneeling and turning to her, she praying and looking up. [E4]

North Frodingham Long village street with restored market cross, a weekly market having taken place until the late 18th century. The church lies ½ mile (0.8 km) to the west, and has a unique dedication to St Elgin, perhaps an error since it was recorded as St Helen's in the 16th century. Cobblestone nave and chancel with pantile roof, mainly from a restoration of 1878, but the stone tower is medieval, although the top part was rebuilt in the late 19th century. Inside, a remarkable Anglo-Saxon shaft and cross head. Church End Farmhouse, the former rectory house, is dated 1619. The massive external brick stacks are probably of that date, although parts of the building are stone and may be medieval. [B6]

Nunburnholme This small Wolds village nestles in a valley below Bratt Wood. To the northeast the site of a small Benedictine nunnery that gave the settlement the first part of its name. The parish church of St James, at the southern edge of the village, has a Norman nave, early 13th-century chancel, and a west tower rebuilt by Temple Moore, 1902, in an early 14th-century style. The interior has a spectacular Norman tower arch and under the tower an elaborate Anglo-Scandinavian cross shaft, dating from the late 9th or early 10th century. Possibly the gift of the warrior who is shown seated with a sword, the cross has both Christian and Viking features. The adjacent Old Rectory was the home for nearly forty years of the naturalist Revd Francis Orpen Morris (1810–93), author of a six-volume *History of British Birds* and many other works, and a pioneer in the campaign for the protection of wild birds. [C3]

Nunkeeling Not very much to see, but a site of historic interest. As the name suggests, there was a house of Benedictine nuns here from 1152 until the Dissolution. Manor House Farm, probably late 17th century, incorporates some stonework, including a buttress, from the nuns' priory. Their church was demolished, but the adjoining parish church, dedicated to St Mary and St Helena, survived. It was rebuilt in 1810, but for decades has been a roofless ruin, with anything of value moved elsewhere. [C6]

Ottringham The tower of St Wilfrid's church with its distinctive broach spire was, like that of neighbouring Patrington, a landmark for ships sailing along the Humber. Recorded in Domesday Book, the church was given to Bridlington Priory in 1130, and probably rebuilt soon afterwards. Now mainly of the 13th and early 14th century, although the chancel arch has its Norman predecessor reused in pointed form. Fine interior with the feel of a great Fenland church. Much of the splendid 15th-century king-post roof remains,

opposite: Norman tower arch and Anglo-Scandinavian cross shaft, St James, Nunburnholme

ST PATRICK'S
PATRINGTON

as do Georgian box pews, numbered and with butterfly hinges. During the Second World War many of the BBC's broadcasts to occupied Europe were sent via the most powerful transmitter in the world, located ½ mile (0.8 km) east of Ottringham. [E7]

Patrington Although a long way down into Holderness, Patrington draws visitors from all over the world to admire one of the most splendid medieval village churches in Britain. St Patrick's was built in the half-century between 1300 and the Black Death, with the soaring spire, which rises to 180 ft (55 m), and the east window both following by 1400. Pevsner wrote of the building's 'sheer architectural beauty', which owed much to 'a unity of exterior and a unity of interior with a calm perfection in each which one never ceases to admire'. Of cruciform plan with transepts and central tower, the building has a superb interior rich in fine stone carving. The nave and transepts are aisled, but not the spacious well-lit chancel, which has on its north side an early 14th-century stone-carved Easter sepulchre with figures of three sleeping soldiers and Christ rising from the tomb with censing angels.

The grandeur of the church is thanks to the archbishops of York, who held the valuable manor of Patrington for over 500 years, and in 1311 obtained the right to hold a market and fair. The small market town was thriving in the late 18th and early 19th century, as shown by the number of good Georgian buildings that line the main streets. At the east end of the broad Westgate the roads diverge, running either side of a close-built area of infilling, where more permanent buildings long ago replaced market stalls. Just over a mile (1.5 km) south is Patrington Haven, where an 18th-century warehouse and other buildings mark the site of a small medieval port, revived in the 1760s but abandoned because of silting up and decline in trade after the opening of the Hull–Withernsea railway. ***Enholmes***, a mile west of the village, is a most impressive model farm (now housing) built in 1849 by William Marshall, of the important Leeds flax-spinning firm. [E7]

Paull On the Humber estuary, with shipbuilding recorded here from the Middle Ages. Lighthouse built 1836, now a private house, replaced by a pair of 'low' and 'high' lights built 1870 a mile (1.5 km) to the southeast. The 14th-century church of St Andrew and St Paul, sited well away from the waters of the estuary that more or less destroyed its predecessor, suffered damage during the Civil Wars. Inside there is some ancient glass, an unusual stone lectern and 17th-century painted inscriptions. In 1542 a gun battery was established at Paull. The present five-sided 'fort', close to the Humber bank, dates from 1861–64 and later. Southeast of the village stands Paull Holme Tower, a three-storey brick structure, probably built in the late 15th century, all that remains of a larger house demolished *c.* 1830. A nature reserve alongside the Humber estuary, Paull Holme Strays (*Yorkshire Wildlife Trust*), offers spectacular views across the South Holderness landscape. [E6]

Lighthouse, Paull
opposite: St Patrick, Patrington

Pocklington One of the most pleasing of East Yorkshire's small market towns, given character by its enjoyable townscape of narrow back lanes and a winding main thoroughfare that follows the route of a hidden stream. The broad, rectangular Market Place is lined with the usual 18th- and 19th-century buildings, the finest a town house of *c.*1700, now the thriving Pocklington Arts Centre. Rather hidden by the houses on the north side is All Saints' church, with a prominent 15th-century west tower, 120 ft (37 m) high. The chancel is also 15th century, the rest chiefly of the late 12th to late 13th century. Inside, the tall tower arch has carvings of leaves and large heads; the north arcade capitals include two men wrestling. In the north aisle a beautiful early 15th-century cross head and in the north chapel a superb Flemish altarpiece, *c.*1520, wood, with intricately carved New Testament scenes. The best monuments are of the late 16th century, to Robert Sotheby and Thomas Dolman, the latter the more unusual, of black marble with incised figures. A recut stone on the external east wall records the death of Thomas Pelling, 'the flying man', who was killed in 1733 when 'abseiling' from the tower. On Chapmangate the handsome Methodist church, 1864, pedimented, with large Doric portico, flanked by contemporary houses for the ministers, and a simpler former Congregational chapel of 1807, refronted 1878.

Pocklington School, to the south of the town, was founded in 1514. Now a public boarding and day school, its pupils have included William Wilberforce and Sir Tom Stoppard. The oldest building dates from 1818, when the school was at a low ebb. Major additions were made from the 1850s onwards as its reputation was re-established. The former railway station, built in 1847, was converted to the school sports hall in the 1970s. To the east of the station is The Balk, with some good large Victorian houses, ending with Burnby Hall and Gardens (*open*), famous for its water lilies, introduced in the 1930s by Major Stewart and his wife, who were great travellers. Their collection of cultural and religious artefacts from around the world is well displayed in a small museum. On the A1079 is the head of the Pocklington Canal, opened 1818, with a restored lock, lock-keeper's cottage and former warehouse. From here take a delightful walk along the canal. [C3]

Methodist church, Chapmangate, Pocklington (drawing by Eugene Fisk)

Huge heads on tower arch, All Saints, Pocklington

Pollington Brick church (St John's) with steeply pitched roof and massive buttresses to the west end, typical of William Butterfield, the architect favoured by William Dawnay, 7th Viscount Downe. It was built in 1855, and, as at Cowick and Henshall (West Yorkshire), commissioned by Dawnay. At the same time Butterfield designed the vicarage and school. The vicarage at Pollington is especially charming, simple red-brick vernacular with double gables. Pollington Hall, a smart three-storey Georgian farmhouse, rises out of the flat landscape overlooking the Aire and Calder Navigation. [E1]

Preston The mother parish, from which the town of Hedon was carved. The busy road through the village loops uncomfortably round the west end of All Saints' church, with its impressive early 16th-century tower. The nave arcades are 13th century, the south aisle and north chapel early 16th, the chancel rebuilt 1870. The church's greatest treasures are the sections of two finely carved 15th-century Derbyshire alabaster altarpieces depicting various scenes, including the Adoration of the Magi. A few good 18th- and early 19th-century houses spread about the large village, including Magdalen House, 1815, and Abbey House Farm and Somerdon House of the 1820s. ***Saltend***, some 2 miles (3 km) southeast, is a vast complex of chemical works that, when lit up at night, make for a dramatic skyline. [D6]

Rawcliffe Once a busy medieval port on the River Aire, revived in the later 17th century, but trade suffered after the Knottingley–Goole Canal was opened in 1826. Georgian and early Victorian houses surround the large village green, in the centre of which is the church of St James, built in 1842 to a design by Hurst & Moffatt of Doncaster. Nave with lancet windows, and tower of grey brick with later stone spire. Plans by Walter Brierley to rebuild in 1906 got no further than the rather contrasting red-brick chancel. The international company Croda (see *Cowick*) was founded in 1925 at the industrial settlement of ***Rawcliffe Bridge***, which developed on the Dutch River and canal. [E2]

Rimswell Small settlement with pleasing Georgian church (St Mary's) of 1801, now redundant. Pale yellow brick, in a Classical style, with windows in round-arched recesses. To the southwest of the village is a local landmark in the form of a white-painted circular water tower, quite architectural, built in 1916 by City of Hull Waterworks. A couple of miles (3 km) south of Rimswell stands South Frodingham Hall. Painted white with black quoins, the result of an unfortunate Victorian makeover, but the plan is still that of the manor house built in the late 16th–early 17th century. [D7]

Rise Hidden among a wooded landscape is Rise Hall (*event venue*), built for Richard Bethell 1815–20, partly encasing its 1770s predecessor. Undoubtedly by Watson & Pritchett, who were responsible for the delightful entrance lodges. The hall, impressive in scale, is a rather austere, Neoclassical building with a huge portico of four giant Ionic columns on the west front, and a very long, quite plain south front, all ashlar-faced. The grand interior, which feels as if it was designed to host society gatherings, with interlinked entertaining rooms and an impressive staircase, was sympathetically restored by Sarah Beeny and Graham Swift. On the edge of the park, landscaped by 'Capability' Brown, are Rise Park, the former Georgian rectory, and All Saints' church, which was rebuilt by R.D. Chantrell, 1845, in an Early English style. Inside is stained glass by Wailes and Kempe & Co., and a series of wall tablets to members of the Bethell family. [C6]

Roos Held from the early 12th century by the Ros or Roos family, who took their name from the village. The Roos estates passed to the Earls of Rutland in the early 16th century. The site of their manor house, or so-called castle, is to the south of the church. A long yew-lined path leads

Rise Hall, Rise

up to All Saints' church, which is entered at the west end through a Victorian porch and mid-15th-century tower. Unusual two-storey vestry with round stair-turret, early 14th century.
Inside is a monument with portrait medallions to Revd Sir Mark Sykes, 1st baronet of Sledmere and rector of Roos, d. 1783, and his wife. Rood screen and reredos by Temple Moore, who also designed the handsome Old Rectory of 1893, in Wrenaissance style.

In 1836 a remarkable discovery was made at Roos Carr: a tiny wooden ship and five 'warrior' figures dating from the late Bronze or early Iron Age. They are now in the Hull and East Riding Museum (see *Hull*). The many months J.R.R. Tolkien spent in East Yorkshire in 1917–18 included time at a camp near Roos, where he is said to have drawn literary inspiration from a woodland glade in which his wife, Edith, danced for him. [D7]

Roos Carr figures, Hull and East Riding Museum

Routh A scattered settlement along the main road, with the small medieval church of All Saints set back on the road to Meaux. The charming pinnacled west tower is of 1904, the rest, including the rendered brick chancel, of the 13th–14th century. Inside is a cross-legged knight of *c.* 1290, an excellent brass of a knight and lady of *c.* 1420, and a good early 18th-century pulpit. Some of the village houses carry the cipher of the Lords Londesborough, onetime owners. [C6]

Rowley Isolated parish church and former rectory, but no evidence for a medieval settlement. St Peter's served a handful of surrounding townships, but in the 1630s its Puritan rector, Revd Ezekiel Rogers, attracted a congregation from further afield. Suspended from his post, in 1638 Rogers took some of his flock to America, where they founded Rowley, Massachusetts. The church they left behind is essentially medieval, although of more than one period, and with the usual Victorian restoration. A modern stained-glass window given by the people of Rowley in America shows Rogers and the ship on which he and his followers sailed. The 13th-century square font came from St Nicholas, Beverley. The south chapel serves as a mausoleum for the Ellerkers of Risby and has instructive marble panels recording the family's history. Rowley Manor, the former rectory (now a hotel) was built in 1710, but the east wing was added in the late 18th century and the west wing after the house was sold in the 1920s. The early 18th-century staircase belongs here, but most of the fittings of interest have been introduced from other houses. Delightful 18th-century rotunda in the grounds, brought from Campden Hill, London.

At ***Risby***, a deserted hamlet about 2 miles (3 km) northeast of Rowley, the garden terraces of the late 17th-century house of the Ellerkers, destroyed by fire towards the end of the 18th century, can be seen from Dunflat Road. In Fishpond Wood to the east are the remains of an 18th-century octagonal Gothick folly overlooking a lake that is now used for fishing. [D4]

Rudston Interesting church (All Saints) with Norman origins, heavily restored in 1861, the date of the elaborate stone reredos with Minton tile panels. It was deliberately built on the pagan ritual site next to the massive Neolithic standing stone that gave the village its name. The tallest in Britain, the lead-capped monolith dominates the churchyard. Among those buried here is the writer Winifred Holtby (1898–1935), who was born at nearby Rudston House. East Yorkshire is the setting for her most famous novel, *South Riding*. East of the village in parkland with lakes is Thorpe Hall (*private*), probably built at the close of the 17th century but with 18th-century and later additions. The estate belongs to the Bosville Macdonalds, and the head of the family is chief of Clan Macdonald of Sleat on the Isle of Skye, some 400 miles (645 km) away. Several Regency outbuildings include an enchanting octagonal dairy. The Hull and East Riding Museum (see *Hull*) has superb Roman mosaics from a villa site at Rudston, including one showing a strangely proportioned naked figure of Venus with flowing locks and mirror, accompanied by a merman. [A6]

Ruston Parva So called to distinguish it from Rudston. The charming, unspoilt yellow-brick and sandstone church of St Nicholas, on a lonely site in fields to the south of the hamlet, was built in 1832. The work was carried out by a local bricklayer cum joiner and cost a very modest £107 10s. Contemporary box pews and pulpit. The font is Norman. [B5]

Saltmarshe The village, in an engaging but rather forgotten area to the south of the M62, lies below the level of the River Ouse. Here you look up to see occasional large ships passing by on their way to and from Goole. In parkland at the west end lies Saltmarshe Hall (*event venue*), built 1825–28 near the site of the old manor house, the home of the Saltmarshe family from the early Middle Ages. The present hall, an austere Neoclassical building, was designed by Watson & Pritchett of York. Well-preserved interior with fine cantilevered staircase. In the grounds a delightful game larder, stables with unusual ice house attached, and impressive walled kitchen garden. To the west

Neolithic standing stone, Rudston

St Nicholas, Ruston Parva

Sand Hall, 1770s with major late 19th-century additions, the home of the Scholfields, who were responsible for the 1850s estate cottages and neat school-chapel to the north in ***Skelton***. [E3]

Sancton All Saints' church is prominent on the hillside above the village, distinguished by its 15th-century octagonal tower, unique in the East Riding. The rest, in early 13th-century style, is a rebuild of 1869–71. Floor slab to Marmaduke, Lord Langdale, d.1661, celebrated for avoiding capture by Parliamentarians by dressing as a milkmaid and riding a cow. The Roman Catholic cemetery adjoining the churchyard has a small memorial chapel to the Langdales. Their home, Houghton Hall (*private*), 1 mile (1.5 km) west, is a perfect mid-Georgian country house in a sublime parkland setting with serpentine lake. Built *c.*1765–68, designed by Thomas Atkinson and the grounds landscaped at the same time by Thomas White for Philip Langdale. A five-bay two-storey centre block is flanked by three-bay pedimented pavilions. [C4]

Scorborough A small village owned by the Hotham family since the 13th century. The hall of Sir John Hotham, who would not let Charles I enter Hull in 1642, was burned down in 1706. The present hall, 18th and mid-19th century, standing on the edge of an extensive moated site, was the home of the Hothams' land agent James Hall, who was responsible for building the superb High Victorian church (St Leonard's) in 1857–59. Designed by J.L. Pearson, it was described by Pevsner as 'small but exquisite with a memorable steeple', and has pinnacles and gables in a French style. The lavish interior displays great originality in use of different coloured stones, light-grey walls with bands of darker grey and red. The bays are divided by polished black marble shafts, with full-height shafts marking the division between the nave and chancel. The excellent east window, and all the rest, by Clayton & Bell. [C5]

Seaton Seaton Hall, a fine grey-brick villa of 1825, and the Black Swan Inn with its 1920s Automobile Association sign are the most prominent buildings in this small Holderness village. At the east end the

road is flanked by a pleasing group of relatively unaltered 18th-century white-painted cottages. Further east on the road to Hornsea are two Victorian estate cottages and the pretty circular Mushroom Cottage of 1812, associated with Wassand Hall (*open occasionally*), which is reached along a tree-lined lane. Elegant white-brick Regency villa with fine interior, built 1813–15 for the Revd Charles Constable, and designed by Thomas Cundy senior of London. The grounds run down to Hornsea Mere, part of the estate. The Georgian walled gardens have been well restored and are open every weekday from April to October. [C6]

Seaton Ross A sprawling village with a mixture of old and new houses. Dial Cottage at North End, with an enormous semicircular sundial, 12 ft (3.7 m) in width, covering much of the façade, is unmissable. There is a similar one on Dial Hall Farm, northwest of the village, and visible from Mill Road. This was the home of farmer, sundial maker and amateur surveyor William Watson (1784–1857), who, in addition to sundials, made two fascinating maps of his local market towns, Market Weighton and Pocklington. They show not only an elevation for each building but also the name and trade of the occupier. Watson made a smaller, more conventional sundial for his village church, St Edmund's, added some years after the rebuilding of 1788. The brick church retains some typical Georgian fittings, including a pulpit with sounding board and reading desk. [C3]

Sewerby A narrow street of cottages, some of chalk and cobble, leads to the early Victorian entrance archway to Sewerby Hall (*open*). Built about 1714 for John Greame, the house was given two-storey bow-fronted wings in the early 19th century, which were heightened in 1848, when a large conservatory was added. The interior, which is fitted out as an Edwardian country house, has some early 18th-century panelling and an impressive cantilevered staircase. The extensive grounds, which include a large walled garden,

opposite: St Leonard, Scorborough

Dial Cottage, Seaton Ross

Sewerby Hall

run to the edge of the chalk cliffs from where, on 23 September 1779, Mrs Greame reported watching the battle of Flamborough Head, when British Navy ships escorting a convoy of merchant vessels were attacked by an American-French naval squadron under Capt. John Paul Jones. To the north St John's church, built 1846–48, designed by George Gilbert Scott in a Romanesque style, has a good period interior with box-like pews, and contemporary pulpit and Royal Arms. Former school nearby is also by Scott. Then come the grounds of Marton Hall, built 1672 for the Creyke family. [A6]

Shiptonthorpe Sympathetically restored medieval church of All Saints. Tower and north arcade 13th century but the south doorway is Norman, as is the naive carving of a bishop with crozier in the porch gable. The church stands at the junction of the busy A1079 and Town Street, where the older village houses are. [C3]

Sigglesthorne St Lawrence's church, considered 'by far the most picturesque in Holderness' by the historian George Poulson in 1840, is a patchwork of brick, stone and cobble. Largely early 13th century, restored by J.L. Pearson in 1848 for the wealthy rector, William Bentinck, Archdeacon of Westminster. Good series of Georgian–early Victorian wall tablets, east window by Clayton & Bell, 1863, and period wall painting of Christ in Glory, 1900, over chancel arch.

Opposite, hidden by trees, the rather grand Old Rectory of 1767, and, in the village, two blocks of early–mid-19th century cottages, much altered, one with Gothick windows, the other with rustic veranda, Tudor hoodmoulds and fish-scale slate roof. To the south is the Italianate Sigglesthorne Hall of *c.* 1820, enlarged by Cuthbert Brodrick *c.* 1850. [C6]

Skeffling The 15th-century cobblestone St Helen's church (redundant) stands alone to the south of the village. Atmospheric whitewashed interior and a chancel roof with carved bosses. Little more than half a mile (800 m) away lies the Humber, which perhaps explains the interesting graffiti of boats on the otherwise plain octagonal font. When last visited there were stones laid out in the north aisle said to have come from an archway at the alien priory of Burstall, which stood near the estuary. [E8]

Skerne Externally St Leonard's church is unremarkable, but the interior has good Norman work including a richly carved chancel arch with zigzag decoration. Venturing inside, one is greeted by a startling sight: two badly retooled 14th-century effigies placed upright, a man and a woman, with a swaddling child between them. On Main Street, at the junction with West End, where Nicholson's Farm has good brick detail, is Rose Cottage. The house has large metal ties in the gable with the initials RA for Richard Arkwright of Willersley Castle, Derbyshire, who purchased the estate in 1792. His father invented the water-powered spinning frame. [B5]

Skidby Skidby Mill, with its black tower and white-painted sails, is a familiar sight to those travelling from the Humber Bridge towards Beverley. Built in 1821 and later raised to five storeys, the windmill and its courtyard of buildings now house the East Riding Museum of Rural Life. It stands just southeast of Skidby village, which has a long main street with some older houses, and an eccentric-looking church (St Michael's) that began as a chapel of ease within the large parish of Cottingham. Stone with much patching and later brickwork, including the top two thirds of the squat tower, added in 1827. Viewed from the west end, it looks rather like a massive chimney stack.

About 2½ miles (4 km) southwest of the village, in an attractive parkland setting, is Raywell House, an imposing three-storey building with later wings, constructed in 1803 for Hull MP Daniel Sykes. On the opposite side of Riplingham Road is Nut Wood and Wauldby Scrogs, an accessible area of partly ancient woodland now managed by the Woodland Trust, where wild garlic and bluebells grow in abundance. [D5]

opposite: Skidby Mill

Skipsea After the Norman Conquest Skipsea became the headquarters of the Lords of Holderness. The impressive earthworks of the motte-and-bailey castle constructed soon after 1071 by Drogo de la Beuvrière, stand in a field to the west of the village, at Skipsea Brough. The massive castle mound, 278 ft (85 m) in diameter and 42 ft (13 m) high, which until drainage in the 18th century was surrounded by the waters of Skipsea mere, is now considered to be an Iron Age earthwork, reused by the Normans. The medieval parish church of All Saints is on a raised site overlooking the former mere. It is predominantly built of cobble, as is so often the case in this part of Holderness, and was heavily restored in the 1860s. Inside is a gravestone of *c.*1400 with two chalices suggesting that it commemorates a priest, but when were two gaming boards and an exchequer table inscribed on it?

Serried ranks of modern caravans along the coast. Until recently also several tumbledown shacks, among them an old railway carriage and the body of a Hull tram, perched precariously on the cliff edge. [B6]

Skipsea Castle

Skirlaugh Built in the opening years of the 15th century, St Augustine's church is regarded as a perfect example of the Perpendicular style of architecture. It looks more or less exactly as it would have done when first built. Lots of buttresses with prominent pinnacles, and no division between nave and chancel, which makes

St Augustine, Skirlaugh

it feel more like a College chapel than a parish church. It was paid for by Walter Skirlaw, Bishop of Durham, son of a local sieve maker. Rowton Villas, now Council offices, was built in 1839 as the workhouse for the local poor law union. Surprisingly grand brick and stucco façade for such a utilitarian building. [C6]

Skirpenbeck A quiet village with some mellow brick houses including Skirpenbeck House, late 18th century with pretty doorcase and Westmorland slate roof, a more sophisticated choice than pantiles. At the east end a modest church, St Mary's, with a stone nave and chancel and rather too slender 18th-century brick

Sledmere House

tower. Inside, a Norman font and unusual 17th-century monument with figures, angels and commemorative verse. [B2]

Sledmere Sledmere is one of the great joys of the East Riding, a place many return to again and again to explore the house, grounds, village and church. Sledmere House (*open*), an elegant, austere H-shaped Classical building, the core from the 1750s, with large wings added to the northwest and southeast fronts in 1789 by Sir Christopher Sykes, 2nd baronet, to his own design with advice from Samuel Wyatt. The interior was remodelled by Walter Brierley when he so successfully reconstructed the house after it had been completely gutted by fire in 1911. His is the grand

imperial staircase, a fitting prelude to the magnificent vaulted library on the first floor, running the length of the southeast front. The library windows look across the landscaped park, created in two stages from the 1750s and sweeping away a sizeable village. The wider landscape includes three eye-catchers originally to be seen from the house, and each other: John Carr's Gothick Sledmere Castle (2 miles/3 km east), and Marramatte (1½ miles/2.5 km west) and Life Hill (2½ miles/4 km south), two model farmsteads designed by Sir Christopher himself, built in 1778. Near the house he designed the octagonal walled gardens, so beautifully presented today. The stable block, originally of 1751, was given its pleasing yellow-brick front in 1818 by Watson &

Pritchett, who were also responsible for the lodges on the main road. The rotunda opposite the lodges was erected in 1840 over the village well. Initially no village was built to replace that swept away, just a few cottages, the Triton Inn and a shop. The two long rows of labourers' cottages on Bridlington Road and pairs of semi-detached estate houses on Croome Road were built in the 1870s. It was in the 1890s that the estate office and clerk's house, clerk of work's house, forester's house and post office were added to become the focal point of the village. A fine series of dark-red brick buildings, Tudor-style with mullioned windows, tall chimney stacks

Waggoners' Memorial, Sledmere
opposite: Chancel, St Mary, Sledmere

and bargeboards. On Garton Road, the delightful half-timbered school and master's house by G.E. Street, 1875, extended by Temple Moore, 1896.

Moore was also responsible for the splendid Eleanor Cross, 1899, at the west end of the village, later transformed by the addition of engraved brass figures into a memorial to men of the 5th Battalion of the Yorkshire Regiment who died in the First World War. Those depicted include workmen from the Sledmere Estate and also Sir Mark Sykes, 5th baronet, who died of Spanish flu at the Paris Peace Conference in 1919. The remarkable drum-shaped Waggoners' Memorial, 1920, nearby, designed by Sir Mark, tells the story of his Waggoners' Reserve through wonderful cartoon-like carvings. Could inspiration for the unusual design have come from the splendid Norman fonts in local churches? Opposite this monument, through the wrought-iron gateway, is the path to St Mary's church. Rebuilt, except for the lower part of the tower, in early 14th-century style in 1893–8 for Sir Tatton Sykes II by Temple Moore, it is the largest and most lavish of the Sykes churches. The quality of the stone carving and woodwork of the interior is superb, with excellent stained glass by H.V. Milner and Burlison & Grylls.

To the north is ***Croome***, a deserted settlement where the medieval earthworks include hillside cultivation terraces known as lynchets. Croome House, a three-storey Georgian farmhouse, has distinctive fenestration including an elegant first-floor Venetian window with stone surround. [A4]

Snaith An engaging small town on the western edge of the present East Riding. Until the early 19th century and the rise of Goole, Snaith was a thriving market town, a role recalled by the street names Beast Fair and Butter Market. Many Georgian buildings, some of the best on Market Place and High Street, including the Downe Arms with its prominent bow windows, and the well-kept group opposite the impressive medieval priory church of St Laurence. In 1100 the church, which served a vast parish originally covering 34,000 acres (13,760 ha) was granted to Selby Abbey, and a subsidiary priory was founded here. It was then rebuilt, but the broad square tower is 13th century, the chancel, with its fine east widow with reticulated (net-like) tracery, early 14th century, and the nave reconstructed in the 15th century. The family chapel of the Dawnays of Cowick Hall, on the south side of the chancel, has a fine table tomb of 1493 and the imposing life-size figure of the 5th Viscount Downe by Sir Francis Chantrey, 1837. Charming bust of Lady Stapleton, 1684, in the chapel of the Stapletons of Carlton Towers, on the north side of the chancel. In a corner of the churchyard is the former Grammar School, built 1620s, rubble stonework and brick, somewhat neglected. Adjoining churchyard on east, the parish lock-up of *c.*1800. The Methodist Church, Cowick Road, 1862, is particularly grand. By Lockwood & Mawson (the architects of Saltaire, West Yorkshire) of red brick and stone, with temple-style façade of full-height Ionic half columns and pilasters. [E1]

Priory Church of St Laurence, Snaith
opposite: South Dalton

South Cave A large former market village lying below the escarpment of the Wolds, where the older houses are of the locally quarried cream limestone. The Market Place, on the Roman road leading from Brough towards York, has a delightful market hall, 1796, two storeys with turret and cupola. The first floor was used as a school, kept by Robert Sharp, whose diaries, published by the British Academy, give an intimate picture of early 19th-century village life. Church Street, with estate housing, Victorian temperance hall, church institute, girls' school and contrasting Methodist chapels (plain pedimented, 1816, and Italianate of red and white brick, pedimented with corner turret, 1877), leads to West End. Here is All Saints' church, 13th–14th century with 15th-century tower. Inside a charming oval charity board, 1809, with painted figures of pauper mother and children, and numerous memorials to the Barnard family. They lived at Cave Castle (*hotel and country club*), the grounds of which are entered through the embattled West Lodge, the pillars topped by bears, the family crest. The house, Gothic castellated, of yellow brick with stone dressings, was built for Henry B. Barnard 1802–09 and enlarged in the 1870s. [D4]

South Dalton The East Riding's most enjoyable estate village, dominated by the soaring spire of St Mary's church, 208 ft (63 m) high, a great landmark in the southern Wolds. Built 1858–61, the church is one of architect J.L. Pearson's finest creations, 13th century in style with geometrical tracery to the windows. The interior is more compact than the exterior leads one to expect, but it abounds in sumptuous carving and other detail, particularly in the chancel. The stained-glass windows are by Clayton & Bell; the best is the east window. Wrought-iron screens by Skidmore of Coventry surround the south chapel, which contains the striking monument to Sir John Hotham, 1689, who succeeded to the baronetcy as a child following the execution of his father and grandfather in 1645 (see *Hull*, Beverley Gate). Sir John is depicted in armour lying on a raised platform supported at the corners by the four virtues, with his skeleton underneath. Below the church nestles a picturesque

group of almshouses, 1874, an L-shaped range with pretty pump house. Opposite is a lodge of 1900, in vernacular revival style by Pearson's son, Frank.

The village is a delight to walk around, with little traffic and a range of housing that provides a guide to East Yorkshire's rural architecture over three centuries. Towards the south end of the main street is Oak Cottage, *c.*1600, timber-framed, now uncommon in this part of the world. Opposite, a whitewashed cottage, early 18th century, has a simple cruck-frame exposed inside. Elsewhere are end-stack Georgian farmhouses, one pantiled with tumbled gables, another with hipped slate roof, and excellent Victorian estate housing. On the road running west is the mock half-timbered village hall (built 1896), the former school of 1848, a cottage with datestone of 1706, and at the end the 18th-century Pipe and Glass Inn. On the south side of the last a public road runs through the parkland of Dalton Hall (*private*), which can be glimpsed in the distance. Built in the 1770s for Sir Charles Hotham, 8th baronet, designed by Thomas Atkinson, it was remodelled for the 5th Lord Hotham in the 1870s. On the west side of the house is an early 18th-century Rococo pleasure garden, virtually intact, with a long avenue leading to a magnificent Classical garden pavilion of the 1730s, attributed to Colen Campbell. At ***Holme-on-the-Wolds***, in the parish, is the site of a small medieval church, the last remnant of which was demolished in 1989. [C4]

Sproatley Although dominated by modern housing, the village boasts one of the best-preserved examples of local vernacular architecture, a single-storey L-shaped brick and pantile cottage with

Early 18th-century bridge, Stamford Bridge

horizontal sliding-sash windows. Probably built in the early 18th century, it stands near the small green, which is dominated by a large chestnut tree. St Swithin's church, rebuilt in the early 19th century and again in 1886, has an early 18th-century organ reputed to have come from Temple Newsam House near Leeds. At the northeastern edge of the village is a former police station and courthouse dated 1849. The Tudor-style mid-19th-century lodge on Park Road was built for the Burton Constable Hall estate. [D6]

Stamford Bridge Almost certainly the Roman settlement of Derventio. It was here that on 25 September 1066 King Harold of England defeated his brother Tostig and King Harald Hardrada of Norway, only days before losing his life at the Battle of Hastings. The 11th-century bridge over the River Derwent was downstream from the present stone one, built in 1727; nearby is a lock constructed at around the same time. The village is on the busy A166 that takes traffic from York towards the coast, and it has been greatly expanded by residential development, but Main Street still has some attractive 18th- and 19th-century houses and a late Georgian Methodist chapel. The small Anglican church, St John the Baptist, 1868, is on Church Road. The massive watermill near the centre, built to grind corn, has been converted to apartments. To the west of the village an imposing railway viaduct, built 1847, with fifteen brick arches and one of cast iron over the Derwent, is now a cycle track. [B2]

Sunderlandwick Nothing more than a scattering of estate houses dating from the mid-19th century, the most visible being the ornate lodge on the A164, whitewashed with stone quoins, hoodmoulds to the windows, fancy bargeboards and a veranda. It stands beside a golf course that incorporates earthworks of a medieval settlement. Hidden away in parkland is Sunderlandwick Hall, an accomplished Neo-Georgian house by Francis Johnson, 1963. Its Italianate predecessor was largely destroyed by fire in 1940, but the 1840s stable block survived. [B5]

Crown property datestone, Sunk Island

Sunk Island Not an island, but a vast expanse of land reclaimed from the Humber estuary from the late 17th century onwards, and therefore Crown property. A bleak, flat but haunting landscape, under a wide sky, unlike anywhere else in Yorkshire. Church and school, but no village, just farms and smallholdings spread over more than 7,500 acres (3,035 ha). Many of the isolated red-brick and slate farmhouses, some with decorative touches including gables and polychrome brickwork, date from 1855–57, and were designed by S.S. Teulon. The elaborate date plaques denoting Crown ownership are unmissable. Some twenty years later a site opposite the school (also by Teulon) was chosen for Ewan Christian's now redundant church and vicarage. His imaginative design for Holy Trinity church, built of homely red brick with Westmorland slate roof, includes a rounded end to the chancel and a separate but linked tower topped with a pyramid roof. The eastern part of Sunk Island became known as the Crown Colony when cottages attached to smallholdings were built for the resettlement of servicemen towards the end of the First World War. It provided the model for Cold Harbour Colony in Winifred Holtby's novel *South Riding* (see *Rudston*). The scheme was not a success. Near the estuary, in woodland, is a First World War battery with gun tower. [E7]

Sutton-on-Derwent Some good 18th- and early 19th-century brick farmhouses and cottages either side of the main street, which runs parallel to the River Derwent. At the north end a late 17th-century stone bridge links directly with Elvington across the river. Nearby is the fine medieval church of St Michael with well-preserved lower part of an elaborately carved Anglo-Saxon cross shaft. The church itself has 12th-century nave arcades; the western arches date from the 14th century, when the lower part of the tower was built. Upper part and clerestory later 15th century. The area known as ***Woodhouse*** to the north has been owned by the Crown since the early 18th century. Pairs of Victorian estate cottages with royal cipher and date 1854. [C2]

Methodist/URC church, Swanland

Swanland A large pond or mere, the focal point of this popular village, is overlooked on the east side by a most delightful Independent chapel (now Methodist/URC), 1804. Grey brick and hipped slate roof, with round-arched and central Venetian windows, and early Victorian gabled wings. Alongside, with half-timbered gable, is the former village institute of the 1920s, given by Sir James Reckitt, the Quaker philanthropist, who lived in Swanland Manor (demolished). On the north side of the pond the mid-Victorian Tudor-style Mere House, and to the south, in a similar style, the former school, now village hall, of 1876, with pretty bell-turret. The five-bay, three-storey Swanland Hall was built in the mid-18th century by John Porter, the first Hull merchant to make his home in the village. [D4]

Swine This small Holderness village should be visited to see its remarkable parish church (St Mary's), the only remnant of a wealthy Cistercian nunnery. It consists of the aisled choir of the nuns' church dating from the late 12th century, with an enormous 15th-century east window, and west tower rebuilt 1787. The interior has a wealth of furnishings and a very fine series of late medieval monuments. The latter are to members of the Hilton family, dating from between *c.*1370 and *c.*1410, three with a knight and lady, one of a knight alone, all tomb-

Hilton family monument, Swine

Norman south doorway, All Saints, Thwing

chests. Eight choir stalls have misericords, with figures including a Green Man and a grotesque wearing a bishop's mitre. The village, the name of which comes from the Anglo-Saxon word *swin*, meaning a creek or channel, was largely rebuilt by the Crown Estate soon after its purchase in 1865 from the social reformer Lord Shaftesbury. The former school and some of the farmhouses and cottages bear the royal cipher and the old smithy has a horseshoe-shaped entrance, now blocked. [D6]

Swinefleet The main street runs alongside the south bank of the River Ouse. St Margaret's church is a rebuild of the late 19th and early 20th centuries. From the east end of the large, overgrown churchyard one can see The Park, a handsome Georgian brick farmhouse with projecting central bay and hipped roof. At ***Reedness***, a strung-out settlement east of Swinefleet, is another nicely proportioned farmhouse, Reedness Hall, of a similar date. [E3]

Thorngumbald The village more than trebled in size in the 1960s. St Mary's church, a jumble of stone and brick, was originally a Norman chapel of ease. Two doorways and a font of *c.*1200, and a Victorian bellcote. Panelling in the chancel, made from box pews, and Royal Arms, amended 1858, survive from a Georgian restoration. Thorngumbald Hall, a large Jacobean-style house of red brick with shaped gables and stone-mullioned bay windows, by B.S. Jacobs, was built in 1880 for a Hull surgeon. [D7]

Thornton Small village once owned by the Earls of Northumberland, with simple 14th–15th-century church (St Michael's) with late Victorian wooden bell-turret. Inside, a pretty early 19th-century organ case and delightful fragment of medieval glass. To the south is the early 19th-century Pocklington Canal with restored Walbut Lock and neat brick bridge [C2]

Thwing It lies in an area rich in prehistoric remains, including Willy Howe, a gigantic round barrow, and the site of a Neolithic henge and Bronze Age hill fort on Paddock Hill. The medieval church of All Saints, which stands on a hillside opposite the village, has a south doorway and chancel arch of *c.*1150 and 15th-century nave.

The tower was rebuilt and much else restored 1898–1901. Inside are memorials to two men born here: St John of Bridlington, commemorated by a stained-glass window, and Thomas Lamplugh (d.1691), Archbishop of York. In a field near the late 18th-century Wold Cottage, 1½ miles (2.5 km) northwest, is a square brick pillar erected by Edward Topham, journalist and playwright, to mark where a meteorite fell in 1795. (The meteorite is now in the Natural History Museum.) At Glebe Farm, in the small hamlet of ***Octon*** (1 mile/1.5 km west), there survives the most complete early farmhouse in the East Riding. Cruck-built, it has been dated to 1670–71. [A5]

Tibthorpe A neat series of 18th- and early 19th-century farmhouses and cottages line the street running west from the main road. To the east is Eastlands, a large Victorian yellow-brick villa. [B4]

Tickton Much new building from the 1970s onwards, when a bypass took the busy coastal road away from the village centre, but the main street retains some character. Several modest farmhouses and cottages, some single-storey, small stone church (St Paul's) with bellcote, built 1844 as a chapel of ease to Beverley Minster, and Tudor-style almshouses at the north end of the settlement dated 1872. Tickton Grange, on the opposite side of the bypass, was built by a Beverley attorney in the late 18th century, but has been much altered. Now a hotel. To the west of the village is ***Hull Bridge***, once an industrial hamlet on the River Hull, quite picturesque with waterside inn and a handful of boats moored nearby. [C5]

Tunstall Fields still separate this sleepy little Holderness village from the sea, which comes ever closer as time passes. The prominently sited medieval church of All Saints, restored 1870s, is chiefly built of cobbles, as are the older houses and farm buildings. [D7]

Ulrome One long street links the two 'ends', each with its vestigial village green in the form of a small grass triangle. At the west end the largely Victorian St Andrew's church is built with stone and cobble from an earlier building. By the sea a rash of caravans, some perilously close to the eroding cliff edge. [B6]

Walkington The main street is divided into East End, with duck pond, and West End. Interesting houses, an eclectic mix, mostly set back from the road behind grass verges. On West End is the most characterful of the old farmhouses, Middle Farm, built of rubble limestone in contrast to the more usual brick. No. 48, on the opposite side, is one of several houses that incorporate random architectural fragments, the trademark of local builder Samuel Lythe, who lived at No. 12 Kirk Lane. All Hallows' church can be reached via Church Walk, a long footpath running off the south side of East End. Medieval origins, including the tower, but a substantial part of it rebuilt in brick in the early 19th century. On the north side of the village Walkington Hall, much altered in recent years, is screened by a long wall, but the ornate Victorian clock tower on the stable block can be seen from Manor House Lane. Walkington Grange, a mile (1.5 km) or so west of the village, is a particularly nice example of an East Riding farmhouse, built after enclosure of the open fields at the end of the 18th century. [D5]

Wansford Now a quiet spot by one of the locks on the Driffield Canal, 200 years ago Wansford was a bustling industrial village with a very large carpet factory. Built by Sir Christopher Sykes of Sledmere in 1789, it was demolished in the early 20th century. Some of the workers' housing remains, as does the Georgian Manor House, once the factory proprietor's home, with a picturesque whitewashed watermill (for grinding corn) nearby. The factory stood between the canal and West Beck, a beautiful clear chalk stream famous for its trout. A footpath runs alongside the stream from the bridge on the Skerne road to Snakeholme nature reserve (*Yorkshire Wildlife Trust*). On the road leading north from the canal, St Mary's church and the former vicarage, school and schoolhouse, designed by G.E. Street for Sir Tatton Sykes, 5th baronet, form a

Watermill, Wansford

St Mary, Wansford

delightful group. The church, built 1867, has a bell-turret with small spire and inside a resplendent Italian Gothic screen, and stained-glass windows by Clayton & Bell. [B5]

Warter An attractive Wolds village, dominated by Victorian estate houses, most set back in large gardens. It was chiefly the creation of the Pennington family, Lords Muncaster and their successors the Wilsons, later Lords Nunburnholme, Hull shipping magnates. Their home, the monumental Warter Priory, demolished 1972, stood over a mile (1.5 km) to the west. At the village centre is a triangular green with a fine carved First World War memorial cross, and a pretty row of cottages rebuilt and thatched *c.* 1930. Nearby is a 1730s farmhouse built of stone from the medieval Augustinian priory. St James' church, 1863, now the Yorkshire Wolds Heritage Centre (*open*), is on the priory site, and there are earthworks in fields to the north.

The church and churchyard contain a remarkable collection of Edwardian Arts and Crafts monuments and stained glass to members of the Nunburnholme family by three men who served as masters of the Art Workers' Guild. Sir George Frampton carved the moving memorial to the young Lady Isabel Wilson, a sublime recumbent figure, formerly in a now demolished mausoleum, and the portrait medallions of Lord and Lady Nunburnholme. His friend Robert Anning Bell designed the glorious stained-glass windows, and Frampton's pupil Gilbert Bayes was responsible for the exquisite 'New Sculpture'

St James, Warter: Stained glass by Robert Anning Bell

Monument to Lady Isabel Wilson by Sir George Frampton

figures in the churchyard. A century later David Hockney painted his celebrated 'Bigger Trees near Warter', made up of 50 panels, on the Wolds to the south. [C3]

Wassand Hall see **Seaton**

Watton Most of the small village lies to the west of the main road, but everything of interest is on the east side. The house long known as Watton Abbey is the remnant of a 12th-century Gilbertine priory, a 'double house' with separate accommodation for nuns and canons. What survives is the prior's lodging, converted to a private house after 1539. Three-storey stone range with undercroft, to which was added in the 15th century an impressive brick range with octagonal corner turrets and a very fine two-storey stone bay window. The surrounding priory site was excavated in the late 19th century. A stream running under the house continues north to a long brick outbuilding with window openings to both floors. Whether it dates from before or soon after the Reformation is uncertain, as is its original function. Uncertainty also surrounds the date of St Mary's church, which overlooks the monastic site. Also of brick, perhaps a post-Reformation build or rebuild using material from the dissolved priory. Incised slab with figure of prior. [C5]

Wawne A low-lying settlement east of the River Hull, with a ferry crossing until the mid-20th century. Suburban Hull now covers fields to the south, but Wawne has just managed to retain its village identity. Several brick and pantile farmhouses, and on Main Street 18th-century cottages attractively remodelled when the adjoining lodge to Wawne Hall (demolished) was built for the Windham family in the early 20th century. On Cedar Close, off Meaux Road, an intriguing white-rendered bungalow, not at all like its neighbours. It was converted a few years ago from a Cold War bunker. Interesting medieval church, St Peter's, late 13th century onwards, stone with brick clerestory. West window with intricate tracery, 15th century. Inside, two damaged incised slabs from Meaux Abbey, a wealthy Cistercian house dissolved 1539. The demolished buildings provided materials for Hull's defences. Artefacts from the extensive site (on private land, a couple of miles/3 km north of the village) include many locally made encaustic tiles in private and public collections. [D6]

Welton One of East Yorkshire's most rewarding villages with its green spaces, stream, former millpond and plenty of charming houses and gardens. The picturesque Wolds setting looking down towards the Humber made Welton (together with ***Melton***, ¾ mile/1.2 km east) a popular choice for Hull merchants looking to build country villas, although the best of these was paid for with West Riding money. Welton Grange, at the west end, is a perfectly proportioned miniature country house, built of honey-coloured stone *c.*1750. St Helen's church, restored or rather rebuilt 1863, has a splendid series of stained-glass windows

Watton Abbey

by Morris & Co., mainly commemorating the Galland family, to whom Burne-Jones, one of the designers, was related. In the churchyard, near the east window, is a gravestone with rhyming inscription to eight-times-married Jeremiah Simpson, who died in 1719 and 'now lies in his cage' under the grass. On Dale Road north of the village is a five-storey watermill converted to a house, and at the top of sylvan Welton Dale a circular mausoleum dated 1818. It was built for the Raikes family, who lived in the largest of the merchant houses, Welton House, demolished 1952 and its landscaped park built on. [D4]

Welwick A fine medieval church (St Mary's), extended in the 14th century, when the aisles and clerestory were added. Of this date too is the grand canopied tomb of a priest, built into the south wall of the interior but in an odd way whereby some of the decorative stonework can be seen from outside. The quality is such that it has been attributed to the same workshop as the splendid 'Percy tomb' in Beverley Minster. A brass set into the floor of the north aisle has figures representing Ann and William Wright, with an inscription recording how they 'lived lovingly together for fifty years'. She died in 1618, he in 1621. Their lives were not without incident, for William was half-brother to Christopher and John Wright, two of the notorious gunpowder plotters who in 1605 attempted to blow up James I and Parliament. The Wrights farmed at Plowland, to the west of the village. On the edge of a field near the B1445, close to the farm entrance, a steel sculpture showing four of the conspirators has been erected – a controversial choice of subject, but intended to celebrate the plot's failure. Welwick Saltmarsh on the Humber is managed by the Yorkshire Wildlife Trust. [E8]

West Ella The East Riding's most picturesque village. The single street is lined with 18th- and 19th-century whitewashed Tudor-style houses and cottages, with arched doorways, hoodmoulds and latticed casement windows, most set back in pretty hedged gardens. In the 1830s the squire, Richard Sykes, transformed West Ella from 'a poor dingy country village ... into one of the prettiest and most picturesque in the country, every cottage, barn, or shed being changed into a thing of beauty'. Sykes' home, West Ella Hall, a much-extended mid-Georgian house, is hidden away at the east end. [D5]

Wetwang A curious name that causes much amusement, perhaps Old Norse meaning a field for the trial of a legal action. One long village street lined with brick and pantile cottages and farmhouses, with back lanes each side, and a small pond. Wetwang House, built in 1795, is the most distinguished of the larger houses. The church of St Nicholas has Norman origins, but the chancel was rebuilt for Sir Tatton Sykes II in 1902, the date of the fine barrel-vaulted roofs and stained-glass windows. Traces of medieval and later wall paintings. In 2001 a builder digging foundations for a small housing development unearthed the skeleton of an Iron Age woman buried with an ornate cart. One of several local 'chariot burials', the hallmark of the Parisi tribe, it represents a time when East Yorkshire was an important cultural centre. [B4]

Whitgift Linear settlement along the south bank of the Ouse. Church of St Mary Magdalene dating from the beginning of the 14th century, slightly sunken and askew at the west end, a reminder that it was built on marshy ground. The rendered brick aisles came later. The tower clock, dated 1919, has the number XIII at the top instead of XII. In his Second World War broadcasts Lord Haw-Haw apparently boasted that German bombers would be able to spot this, so low would they be flying on their route between the docks at Hull and Goole. Further east is Whitgift Hall, *c.*1700, a handsome five-bay house with hipped roof, brick enhanced with stone dressings. To the northeast, on the riverbank, is a lighthouse, a curious sight so far inland. Only 46 ft (14 m) high, but still a marker for shipping on the tidal Ouse. [E3]

opposite: Lighthouse at Whitgift

Wilberfoss The village where the family of William Wilberforce originated. A small Benedictine nunnery here had in its last days a reputation as a place of education for upper-class girls, one of whom was Thomas Cromwell's granddaughter. The chancel of the parish church, dedicated to St John the Baptist, may be on the site of the nuns' church. Norman in origin, the south arcade 13th century, south aisle and tower mid-15th century, and north aisle added 1993. Fragment of medieval stained glass in the east window, and a worn 15th-century brass of a man in armour and his wife. The stream nearby is crossed by an early stone footbridge. [C2]

Willerby Suburban Hull, but Main Street still feels a little like a village. Willerby Hall was described as lately built in the early 18th century, but the authenticity of its shaped gables is open to debate. [D5]

Winestead Birthplace of the poet Andrew Marvell (1621–78), whose father was rector here. The rectory was rebuilt in the 18th century. The medieval church of St Germain, on its own across a field, is far more rewarding than its humble exterior might suggest. Largely cobble-built and with some Norman work, the rest 14th and 15th century, it was well restored by Temple Moore. Excellent fittings, including 15th-century choir screen, 17th-century pulpit and charming Jacobean-style pews. The south chapel has memorials to the Hildyard family, lords of the manor from the 15th to the late 19th century. The finest is that to Sir Christopher Hildyard, d.1602, tomb-chest with figure of a knight. Of the family's Georgian Red Hall, at the north end of the village, only the handsome stable block of 1762 remains. White Hall (*private*), to the west of the church, is an elegant grey-brick Greek Revival villa built for Arthur Maister, 1815. [E7]

Withernsea Withernsea has seen better days, as have so many English seaside resorts. In its Edwardian heyday the many visitors, and the Hull businessmen and professionals who made their home here, came 'for the sake of the sands and the bracing air rather than in search of the picturesque' (J.E. Morris, *Little Guide*, 1906). The sea, sand and bracing air still attract. The town was formed from two medieval settlements, Owthorne and Withernsea, the greater part of which had long disappeared into the sea when Hull merchant Anthony Bannister proposed to develop a resort here at the end of his Hull and Holderness railway, opened 1854. Plans were drawn up for a grid of streets with grand Classical terraces designed by Cuthbert Brodrick, architect of Leeds Town Hall. The main streets were laid out but few houses built, and the town grew slowly. Brodrick designed the railway station and the very grand Queen's Hotel, 1855, both demolished in

Lighthouse, Hull Road, Withernsea

recent times, the latter having become the town's hospital (Community Hospital built on its site).

The former parish church of St Nicholas stands in a packed churchyard, behind the hospital and reached via Park Avenue. Consecrated in 1488, as a replacement for one washed into the sea, the church was unroofed by a storm in 1609 and subsequently abandoned. An impressive ruin on the opening of the railway, it was successfully restored by Brodrick, 1859. Chiefly cobble-built with a fine ashlar chancel, and architecturally the best building in the town, the church is now redundant and its future uncertain. St Matthew's, on Hull Road, a good brick 1930s church, stands opposite a showier Italianate Methodist church of the 1870s. On the seafront are two castellated turrets that formed the entrance to a pier, 196 ft (60 m) long, built 1877. Much damaged by frequent storms, the remnant was finally taken down in 1904. The town's chief landmark, the lighthouse on Hull Road, built 1893, is 127 ft (39 m) high. Now a museum (*open in summer months*) with displays about the RNLI, local history and the Withernsea-born film star Kay Kendall. [D8]

Withernwick St Alban's church built in 1855, cobble with regular bands of brick, and stone buttresses. Bell-turret on gable end of nave, where it joins the slightly lower chancel. On Main Street the chapel-like former Ancient Order of Foresters'

Entrance towers to lost pier, Withernsea

Hall, built in 1890, demonstrates the strength of the friendly society movement in rural East Yorkshire. Buildings associated with mutual aid organizations are found more often in urban communities. [C6]

Wold Newton The most northerly village in the East Riding. Large green and pond. The earlier houses are built of chalk. Small church of All Saints with a pretty wooden bell-turret. The south doorway, chancel arch and font are Norman, with chancel and north aisle of the 1850s. Sympathetically restored in 1899 by Temple Moore, who inserted the wooden posts to support the turret. Commandment boards, etc., and Royal Arms of 1839, and late Victorian stained-glass windows by C.E. Kempe. Village Hall, originally Wesleyan chapel of 1839, with Gothick windows. The American science-fiction and fantasy author Philip Farmer's Wold Newton Family is a group of well-known heroic and villainous literary figures that he claims descended from those present when a meteorite landed near the village in 1795 (see *Thwing*). [A5]

Wressle Standing majestically near the River Derwent, Wressle Castle (*private, occasional open days*) is best known to many as an impressive ruin glimpsed from a moving train on the Hull to Selby line. It was built in the 1380s for Sir Thomas Percy, Earl of Worcester, who was executed in 1403 for rebelling, with his nephew Henry ('Hotspur'), against King Henry IV. In the late 15th and early 16th century it was a favourite residence of Henry 'the Magnificent', 5th Earl of Northumberland (see *Leconfield*). The castle, as built, was similar to Bolton Castle, North Yorkshire, in that it consisted

Wressle Castle before recent conservation work

St John of Beverley, Wressle

of four ranges around a large courtyard with four massive corner towers. At Wressle there was also a five-storey gatehouse in the middle of the east range. Built of fine ashlar stone, and considered by John Leland to be 'one of the most proper beyond the Trent', it was largely demolished under Parliamentarian orders in 1648–50, leaving, as now, the south range with towers at each end. It was then occupied as a farmhouse until gutted by fire in 1796. The farmer, no doubt delighted, got a new house alongside. To the south stands the plain brick church with a rather thin tower. It was built in 1799 on the site of an earlier church, and is dedicated to St John of Beverley. Simple interior with pretty organ case. [D2]

Yapham Originally a chapel of ease within Pocklington parish, the little church of St Martin has a rustic charm, more like a barn to which porch and wooden louvred bellcote have been added. Most of the fabric dates from a rebuilding of 1778. The inscription on the heart-shaped plaque set into the porch is difficult to read, but seems to have the initials of the churchwardens who probably supervised the work. The simple interior, an uninterrupted space, has a Georgian pulpit and communion rails. The Victorians chopped up the box pews to make the present ones, which, when last visited, were painted a rather outlandish bright blue. [B3]

Yokefleet A small village of Georgian farmhouses and Victorian estate cottages alongside the River Ouse. The elaborate Gothic red-brick Yokefleet Hall, built 1868–74 for Philip Empson, was one of the last works by the architect Cuthbert Brodrick before he retired to France with his mistress. Birthplace and childhood home of the poet and literary critic William Empson (1906–84). [E3]

St Martin, Yapham

Central Hull and Old Town

1. Hull Truck theatre
2. St Stephen's Centre
3. Paragon Interchange
4. Prospect Centre
5. Library
6. St Charles (R.C.)
7. New Theatre
8. History Centre
9. Charterhouse
10. North End Shipyard
11. Hull College
12. Guildhall
13. Maritime Museum
14. Queen Victoria Square
15. City Hall
16. Paragon Arcade
17. Art Gallery
18. Princes Quay
19. Bonus Arena
20. Trinity House
21. Trinity Square
22. Grammar School
23. Hull Minster
24. Hepworth's Arcade
25. St Mary's Church
26. Museum Quarter
27. Wilberforce House
28. The Dock
29. The Deep
30. Murdoch Connection

City of Hull (Kingston upon Hull)

'Hull is part of the county of York, but it seems to be sort of a kingdom of its own, with an identity of its own. It is a remarkable place with an individual character.' So wrote Herbert Morrison, wartime Home Secretary and High Steward of Hull. Hull's individuality and independence are in part thanks to its location, which many commentators refer to as 'isolation', at the end of a 40-mile (64-km) cul-de-sac. It may appear cut off from London and the south, but as a port it is not isolated from the wider world, a fact that is reflected in its history, community and buildings.

The city has its origins in the settlement of Wyke, sited at the junction of the River Hull and the broad Humber estuary, established by the wealthy Cistercian abbey of Meaux (6 miles/10 km north) in the later 12th century. A flourishing wool-exporting port by the 1190s, it was relocated a little further east to its present site in the mid-13th century, following the realignment of the River Hull. In 1293 King Edward I, pursuing his campaign against the Scots, acquired Wyke as a base, and renamed the port Kingston upon Hull, which is still the city's official name. A new town was planned and a high brick wall and ditch constructed on three sides, the River Hull providing protection on the fourth. The port prospered through trade with the Low Countries and the Baltic, exporting wool, cloth and lead, and importing timber, corn, flax and iron, as well as wine from Bordeaux. Late medieval decline was followed by a revival in fortune from the late 16th century, interrupted by the Civil Wars, when Hull became the only Parliamentarian stronghold in Yorkshire. Then followed a golden age for Hull's merchants with the end of the dominance of the Dutch in trade with Scandinavia and the Baltic. They replaced their timber-framed mansions and counting houses on High Street with smart new brick houses, some of which survive, and revelled in a lively social life. William Wilberforce recalled that in his youth in the 1760s–70s Hull 'was then as gay a place as could be found out of London. The theatre, balls, great suppers, and card-parties were the delight of the principal families.'

As the marketing centre for Holderness and North Lincolnshire, the town was well supplied with shops and services. It had a vast hinterland, reached via the rivers Trent, Ouse and Aire and by an increasing network of canals. Through the port passed many of the raw materials for, and products from, the Industrial Revolution occurring in the Midlands and the North. Add to this the growth of the whaling industry and it was inevitable that the River Hull, where the merchants had their private staiths (wharfs), became congested. Pressure for increased accommodation for shipping and for a legal quay resulted in the opening in 1778 of what was then the largest inland dock in Britain, later named Queen's Dock (now Queen's Gardens). It was followed by Humber Dock (now Hull Marina), 1809, and Junction (later Princes Dock) in 1829. They were built along the line of the town walls, which were demolished to make way for them. The docks thus preserve the boundaries of the medieval town in the city's present layout. With the walls gone the town expanded to the north, where some of the fashionable Georgian terraces survive, and to the west.

KINGSTON UPON HULL

Hull rooftops | *opposite:* Hull Marina and tower of Hull Minster

The railway arrived in 1840, and the all-important fishing industry shortly afterwards, which, together with shipbuilding, seed-crushing, paint manufacture and the short-lived cotton mills, turned Hull into a boom town. New docks were built along the Humber for timber, coal and other goods to the east of the River Hull and primarily for fishing to the west. A rivalry developed between the communities living in the close-built terraces and court housing off Holderness Road on the east side, and those living off Hessle Road, many of them trawlermen, on the west. The rivalry remains today, focused on Hull's two Super League rugby sides, Hull FC (west) and Kingston Rovers (east).

Many fine buildings were erected in the rapidly expanding Victorian town. Most of the numerous churches and chapels then built have gone, but the grand banks, with new uses, and other commercial buildings, ornate public houses and some of the splendid Board Schools and middle-class houses survive. Ranked as the third port in Britain after London and Liverpool, Hull was finally granted city status in 1897, just a couple of years after its Yorkshire rivals, Leeds and Sheffield. In a great display of civic pride, the centre was replanned, with a public square, new streets, a very grand City Hall, Guildhall and Law Courts, and much more. Private philanthropy led the way in improved housing, with James Reckitt's Garden Village, and between the wars Thomas R. Ferens of Reckitt's funded the superb Art Gallery and the first stage of the University.

Hull was the second most heavily bombed city in Britain during the Second World War, with the loss of some 1,200 lives and the destruction of great swathes of the city, including many fine buildings. If the ambitious Abercrombie Plan for the city's reconstruction (published 1945) had been fully implemented, much more would have been lost, including a large part of High Street. Post-war redevelopment added little of great merit to the city centre, but much was in a tasteful Neo-Georgian retail style that has worn well. The scars of the war lasted for decades. Many of the damaged historic buildings in the Old Town were cleared away in the 1970s, but there and elsewhere empty sites still await development. After the collapse of the fishing industry and industrial decline in the 1970s–80s, Hull has begun to show signs of resurgence in the 21st century, with great hopes for its role in the 'green power revolution'. High-quality buildings

Hull Maritime Museum | *opposite:* City Hall and statue of Queen Victoria, Hull

such as The Deep and Hull History Centre encourage optimism for the city's future landscape, and its recent UK City of Culture status gave the community pride in their home town and great encouragement to its thriving cultural and artistic life. Hull has the best collection of museums and art galleries of any place of its size in Britain, all free and open every day. It is a city proud of its heritage.

One of Hull's greatest strengths is that it is on a human scale. The streets are not dominated by tall buildings. Many are spacious and pedestrianised, and where they are narrow, in the Old Town, they are quiet, with little traffic. It is a city to enjoy on foot. Any exploration should begin at ***Queen Victoria Square***, the heart of the city, laid out in 1901–02 as part of architect-mayor Alfred Gelder's ambitious plan to give Hull a centre in keeping with its recently acquired city status. In this he was highly successful by providing a perfect setting for the grand Edwardian Baroque ***City Hall*** and the iconic former Dock Company Offices (***Maritime Museum***). The latter, built 1868–71 to the designs of an obscure architect, Christopher G. Wray, was cleverly conceived for an awkward triangular site. Venetian-style with tall domed drums at each corner, and much decoration on a maritime theme throughout, even on the railings. City Hall, built 1903–10, fills the west side of the square, and was designed by the skilled city architect Joseph H. Hirst. The balcony on the entrance front, backed by a giant recessed portico, has been the scene of many public celebrations. Inside are a flamboyant staircase and a vast concert hall, designed with advice from the celebrated theatre architect Frank Matcham – and it shows. Much more restrained on the south side is the wonderfully austere Classical ***Ferens Art Gallery*** by S.N. Cooke and E.C. Davies, 1927. Superb, cool interior with a remarkable picture collection. It contrasts with the adjacent extravagant brick and terracotta Renaissance façade of the Punch Hotel, 1896, by Smith, Brodrick & Lowther, and the former bank, 1898, by B.S. Jacobs on the opposite corner, with its pretty cupola. Lastly, in the centre of the square, a statue of Queen Victoria, 1903, by H.C. Fehr. There was an outcry when public lavatories were installed below her in 1924.

The three walking tours that follow all start from Queen Victoria Square. The longest and most detailed covers the Old Town, an area that must be explored to appreciate the rich history and architecture of the city.

VICTORIA DEI

Walk 1

The Old Town

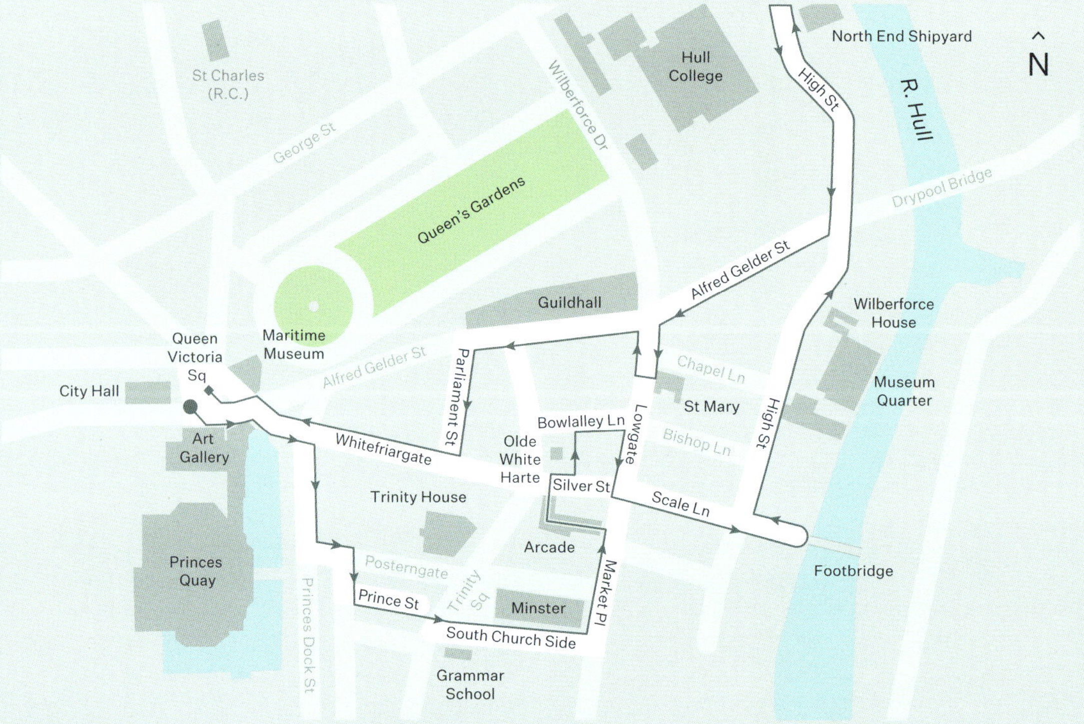

From ***Queen Victoria Square*** go east to the site of the 14th-century ***Beverley Gate***, the entrance to the medieval walled town. Here the town's governor, Sir John Hotham, turned away King Charles I on 23 April 1642, on the orders of Parliament, to prevent the king from getting hold of the Hull arsenal, the most important collection of arms and ammunition outside the Tower of London. This was later considered by the Royalists to be the first act of the Civil Wars. The brick foundations of the gateway and part of the town walls are exposed to view. Turn right along ***Princes Dock Street***, with a fine range of late Georgian–early Victorian buildings on the left, including the pedimented former Ferres Almshouse (Roland House) and the arched entrance, 1842, to the Trinity House courtyard, which provides a view of the austere west front of H.F. Lockwood's Trinity House chapel, 1839–43. On the right is Princes Dock, mostly taken up by the large ***Princes Quay shopping centre***, opened 1991, by no means as disastrous as it might have been. Imaginative and dramatic aluminium and glass exterior, with posts and cables, giving it a semi-nautical feel, best appreciated when lit up at night.

Take the first left down ***Posterngate***, with well-converted warehouses on the south side. (Note the pattern of small fish inset in the brick footpath on the right, part of the excellent ***Fish Trail***, providing an original and entertaining way of marking a route around the Old Town. Copies from Tourist Information Centre or online.) Then right down

Princes Quay shopping centre, Hull

Prince Street, Hull

Dagger Lane, and next left into ***Prince Street***, a delightful curving street laid out in the 1770s, with a terrace of three-storey Georgian houses on the north side. Emerging through the archway at the end into ***Trinity Square*** one is rewarded with a stunning view of the outstanding west front of ***Hull Minster*** (Holy Trinity).

One of the greatest medieval town churches in Britain, Hull Minster is 285 ft (87 m) long and 75 ft (23 m) wide in nave and choir, and the tower is 150 ft (46 m) high. Building began soon after Edward I established his 'new' town in 1297, and it replaced the existing chapel of Wyke. The transepts and the lower part of the central tower are of *c.*1300–20, and the aisled choir of *c.*1340–70, all brick with stone for the window tracery and other details. The nave, rebuilt *c.*1380–1420, and the upper section of the tower, *c.*1490–1520, are of stone. Evidence suggests that royal masons were involved in the building of the transepts and choir, possibly funded by the king, and that the nave was paid for by Hull merchants, in particular the prominent De la Pole family.

Inside, the grandeur of the building is best appreciated standing at the west end looking

Hull Minster from south-west

east, with the light flooding in through the large Perpendicular windows of the nave highlighting the scale and elegance of the slim pillars. The capitals are carved with a great range of figures, including mermaids, eagles and winged monsters. The nave was clearly designed to echo the existing choir, which also has high arcades and clerestory. Among the furnishings are an exceptional late 14th-century font of coralloid marble, covered with lively carvings, a superb Rococo altar table of 1753, and a large painting of the Last Supper of 1711 by a French artist, James Parmentier, who lived for a time at Hull. From the restoration of the church in the 1840s are the impressive Gothic stone pulpit and the carved oak pews now in the nave aisle, and from the 1860s–70s restoration the choir fittings designed by George Gilbert Scott. The church is packed with memorials to the merchants and other townspeople. In the south aisle of the choir are two 14th-century canopied tombs, one with the stone figures of a merchant and his wife, the other with a more elaborate canopy carved with angels and 24

Hull Minster looking west along nave before removal of pews

shields, including the arms of the De la Poles. The choir and its aisles are floored with many 17th- and early 18th-century black ledger stones carved with deeply incised coats of arms. These gravestones of Tournai marble were imported into Hull in large numbers from the Low Countries. There is much stained glass, all of it of the late 19th–mid-20th century. The finest two windows, designed by the Arts and Crafts artist and Socialist Walter Crane, are in the south aisle of the nave. Both were made by J. Silvester Sparrow, who was also responsible for the striking window depicting the Crucifixion in the south transept.

On the south side of Trinity Square the Elizabethan brick ***Grammar School***, now Hands on History museum, had among its pupils the poet ***Andrew Marvell***, whose statue is nearby, and ***William Wilberforce***, the emancipator. ***Trinity House***, on the northwest corner of the square, has a remarkable complex of Georgian buildings *(for visits see website)*. It began as a religious guild in 1369, became a guild of mariners in the mid-15th century, and received a

Stained glass by Walter Crane, Hull Minster

royal charter in 1541. In the 17th and 18th centuries it took increasing control of shipping and navigation on the Humber and along the east coast. The present buildings are arranged around a courtyard; on three sides the former almshouses of the 1750s, the entrance front having a grand pediment filled with an elaborately carved Royal Arms, and on the fourth side a courtroom and council chamber of 1773, with splendid interiors. Opposite Trinity House is an ornate Victorian pub, and along ***North Church Side*** the nicely detailed Baroque Edwardian ***Market Hall***, 1904, by Joseph Hirst, with a ground-floor arcade and tall copper-domed campanile.

From Trinity Square go east along the south side of the Minster, to what was once a very bustling ***Market Place***, the location of a large twice-weekly market, and the principal inns and shops. Now all have gone, leaving the golden equestrian statue of William III by Peter Scheemakers, erected 1734, in splendid isolation. Here, as with Queen Victoria above, the monarch stands guard over public lavatories (closed), listed owing to the wonderful interior of ceramic columns and Art Nouveau tilework. Go north along Market Place, with the tower of St Mary's church (see below) in the distance. On the left is the truly delightful ***Hepworth's Arcade***, with elaborate Continental Renaissance façade, by Gelder & Kitchen, 1895, for Leeds tailor Joseph Hepworth. Go through the L-shaped arcade, with its fabulous two-storey interior with fluted pilasters, half columns, glazed barrel-vaulted roof and small independent shops, to ***Silver Street***. Here are three unmistakable former Victorian–Edwardian banks, the grandest – of Portland stone with heavy moulded rustication to the ground floor – on the corner of ***Land of Green Ginger***. This intriguing street name gave Winifred Holtby a title for a novel. On the north side of Silver Street an alleyway leads to the Olde White Harte, *c.*1660, in the Artisan-Mannerist style, displaying a free use of Classical details. Inside is 17th-century woodwork including staircase and panelled 'plotting chamber'. The latter is so called because it was there that the successful overthrow of the Catholic governor when the Protestant William of Orange landed in 1688 was planned, not the barring of Charles I in 1642, as is claimed. The alleyway continues through to ***Bowlalley Lane***, lined with late Victorian offices, and at the east end, on the corner of Lowgate (the extension of Market Place), the Italianate former Exchange by William Botterill, 1866, considered on opening as 'one of the chief ornaments of the town'.

Go south down ***Lowgate*** and left onto ***Scale Lane***, which leads down to the ***River Hull***. Some early 20th-century offices with period façades and lettering, the ornate Jacobean Revival Manchester Arms, 1898, and next door the city's only surviving medieval timber-framed building, probably 15th century, jettied and gabled to the street. Cross High Street and continue along Scale Lane Staith ('staith' meaning wharf or landing stage) and on to the stylish and exciting ***footbridge*** by McDowell & Benedetti, 2011, over the River Hull. From this unusual swing bridge, which you can ride on as it opens, there are great views along the river. The scene changes with the tides, as mud banks emerge then disappear, but boats are rare. To the south, ignoring the unfortunate Premier Inn, are the Tidal Barrier and The Deep (see below), to the north on the west side a few surviving Georgian and Victorian warehouses, and on the east side the red-brick and stone Trinity House buoy shed, 1901, and the stone-walled entrance to the Victoria Dock of 1850.

Statue of King William III (King Billy), Hull

Georgian warehouses, River Hull

Back down Scale Lane Staith, turn right on to ***High Street***, which is untypical of its name. This is not a shopping street but the commercial centre of the port from the 14th until the early 20th century, and where the merchants lived until the late 18th century. Most had their homes and counting houses on the east side, backing on to a yard or garden, and their private wharf or staith on the River Hull. Go north along this delightful, narrow street that curves to follow the line of the river. It is full of Dickensian atmosphere, especially the glimpses up the alleyways on the right, understandably a favourite location for film-makers. One passageway alongside No. 41, accessible in working hours, leads to the remarkable remnant of ***Crowle House***, dated 1664. An elaborate tower-like three-bay frontispiece of brick, Artisan-Mannerist, the centre bay flanked by tapering Corinthian pilasters, with stone jewelling. A little further on is the former Pacific Club, 1901, meeting place of the Old Town merchants, Jacobean Revival, of red brick and terracotta, materials favoured by its architect,

Blaydes House, Hull

B.S. Jacobs. Opposite is narrow Bishop Lane, a quaint street with stone setts. Here there is a mid-Georgian terrace, Victorian offices and, on the High Street corner, an imposing late 18th-century three-storey house with basement, now a restaurant. Next, on the east side of High Street, is a range of early 19th-century warehouses, successfully converted to student accommodation, then the large Italianate stone façade of the former Corn Exchange, 1856, with fluted Corinthian columns flanking the high-arched entrance. In contrast, the rather plain brick façade of ***Maister House*** (*National Trust*) opposite hides the most exciting interior of any domestic building in Hull. Built in 1745 by Henry Maister, MP and wealthy Baltic merchant, with advice from Lord Burlington. The remarkable staircase of stone, with a wrought-iron balustrade by the celebrated Robert Bakewell, has been attributed to William Kent. It rises around three sides of a spacious hall to a first-floor landing. A door leads to a separate staircase giving access to a square gallery with iron balustrade on the second floor, above which is an octagonal turret with glazed roof lantern. The stucco is work by Joseph Page, plasterer and architect, who evidently oversaw the house's construction.

Next comes the ***Museum Quarter***. Set back on the right, the ***Hull and East Riding Museum*** provides an excellent introduction to the history of the area from prehistoric times to the end of the Middle Ages. The Roman galleries with superb mosaics from local villas and the reconstructed Iron Age settlement are the highlights. At right angles and backing on to the river is the purpose-built ***Streetlife Museum***, with an enjoyable and extensive display of a great range of vehicles from stagecoaches to trams, bikes and cars in period settings. To the north, and best entered from High Street, is ***Wilberforce House***, built *c.* 1660 for the merchant Hugh Lister, with an elaborate Artisan-Mannerist rusticated brick façade. The three-storey projecting porch has indented Corinthian pilasters decorated with stone 'jewels'. Good mid-17th century and Georgian interior, including a grand staircase with fine plasterwork. The birthplace in 1759 of William Wilberforce and now a museum telling the story of the brutal transatlantic slave trade and its abolition, as well as modern slavery. The museum incorporates the pair of mid-18th-century houses next door, where there are displays of Hull silver, clocks and the collection of the East Riding Regiment.

From Wilberforce House go north, glimpsing in a large courtyard on the right the rear of Pease Warehouses of 1745 and 1760. Then cross Alfred Gelder Street (the intriguing Meccano-like ***Drypool Bridge***, a rolling lift bridge of 1961, on the right) into what is sometimes called Little High Street. On the right is ***Blaydes House*** (*usually accessible on Heritage Open Days*), another fine Georgian merchant's house. Between the chimney stacks on the south gable is a lookout so that the owner could see his ships on the river. The Blaydes family were both merchants and shipbuilders, and in their yard nearby or at Hessle they built the *Bethia*, which became the *Bounty* of mutiny fame. Further north is the charming former late Georgian Dock Office, and alongside it the North End Shipyard (originally the entrance to Queen's Dock), which is being restored and will house the *Arctic Corsair*, Hull's last surviving sidewinder trawler, with visitor centre.

Turn back down Little High Street and right onto ***Alfred Gelder Street***, past the mock half-timbered White Hart with wonderful original curved ceramic bar, and the postmodern domed Crown Court, to ***St Mary's church, Lowgate***. Hull's other medieval church (*usually open Thursdays and Fridays 11 am–2 pm*) was built in the early 14th century on the only land in the town not acquired by Edward I. Rebuilt from the 1390s, partly in brick. The west tower collapsed in the early 16th century; a new tower built in 1697 was, like the rest of the church, faced in ashlar when George Gilbert Scott, cousin of the vicar, restored the church in the 1860s. Scott also added a second south aisle, porch and vestry, and made the walkway through the tower, to save it from demolition when the road was widened. On entering you are struck by the church's width, and by the forest of pillars. The Victorian–Edwardian furnishings reflect the fact that this was the centre of Anglo-Catholicism in the city. Screens and organ case by Temple Moore, and excellent stained glass by Clayton & Bell. Monuments include an incised brass of an early Tudor woollen draper and his family, and the bust of a wealthy merchant, William Dobson, d.1666.

St Mary, Lowgate, Hull

Opposite on Lowgate are the superb Ocean Chambers of 1901 by W.S. Walker, and the former ***General Post Office***, a vast Edwardian Baroque building, part now reduced to a public house with the most original name of Three John Scotts, commemorating three successive vicars of St Mary's. In both scale and architectural merit, the Post Office is outshone by Hull's grandest show of civic pride at the height of its Edwardian prosperity, the stupendous ***Guildhall and Law***

Mural by Harry Watson in Council Chamber, Hull

'Law' by Albert H. Hodge over entrance to Guildhall, Hull

Courts, 1905–16. An amazing colonnade of giant Composite columns stretches out along Alfred Gelder Street, of fifteen bays on each side of an enormous three-bay central block. Here, above the main entrance to the Law Courts, is the figure of 'Law' on a boat, by Albert Hodge, who was also responsible for the monumental sculptures topping each end of the building. Designed by the young Edwin Cooper, who after completing the Law Courts and Council offices persuaded the Council to replace Cuthbert Brodrick's Venetian-style Town Hall, less than 60 years old, at the east end, with his more restrained Guildhall. It is dominated by a tall clock tower finished with the Greenwich time ball, designed to drop down the pole at a pre-determined time to allow ships to check the setting of their chronometers. A restricted ceremonial entrance hall leads to a rather hidden grand marble staircase, and along narrow mahogany-lined office corridors to the sumptuous council chamber. In the open area fronting the Guildhall entrance, the statue of the shipping magnate and MP Charles Wilson, Lord Nunburnholme, *c.*1910, by Derwent Wood, is overlooked by the Edwardian City Hotel and Maritime Buildings, more admirable works by W.S. Walker.

Leaving the Guildhall, continue along Alfred Gelder Street then turn left into ***Parliament Street***, the most complete Georgian street in the city. It was laid out in 1796, and soon afterwards developed with 28 three-bay, three-storey terraced houses with handsome pedimented doorcases, most of which remain virtually intact. Almost all the properties were solicitor's or accountant's offices in 1892, and solicitors still predominate. The view at the south end of the street is filled with the ambitious ***Neptune Hotel*** on ***Whitefriargate***. The seven-bay façade was designed by George Pycock to impress, with a Venetian window over the central archway, tripartite windows with lunettes over, under blank arches, at each end, and the rest round-headed with Adam-style panels above. On the first floor is a large assembly room with elegant plaster ceiling. Built as a speculation by Trinity House in 1795, it never succeeded as a hotel. It was the Custom House for much of the 19th century, and latterly a shop.

Whitefriargate, the main east–west route in the medieval town, was one of the principal shopping streets, but has suffered disastrously from the relocation of retail, in stages, further west. Here you must look up above the modern shop fronts, especially on the south side, redeveloped by Trinity House in the late Georgian period. The eleven-bay block at the east end, with central pediment, was built for Smith's Bank, 1829–30, designed by Charles Mountain junior, as was the seven-bay range with pilasters and tripartite sashes towards the west end. In contrast, the north side of the street has Victorian and Edwardian banks and a great display of 1930s shop façades ranging from the 'Moderne' former BHS to impressive Greek Revival stone-faced former Marks & Spencer, ending at the corner with a typical Burtons of polished black marble with Art Deco touches. Then it is just a short distance to Queen Victoria Square.

Parliament Street, Hull

Walk 2

To the waterfront

From ***Queen Victoria Square*** go east, past the sunken site of Beverley Gate, and turn right down Princes Dock Street with Princes Dock on the right, following the line of the medieval town walls marked out along the dockside with coloured brick. At the end is the disastrous Castle Street (A63), opened in 1981, cutting through the Old Town and taking heavy traffic to and from the docks east along the Humber. Cross on the striking futuristic footbridge, 2020, named ***Murdoch Connection*** after the pioneer suffragist Mary Murdoch, d.1916, the city's first female doctor, to the ***Hull Marina*** (formerly the Humber Dock, opened 1809). Lively with many yachts, and the estuary as a backdrop, this is a good place to appreciate the city's maritime heritage. Walk along the east side to vibrant ***Humber Street***, where decaying fruit warehouses have been transformed into small shops, cafes, galleries and performance venues. The area south from here was reclaimed from the Humber in the early 19th century, a fact that is reflected in the names Wellington and Nelson for the new streets.

A short diversion off to the right at ***Wellington Street*** takes you across the lock between the dock basin and dock to ***Humber Quays***, a well-planned office complex with quiet square and short esplanade with views along the estuary. A sculpture of a migrant family, by Neil Hadlock, erected in 2001, commemorates the 2.2 million

View across Marina, Hull

Murdoch Connection footbridge, Hull

transmigrants, chiefly from Scandinavia, Germany and Russia, who, landing near here, passed through Hull, most on their way to America. Back on the east side of the dock basin, continue south to ***Nelson Street***, a delightful, unexpected oasis alongside the Humber. From Victoria Pier ferries crossed to New Holland, Lincolnshire, until the opening of the Humber Bridge in 1982. At the west end of the street is the well-preserved Minerva Hotel, 1829, and at the junction with Queen Street the handsome Pilot Office, 1820. In between is the former Manchester, Sheffield & Lincolnshire Railway Company station of 1880. There were never any trains, but the company ran the ferry. More listed public lavatories, 1930s, with good tiled interior, and two statues, one to the medieval merchant William De la Pole, first mayor of Hull, the other by the sculptor Steinunn Thorarinsdottir in 2006, looking across the junction of the River Hull and the Humber to The Deep. From the latter statue take the clever cantilevered ***footpath*** alongside the river passing

Tidal Surge Barrier, River Hull looking through to Millennium footbridge and The Deep aquarium

a former dry dock, successfully converted to an open-air performance area. Cross the river by the elegant lifting *footbridge*, with the imposing ***Tidal Surge Barrier*** by Shankland Cox, 1980, on the left, to ***The Deep*** aquarium. Designed by Terry Farrell and opened in 2002, this remarkable building has become the icon for Hull's resurgence in the 21st century. Clad in aluminium and glass panels, which reflect the changing light, it juts out dramatically over the estuary like the prow of a ship, although in fact the architect saw it as a cliff-like slice of rock.

(There is an enjoyable walk eastward from The Deep on a well-planned ***promenade*** alongside the Humber, running south of Victoria Dock Village. This successful large-scale housing development was built on the site of the former timber dock in the early 1990s. As well as great views along and across the estuary, the walk takes in remnants of the dock, opened 1850, including a slipway and winding house, and an impressive dock basin, and ends with sight of the amazing towers of wind turbine shafts being assembled on Alexandra Dock.)

From The Deep go back across the footbridge and walk north alongside the River Hull past the Tidal Barrier and under the A63. From here go along the ***wooden sidewalk***, noting the inlaid eels that are part of the excellent Fish Trail, up to the Scale Lane footbridge. Then turn left to go along Scale Lane, Silver Street and Whitefriargate back to Queen Victoria Square.

opposite: The Deep aquarium

Walk 3

The Northern Suburb, Paragon Station and Anlaby Road

Starting at ***Queen Victoria Square***, go east to ***Queen's Gardens***, created in the 1930s by infilling the Queen's Dock. A welcome large green space in the centre of the city, a restful spot as well as the scene of lively concerts and many other gatherings. Walk through the gardens, from the tall white net-like sundial sculpture *Solar Gate* by Tonkin Liu, 2017, to the east end, which is dominated by a Doric column 90 ft (27 m) high, of 1834, topped by a statue of Wilberforce. This stands in front of Sir Frederick Gibberd's under-appreciated Hull College, 1962.

Now turn north along ***Wilberforce Drive*** and left on to ***George Street***, and the beginning of the Northern Suburb, which developed with housing for the emerging middle classes after the opening of the first dock in 1778. Streets were laid out on land belonging to the Dock Company, with the grandest houses on Charlotte Street, now the eastern end of George Street, built for wealthy shipowners and merchants wanting to escape the noises and smells of the overcrowded High Street. Most were badly damaged in the Blitz, and the impressive terrace of fifteen houses was cleared except for two elegant mansions: No. 85, built for William Osbourne, timber merchant, who founded the small Scottish port of Kingston-on-Spey; and No. 83, built for Philip Green, whose ships carried goods from the Baltic. His brother Joseph acted as agent at Königsberg (Kaliningrad), where he was a great influence on the ideas of his close friend the philosopher Immanuel Kant. Another resident of Charlotte Street was Charles Lutwidge, Collector of Customs and grandfather of Lewis Carroll. Turn right into ***Grimston Street***, leading to ***Worship Street***, where, north of the Old English Gentleman pub (part of a short terrace of 1806), is the ***Hull History Centre***, 2009, visually and culturally a great boon to the city. Designed by Pringle Richards Sharratt using 24 curved laminated-timber beams to create an elegant, wide aisle, roofed with an undulating series of inflated cushions. The colourful fibreglass toad sitting outside was one of many placed around the city in 2010 to mark the 25th anniversary of the death of the poet Philip Larkin.

(At this point a diversion can be taken to see the exterior of ***Charterhouse Hospital***, Charterhouse Lane, north of the busy Freetown Way, a wonderful complex of 17th- and 18th-century buildings. Founded in the 14th century by the De la Poles, demolished at the beginning of the English Civil Wars, then rebuilt – including the surviving Master's House, on the south side, with shaped gable – in the 1650–1660s. The main almshouse and chapel on the north side are as rebuilt in 1778–80, a handsome building, seven bays with projecting three-bay wings. The centre three bays are pedimented, with semicircular Doric porch, and above an open Ionic cupola. The chapel retains its delightful Georgian interior, with box pews and an exceptional carved pulpit, with sounding board. The poet ***Andrew Marvell*** spent much of his childhood here when his father was Master.)

South of Hull History Centre turn right into Jarratt Street, with a good run of Georgian houses on the south, and on the north the side wall of the ***New Theatre***, built as the Assembly Rooms, 1830–34, by Charles Mountain junior. The main entrance of the theatre, with its giant Ionic portico, is on the pleasant ***Kingston Square***. Laid out in 1801, this faint echo of a London square, with a central railed garden, lacks the grand houses. Neat, modest terrace on the north side. On the west the stone façade of Hull Medical School, 1833, incorporated into a recent block of flats, and three early to mid-19th-century houses and the more ornate Victorian hotel, once the home and workplace of Madame Clapham, a dressmaker with an international reputation. A former Victorian brewery, successfully recycled as offices, dominates the south side and adjoins one of Hull's great surprises, ***St Charles Borromeo***

Wilberforce Monument, Hull

Charterhouse Hospital, Hull

Roman Catholic church. The restrained stuccoed façade contrasts with what has been described as 'one of the most opulent and dramatic interiors of any 19th-century church in England – a fantastical Roman church with a heavy touch of the Austrian rococo' (Christopher Martin, *A Glimpse of Heaven*, 2006). Built in 1829, it was transformed first in 1835 by J.J. Scoles, who created the remarkable sanctuary with elaborate sculpted Holy Trinity; in the 1890s came the dome with lantern lighting the high altar, with every surface painted with scenes and figures by Henry Immenkamp.

The south side of ***Albion Street*** (the continuation of Jarratt Street west of Bond Street) was largely destroyed in the war, including Brodrick's splendid Royal Institution, but the north side retains its long, impressive terrace of elegant 1790s town houses, most three bays, three-storey with basements. Further west, set back, is the stone-faced Albion House, *c.*1846, still Georgian in character. Next comes the Edwardian Baroque ***Central Library***, by J.S. Gibson, with octagonal corner tower of brick and stone bands, reminiscent of J.F. Bentley's Westminster Cathedral, and a grand pedimented entrance portico with large round-arched window lighting the original reading room on the first floor. Then turn left along ***Prospect Street***, with a rather mean statue of the Hull-born pioneer aviator ***Amy Johnson***, and its continuation ***King Edward Street*** to the junction with Jameson Street. On the former BHS store is the wonderful large Three Ships mosaic (future uncertain) by Alan Boyson, 1963. Turn right into ***Jameson Street***; on the south side a mixture of showy early 20th-century buildings, including King Albert Chambers, Flemish Renaissance with Belgian hand-painted tiles in entrance, and more restrained 1950s Neo-Georgian. In contrast, at the west end facing Ferensway is the splendid former Hammonds (later House of Fraser) store, by T.P. Bennett, 1950–52, with its angular shape and alternate layers of glass and white walls, the most original of the immediate post-war buildings. ***Ferensway***, opened 1931, was planned as a grand 'boulevard' lined with Neo-Georgian offices, shops, cinemas and flats. Something of what was intended can be seen north of Brook Street, but the war came and work ceased. Much of the early 21st-century redevelopment on the west side pays no attention to its setting and is visually disastrous. The St Stephen's development has been described as 'spectacularly wrongheaded' (Adrian Jones), and the eleven-storey Holiday Inn as 'woefully inept ... a disfigurement of an otherwise superb skyline' (Owen Hatherley). ***Hull Truck Theatre***, by Wright & Wright, 2009, is by far the best building here, with the lavender-blue cone of the Albermarle Music Centre adding a frivolous touch.

South of St Stephen's is Paragon Station, referred to as ***Paragon Interchange*** since the successful

Original 1840s station, Anlaby Road, Hull

Philip Larkin by Martin Jennings, Paragon Station, Hull

integration of the new bus station in 2007. The station and adjacent Italianate ***Royal Hotel*** (formerly Royal Station Hotel) are by G.T. Andrews, 1846–49, but the former tiled booking hall, the delightful Art Nouveau kiosk and the stunning five-span station roof are of the major Edwardian extension by William Bell. From the station concourse go past Martin Jennings' statue of ***Philip Larkin*** to the side entrance and turn right to see the original 1840s station overlooking the car park on Anlaby Road. For Simon Jenkins it is 'second only to Huddersfield as a survivor of the great age of station classicism': forgotten, but remarkably complete, with central porte cochère, wings and corner pavilions. The long, low, rather bleak cream-brick building at the southwest corner of the car park was the Victorian waiting room for emigrants about to board trains for Liverpool. It stands on ***Anlaby Road***, where to the east are two more cheerful buildings, the ***former Tower Cinema***, 1914, of ornate green and cream faience with domed corner towers, and the ***former School of Art***, 1904, by E.A. Rickards. The latter has bands of brick and stone, pedimented centre with semicircular two-storey porch, decorated with caryatids and a mosaic portraying the triumph of the arts over ignorance. Opposite is the simpler 'pre-Deco' former Regent Cinema of 1910. Turn left up ***Ferensway***, then right on to ***Paragon Street*** (south of the city's cenotaph and Boer War memorial), glancing into ***Paragon Arcade*** on the right, a Venetian Gothic delight by Alfred Gelder, 1892, with delicate cast-iron arches. Finally pass along the north side of ***City Hall*** – shops below, and above panels with carved portraits of great artists, for here was the city's first art gallery – to Queen Victoria Square.

Former School of Art, Anlaby Road, Hull

Paragon Arcade, Paragon Street, Hull

Around the City

Now for a few of the key buildings and places of interest away from the centre of the city.

First, going NORTH on ***Beverley Road***, once favoured as a place of residence for the port's middle classes, with handsome terraces and neat rows of villas, some intact, others mutilated with unsightly additions and alterations. Among the more notable buildings are, on the west side, the distinctive former ***Trafalgar Street Baptist Church***, 1906, flint-faced with red-brick dressings, in a rather free Perpendicular style with Art Nouveau touches, and on the east side the remnant of the Gothic Kingston College, 1837, by H.F. Lockwood. Further north is the burnt-out shell of the ***National Picture Theatre***, 1914, protected as a Second World War bombsite. A circuitous detour down Fountain Road, on the right, leads eventually to the impressive ***Northumberland Court***, 1880s, extensive almshouses by Smith & Brodrick with Tudor gatehouse and a remarkable, tall Arts and Crafts tower. Even further on is the delightful ***Wilmington Swing Bridge***, which carried the Victoria Dock branch railway over the River Hull, and two massive early 20th-century brick silos. Back on Beverley Road, buildings that stand out include the late Gothic former Northern Library of 1895 and the former Stepney railway station, 1852, an early work by William Botterill. His later partner John Bilson, a still much-respected expert on medieval architecture, was responsible for the nearby Stepney Primary School, 1886, with its shaped gables and cupola, a surviving example of the firm's many excellent Queen Anne-style Board Schools in the city. Next door is the elaborate copper-domed Edwardian Baroque ***public baths*** by Joseph Hirst, with Art Nouveau tiling in the entrance hall. Opposite are four neat mid-Victorian grey brick villas, still with front gardens, then comes ***Pearson Avenue***, and the stunning recently restored cast-iron 'triumphal arch' that gives access to ***Pearson Park***. Opened in 1862, Hull's first public park was given to the town by shipowner Zachariah Pearson. He retained the land around the boundary, on which were built in the 1860s–70s a series of detached and semi-detached villas in a mixture of styles. The popular park has a lake, rebuilt conservatory and bandstand, and statues of Queen

Wilmington Swing Bridge, Hull

'Triumphal Arch' and entrance gates, Pearson Park, Pearson Avenue, Hull

Victoria and Prince Albert, 1860s, by Hull-born sculptor Thomas Earle. The Oriental-style cupola, on the western edge of the park, came from the top of Cuthbert Brodrick's 1860s town hall. Nearby, the top flat of No. 32, one of an unassuming semi-detached pair, was the home of ***Philip Larkin*** 1956–74, and the inspiration for his poem 'High Windows'.

Off ***Princes Avenue***, the road that runs along the west side of the park, are ***'The Avenues'***, Hull's principal late Victorian middle-class development, a popular residential area with four main tree-lined streets running east–west. Originally planned with six elaborate cast-iron fountains at the junctions, but there are now only two, one where Salisbury Street meets Westbourne Avenue and another – an excellent modern copy – where it meets Park Avenue. Between the fountains are the earliest and architecturally most significant houses on The Avenues, a group of eight designed by the troubled but brilliant George Gilbert Scott junior for his cousin John S. Cooper, a Hull solicitor, built 1877–79. Queen Anne style, hipped roofs, shaped gables, tall stacks, white-rendered panels framed in red brick with plenty of stucco decoration. (Scott also designed a church for the Avenues' residents, St Augustine's, demolished, which was eventually built by his pupil Temple Moore. Moore was also responsible for ***St Mary's Sculcoates***, Sculcoates Lane, off Beverley Road, 1916, which has a superb austere interior and a font that started life as an impressively large mid-Georgian wine cooler.) The Avenues have a scattering of blue plaques, including ones to the novelist Dorothy L. Sayers, a short-term resident; the Hull-born actor Ian Carmichael, who played her most famous character, Lord Peter Wimsey; and the pioneer aviator Amy Johnson.

Further north, reached via Newland Avenue or Beverley Road, is ***Cottingham Road*** and the large well-kept campus of the ***University of Hull***, with some of the city's best 20th-century buildings. Founded as a University College in 1927, it gained independent status in 1954, making it England's 14th-oldest university. The campus now includes the complex of early Georgian-style buildings of

Fountain, Park Avenue, Hull

the Municipal Training College (later University of Humberside), 1909–13. The first University College buildings, of 1928, are rather duller Neo-Georgian, in dark red brick. Many of the later buildings owe much to Sir Leslie Martin, of Royal Festival Hall fame, who was appointed as University Architect in 1958. He designed the Middleton Hall and commissioned a number of innovative architects for other buildings, including Peter Moro for the Gulbenkian Centre, 1966–68; and Castle, Park, Dean, Hook for the multistorey Brynmor Jones Library, 1966–69, which dominates the site. It incorporates the 1950s library building, where the university's outstanding collection of British art 1890–1940 is well displayed in a very pleasant gallery (*gallery open every day, visitors welcome – check University Library website*).

Three main roads run WEST from the city. These are, north to south, Spring Bank, Anlaby Road and Hessle Road. Beginning at the south end of Beverley Road, ***Spring Bank*** has remnants of early Victorian terraces on the south and late Victorian on the north. Here were the Zoological Gardens, 1840–62, with exotic buildings and animals, of which the Polar Bear pub with impressive ceramic bar is a reminder. Round the corner on Spring Bank West is ***Hull General Cemetery***, laid out in 1847, an atmospheric place with plenty of trees, bushes and evocative memorials. South of the street is ***Hymers College***, in a successful Free Jacobean style by John Bilson, 1893, brick with stone bands and details and handsome clock tower. A mile (1.5 km) further on, reached via Springhead Avenue off Willerby Road, is ***Springhead Pumping Station***, 1862–64, a monumental Italianate building with spectacular interior with Cornish beam engine supported on four massive Roman Doric cast-iron columns (*open – see website*).

Anlaby Road, from Park Street going west, is dominated on the south by a procession of five 1960s tower blocks, and on the north by ***Hull Royal Infirmary***, 1962–67, by Yorke, Rosenberg & Mardall, fourteen storeys, the city's tallest building, very period. Opposite is one surviving early Victorian villa, and down Linnaeus Street (the site of the

Hull General Cemetery, Spring Bank West, Hull

Botanic Gardens) the former ***Western Jewish Synagogue***, 1902, by B.S. Jacobs in his usual red brick and terracotta. Past the big road junction, on the left, is Coltman Street, laid out *c.*1840, lined with good examples of mid-19th-century lower middle-class housing. Then more elaborate 1870s houses, of cream brick with shaped gables, on the north side of Anlaby Road. Opposite is ***St Matthew's church***, 1870, by Adams & Kelly, grey brick, with prominent tower and spire, redundant and future uncertain. Over the flyover to ***West Park***, 1885, with the delightful half-timbered ***Carnegie Library*** (now Heritage Centre) by Joseph Hirst, 1905, at its entrance. To the north is the stylish ***MKM Stadium***, 2002, the home of Hull City Football Club and Hull FC Rugby Club. A mile (1.5 km) further along Anlaby Road are the Lee's Rest Houses, 1914–15, by Henry Hare, a wonderful early

Georgian-style complex arranged round a large garden square with a pretty dovecot-like pavilion in the centre. Nearby is the very pleasant ***Anlaby Park Garden Suburb***, layout and houses by the architects of Hull Garden Village, Runton & Barry, 1911 onwards.

The first part of ***Hessle Road*** is now the busy A63, with nothing left of the old street but two pubs, the grey-brick Vauxhall Tavern, 1812, with gently bowed windows, a contrast to the showy Alexandra Hotel, 1895, mock-timbered, faience and terracotta. The street really begins when it diverges from the A63, past the flyover, with the extravagant Premier Stores, 1898, by Alfred Gelder, and opposite the Romanesque former Primitive Methodist chapel, 1881. There are a couple of Art Deco shops, a French Renaissance red-brick bank, a branch library by Gelder, 1894, on the Boulevard, with good interior, and a series of late Victorian pubs, ending with the Dairycoates Inn, in a striking green and brown faience. On the corner of the Boulevard, the ***Fishermen's Memorial*** to those lost in the Dogger Bank Incident of 1904, when a fleet of trawlers was mistakenly attacked by a Russian gunboat, is a reminder that this still vibrant shopping street was once the hub of the fishing community who lived in the terraces, long demolished, south of the road. The main fishing dock, St Andrew's, has been filled in for a shopping centre, with only its entrance from the Humber and some increasingly derelict offices remaining. Towards the western end of Hessle Road is ***Pickering Park***, 1909–11, with great wrought-iron entrance gates flanked by Tudor-style almshouses, all by Hirst.

Going EAST from the city Holderness Road and Hedon Road are the main routes. ***Holderness Road*** begins with ***Witham***, largely a wasteland of offices and car showrooms, with the exception of a pretty former Board School off to the right on Malton Street, 1888 – by Botterill & Bilson, stepped gables and cupola – and a couple of Victorian pubs. Opposite the Windmill Hotel (remodelled 1902, with fine multicoloured faience to ground floor) is Dansom Lane, where Hull's best known firm, Reckitt's, later manufacturers of iconic brands such as Brasso and Dettol, established a starch works in 1840. The global giant Reckitt Benckiser (RB) still has a presence here. James (later Sir James) Reckitt established Hull's first free library on Holderness Road in 1888. The Venetian Gothic-cum-Tudor building by Alfred Gelder (now converted to apartments) stands forlornly next to the showier ***East Hull Baths*** by Hirst, 1898. Dutch Renaissance, bands of red and yellow, and scrolled and broken terracotta pediments, with a good tiled entrance hall. Then comes half a mile (0.8 km) of shops, with no buildings of note, until Chestnut Villas, a terrace of four unremarkable, middle-class houses recently listed because the architect Alfred Gelder lived in No. 365, and his friend and client Joseph Rank, founder of the milling firm, lived in No. 371. It was here that the film magnate ***J. Arthur Rank*** was born in 1888.

A little further on, just past a statue of James Stuart, a local Liberal politician, Village Road leads to the delightful ***Garden Village***. No doubt inspired by his fellow Quaker industrialists George Cadbury and Joseph Rowntree, founders of Bournville (Birmingham) and New Earswick (see *City of York Villages*), James Reckitt declared in 1907 that he intended 'to establish a Garden Village, within a reasonable distance of our Works, so that those who are wishful might have the opportunity of living in a better house, with a garden, for the same rent that they now pay for a house in Hull – with

The Oval, Garden Village, Hull

the advantages of fresher air, and such Clubs, and out-door amusements, as are usually found in rural surroundings'. The Hull architects Runton & Barry were commissioned to design the layout and buildings on 130 acres (53 ha), part of the land of Holderness House, a large grey-brick Jacobean Revival mansion of 1838. The Garden Village was officially opened on 2 July 1908, and over 500 houses had been completed by July 1913. Twelve tree-lined streets, most named after trees or shrubs, in a mixture of curves and straight lines. Although described at the time as 'not self conscious and aggressively and irritatingly artistic and arty-and-crafty', the houses – many roughcast, some with tile-hanging or timber framing to the gables – are clearly influenced by the Arts and Crafts movement. The painted rendering, overhanging eaves, decorative gutter brackets, sloping clay-tile roofs and tall chimney stacks of some of the first-class housing on The Oval are all features favoured by one of the movement's leading exponents, Charles Voysey. The Wrenaissance style of the Club House and the Shopping Centre, 1909, with its domed clock tower, are quite a contrast. Half-timbering was the chosen style for three sets of almshouses around the village. Further east on Holderness Road, past the 1950s St Columba's church, is ***East Park***, opened 1887, entered through a 1960s Brutalist gateway. The park retains some original features, including the rocky Khyber Pass, and a 1920s water chute into the large lake, formerly a brick pit.

Hedon Road, very busy, serves King George and Queen Elizabeth Docks and south Holderness. Little of interest except Hull Prison, 1865–70, in what a contemporary termed 'carpenter's Gothic', and adjacent large cemetery, 1870s, with early crematorium, 1900, and columbarium. Immediately south of the prison is ***Alexandra Dock***, where the tower of the 1880s hydraulic engine house is dwarfed by the giant turbine shafts assembled here, part of the ambition for Hull's future as a world-class centre for renewable energy. (Further east is the late Victorian Gothic Marfleet church, St Giles, in a surprisingly rural setting.)

To the northeast is ***Sutton-on-Hull***. Part of Hull since 1929, but retaining its village character in the streets around the medieval church of ***St James***. Stone chancel but tower, nave aisles and clerestory in brick, probably largely from the rebuilding of 1347, when the church was made collegiate. Inside is a mid-14th-century tomb-chest monument to Sir John de Sutton, who provided funds for the work, although the chancel was paid for by the rector. Major restoration in 1867, the date of much of the interior. Also on Church Street is a particularly handsome Methodist church, 1859 but earlier in style. Two sets of almshouses on College Street, both early 19th century, one with attractive pediment with oval plaque.

The older houses include the sympathetically restored single-storey Victoria Cottage (No. 25 Lowgate), probably late 17th century, an unspoilt example of a housing type once common in the area. Plenty of large houses in and around the village built for Hull merchants from the later 18th century onwards, including Sutton House on Lowgate, 1770s; Netherhall on Wawne Road, *c.*1810; and on Salthouse Road Dunbar House (formerly Sutton Grange) and Tilworth House (now a hospital), both *c.*1815.

left: Cream telephone boxes, Lowgate, Hull
opposite: Signs from the streets of Hull

BAKER-STREET

THE
MANCHESTER ARMS

WM JACKSON & SON LTD
GOLD MEDAL
PORK PIES CHOCOLATES WEDDING CAKES

CITY-HOTEL

T.C. BULLESS.

Central York

1. York St John University
2. Treasurer's House
3. York Minster
4. Theatre Royal
5. Art Gallery
6. St Olave
7. St Mary's Abbey
8. King's Manor
9. Yorkshire Museum
10. York Explore (Library)
11. Barley Hall
12. St Anthony's Hall
13. DIG
14. Mansion House
15. Guildhall
16. All Saints
17. Railway Station
18. Bar Convent
19. Holy Trinity
20. Baile Hill
21. Castle Museum
22. York Castle
23. Clifford's Tower
24. Fairfax House
25. Jorvik Viking Centre
26. Merchant Adventurers' Hall
27. St Denys
28. St George (RC)
29. St Margaret

City of York

'York is the second city of England, the most beautiful of this region and indeed of the whole North, as well as its principal fortress. It is pleasant, large and strongly fortified, adorned with private as well as public buildings, crammed with riches and with people, and famous as the seat of an archbishop.' This description by William Camden in the late 16th century could apply to York at many times in its long history, for much of which it was indeed England's second city.

It was founded in AD 71, when the Roman Ninth Legion chose a site on the northeastern bank of the River Ouse to establish a fortress. Later a civilian settlement grew up on the other side of the river. Roman York, Eboracum, became a provincial capital, and was used as a base by the Emperor Septimus Severus, from 204 until his death in the city in 211. The Emperor Constantius also died at York, in 306, following which his more celebrated son Constantine, then present, was acclaimed his successor there. Almost nothing of the Roman fortress survives above ground, but the outline of its plan is still evident. The section of the city wall from Bootham Bar to Monk Bar is built on the line of the Roman defences, and Stonegate and Petergate follow the route of two of the principal streets of the fortress. Little is known of York from the end of Roman rule in the early 4th century until the early 7th century. Urban life had ended, but there were still the walls and some buildings of Eboracum standing in 627, when Paulinus baptised King Edwin of Northumbria at a site probably near the present Minster. For two centuries the city was an important centre of the Northumbrian kingdom, and through Alcuin, master of the cathedral school (and later in the court of Charlemagne), and others it became significant in the region's cultural renaissance.

Two centuries of Anglo-Scandinavian rule followed the entry of the Viking army into York in 866. During this period it became the largest city in England after London, a successful trading community and regional capital. Christianity flourished, but little is known of the cathedral and there were more than half a dozen parish churches and another Minster, Christ Church.

Most of the present information about the lives of the residents, and trades and industries, comes from excavations, the results of which are so skilfully and entertainingly explored in the Jorvik Viking Centre, Coppergate. Following the Norman invasion, met with opposition at York, William I built castles on either side of the River Ouse, and the Minster, which had been burned down, was rebuilt from the late 1070s on a new site. Monastic houses, including St Mary's Abbey, friaries and many churches were built, new streets laid out and the circuit of stone walls all but completed by the end of the 13th century, giving the city a form that remained little altered well into the modern period. Between 1298 and 1337, while kings Edward I, II and III were engaged in fighting the Scots, they often made York their base, and the city served as the country's second capital. In 1298 Parliament was held in the Minster's chapter house, and for the next six years the key royal courts of Exchequer and King's Bench were housed in the castle.

In the century following the disastrous Black Death of 1349 York prospered from clothmaking and overseas trade. The greater part of the present Minster was built, many churches were enlarged and rebuilt, and the halls of the Merchant Adventurers and Merchant Taylors were built, with the Guildhall and St Anthony's Hall begun at the very end of the period. Of York's many surviving timber-framed buildings, a good proportion are dated, wholly or in part, to between 1350 and 1450. All changed in the late 15th century as long-distance trade and the textile industry went into decline, the latter gravitating to the West Riding. York was in crisis; its population had dropped a third by the early 16th century, and its ranking among provincial towns slipped to fourteenth. The changes brought about by the Reformation were a further blow, with the dissolution of St Mary's Abbey and other religious houses. However, one result of the Pilgrimage of Grace, initially a surprisingly successful rising against both religious changes and the actions of central government, was the establishment in 1539 of the Council of the North, with meetings at York. The King's Manor became the permanent home of the Council in 1561, the same year that the Northern Ecclesiastical Commission was set up in the city. These and 'five old-established church courts and the shire and city courts made York a miniature Westminster' (D.M. Palliser, *Tudor York*, 1979). With gentry, lawyers and others attending from all over the north, the city began to prosper as the administrative and social centre of the region. Overseas trade revived under the control of the Merchant Adventurers, who benefited from a royal charter in 1581. Many substantial timber-framed houses were built, some of which survive.

The abolition of the Council and Ecclesiastical Commission in 1641, and the effects of the Civil Wars, during which Charles I set up court in the city for five months in 1644, were a temporary setback. In the 1660s York ranked second to Norwich among provincial towns, and the next century became considered as the city's 'Golden Age', rivalling its heyday with the cloth trade in the 14th–early 15th century. But, as the historian Francis Drake noted in the 1730s, 'the chief support of the city' was 'the resort to and residence of several country gentlemen with their families in it. These have found by experience that living at York is so much cheaper than London, that it is even less expensive than living at their own houses in the country ... there is no place, out of London, so polite and elegant to live in as the City of York.' Race meetings were established on Knavesmire in 1730, Lord Burlington's Assembly Rooms were opened and the New Walk, a promenade along the River Ouse, laid out in 1732, and the first theatre built two years later.

A handsome new prison and court buildings were erected at the Castle, where the twice-yearly assizes were held, described by the writer Sydney Smith as occasions of 'a great deal of dancing and provincial joy'. To house the families of the gentry, doctors, lawyers, merchants and clergy, splendid Georgian mansions were built on Micklegate, Bootham, Castlegate and elsewhere, designed by skilled local architects such as John Carr and Thomas Atkinson.

By the early 19th century, when it was no longer the most populous town in the region (overtaken by West Riding industrial towns and the port of Hull), York had more the feel of a comfortable cathedral city and a marketing and trading centre.

Georgian mansions, Micklegate, York
opposite: North transept of Minster, York

It was now a town of families of prosperous tradesmen and professionals, and annuitants, attending church or one of many Nonconformist chapels, the annual Music Festival, or meetings of the York Philosophical Society, rather than the races or the theatre. Their new homes were on The Mount, with terraces off, or at Clifton. Another York was described by T.J. Maslen, who, on a visit in 1843, found a 'small filthily-dirty, confined town ... full of little, narrow, ugly crooked streets, of mean, poor, shabby, ill-looking houses ... intersected by hundreds, I might say thousands of filthy, "cut-throat looking" lanes, courts, and alleys.' The railway had just arrived, which over time was to transform the economy and landscape of the city. As well as employing large numbers in its workshops, the rapid expansion of the rail network, based on York, assisted the growth of the city's other main industry, confectionery.

Jorvik Viking Centre, York

There were three firms: Terry's, founded in the 18th century, and Rowntree's and the smaller Craven's, both established in 1862. A third of those employed in York in 1951, when the population reached a peak of 105,371, worked in confectionery or for the railway.

These industries went into rapid decline in the later 20th century, to be replaced by tourism, the city's mainstay today. Although the historic buildings and townscape had long been appreciated, it was not until the publication in 1969 of *York: A Study in Conservation* (the Esher Report) that the idea of 'heritage' as the key to economic development was widely understood and pursued. The work of York Civic Trust, founded in 1946, was vital in both saving buildings and promoting the city's heritage, and also laid the foundation for the University of York, 1960, to be joined later by York St John University. In addition to the long-established Yorkshire and Castle Museums and the Art Gallery, the city now has many tourist attractions, including the ***National Railway Museum***, Jorvik Viking Centre, Fairfax House, Barley Hall, Bar Convent, the Chocolate Story and the Mansion House. Following its major restoration 1967–72, and the opening of the undercroft, York Minster has also embraced tourism more fully.

J.B. Priestley in *English Journey* (1934) wrote, 'York is, of course, the guide-book man's paradise, and not without good reason, for if you want the past, here it is, weighing tons.' More of a nightmare than paradise for the writers of this guidebook: how to do justice to this historic city in a few thousand words and a handful of pictures. Descriptions of the major buildings are followed by a walk round the walls, four detailed tours within the walls, and two excursions outside. Much has been left out, particularly in the suburbs.

York Minster: York Minster, or, to give it its formal title, the Cathedral and Metropolitical Church of St Peter in York, is one of the greatest churches in Northern Europe, both in size and splendour, and it contains the most important collection of medieval stained glass in Britain. At a distance, although sited on only a slight eminence, it appears to rise

National Railway Museum, York

York railway station

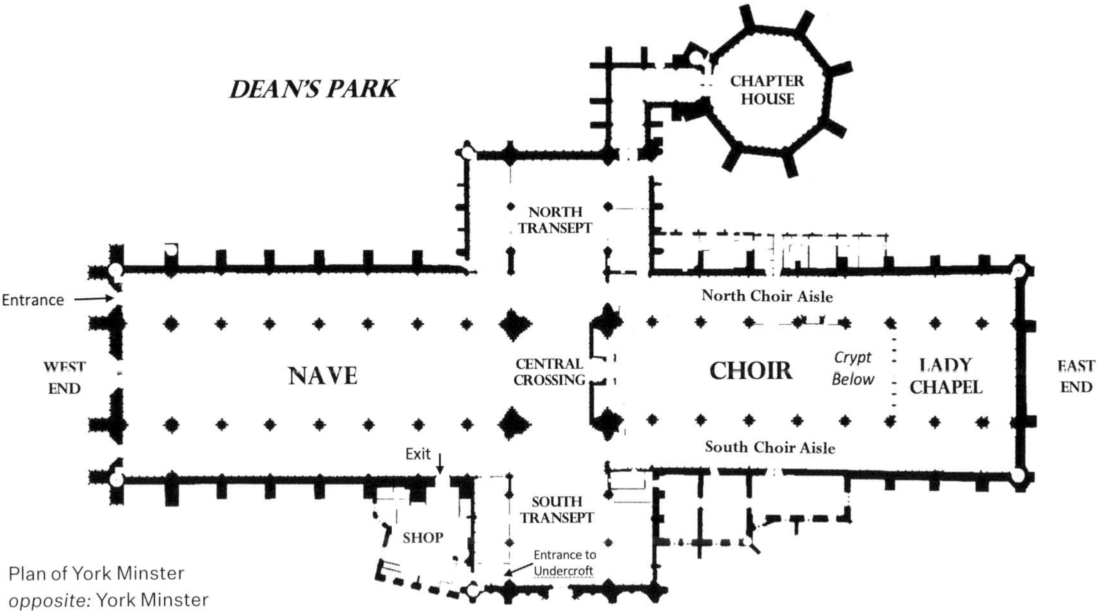

Plan of York Minster
opposite: York Minster

up out of the low-lying Vale of York, but within the city one often gets just enchanting glimpses of the Minster down narrow close-built streets.

There was an Anglo-Saxon cathedral here, built by Paulinus soon after his conversion of King Edwin of Northumbria in 627. It probably stood just north of the present building, which lies in what was the northern quarter of the Roman fortress on the site of the great Norman cathedral completed *c.*1100. Nothing of this Norman building survives above ground, except reused fragments, but its form and extent dictated the layout of the present Minster. From a rebuilding begun in the late 12th century until the late 15th century, there were few periods when the Minster would not be, in part, covered with scaffolding, much as with the ongoing conservation work today.

Exterior: Before entering the Minster at the west end, explore the exterior in a clockwise direction, beginning in ***Dean's Park*** on the north side. The transepts (see plan) are the oldest part, constructed *c.*1220–60, with the distinctive narrow lancet windows of the Early English period so striking on the north façade, where the five tall lancets are topped by a gable with five smaller tiered lancets. Next came the great octagonal chapter house, with its high conical roof, one of the architectural glories of the Minster. Attached to and reached through the north transept, it was built *c.*1280–90, with large traceried windows,of the Decorated period, filling the spaces between the tall buttresses. As the chapter house was being finished work was starting on rebuilding the nave, now with aisles. Beginning at the transepts in *c.*1290, the nave was reaching completion at the west end 60 years later, when work would have been interrupted by the Black Death. The aisle windows, and those of the clerestory above, are again in the Decorated style, similar to but simpler than those of the chapter house.

Now walk round to the east end. The foundation stone for the rebuilding to the east of the transepts was laid in 1361. First came the addition of the grand three-bay Lady Chapel with its wonderful nine-light Perpendicular east window. Even more glorious since it was repaired as part of the 21st-century restoration of the whole east front, demonstrating the expertise of the craftsmen of the Minster Stone Yard and the York Glaziers Trust. Continue to the south side, where can be seen the clerestory of the Lady Chapel with its unusual second screen of tracery. The new choir, beginning with the southeastern transept with its tall five-light window, was skilfully fitted in between the Lady Chapel and the crossing tower, *c.*1395–1425. The latter, then under construction, was a replacement of a tower that had collapsed in 1407. Passing the modern statue of Constantine, stand in front of the south transept. The façade is much grander, with its lovely rose window and pepper-pot turrets, than that of the contemporary north transept, because this was designed as an entrance to the Minster from the medieval city. Finally to the highly ornamented west front, where the superb restored Decorated stonework of the central doorway (with new work of 1996–98 by Rory Young) and the wonderful flowing curvilinear tracery of the great west window, of the 1330s, is successfully complemented by the decorative detail of the pinnacled Perpendicular stage of the towers of the 1440s–50s. The addition of the much plainer upper stage of the central tower by the early 1470s marked the completion of the rebuilding of the Minster.

Interior: On entering, go and stand at the west end of the ***Nave*** and look down the whole length of the building, a tremendous sight. The width and height of the nave are breathtaking, especially when it is empty of seating. The tall columns supporting high pointed arches are widely spaced, the aisles are broad, and the large windows of aisle and clerestory flood the building with light on a bright day. The stained glass is chiefly 14th century, the best at the west end, especially the great west window, the upper part portraying the five Joys of Annunciation, Nativity, Resurrection, Ascension and Coronation. The nave is remarkably clear of monuments, with the original burial place of St William, marked by a slab, set in the geometric-style black marble and York stone floor of the 1730s, designed by Lord Burlington and William Kent. Next go to the ***South Transept*** and descend into the excellent ***Undercroft Museum***, where, between the 1960s concrete foundations, archaeological finds and historic artefacts, with interactive displays, tell the story of the Minster, its site and the city. Return to the ***South Transept***, the earliest part of the present building to be completed, lit from the south by lancets and a rose window. Of three storeys, with pillars of stone and Purbeck-marble shafts. Also of Purbeck marble is the effigy of Archbishop Walter de Gray, 1255, in the east aisle, under a gabled canopy supported on nine Purbeck-marble shafts, the most important monument in the Minster. Nearby monuments to two more 13th-century archbishops, de Bovill and de Ludham, and ones to Dean Duncombe, 1880, designed by G.E. Street, and to Archbishop Thomson, 1890, shown with his pet dog Scamp.

Now to the ***Central Crossing*** to look up at the striking roof vault and at the 15th-century choir screen with statues of fifteen kings of England, from William the Conqueror to Henry VI. Then to the ***North Transept***, with yet more Purbeck marble and the great Five Sisters window with its original grisaille glass (grisaille is painting in shades of grey). The legend behind the window is recounted in Dickens' *Nicholas Nickleby*. The transept west aisle is crammed with military memorials; the east aisle has the tomb of Archbishop Greenfield, 1315, with one of the earliest monumental brasses in England. Nearby is a clock with 16th-century men at arms that strike the hours. At the north end of the transept a large astronomical clock, installed 1955, almost hides the way to the ***Chapter House***, reached through the L-shaped vestibule. The entrance, through a double doorway with carving of Virgin and Child and wooden doors with original wrought-iron decoration of curling spirals and dragons, opens into a great open octagonal space, with seats under canopies for the Dean and Chapter around the edge. One of the most richly decorated parts of the Minster, the large traceried windows are filled with stained glass depicting the life of Christ and the saints.

Back to the North Transept and into the ***North Choir Aisle***. Here the monuments really begin, the earliest that to the infant Prince William of Hatfield, d.1337, son of Edward III and Philippa,

opposite: The nave, York Minster

Chapter House ceiling, York Minster.

represented as a young boy. Other recumbent figures on table tombs are the Archbishops Savage (1507), Harcourt (1847) and Musgrave (1860). Semi-recumbent with his elbow resting on cushions is Archbishop Sterne (1683), ascribed to the carver Grinling Gibbons. More impressive are the Georgian monuments to Thomas Wentworth by William Kent, carved by Guelfi; to Vice-Admiral Henry Medley, by Henry Cheere; and to Sir George Saville, by John Fisher of York. Note the reference to the *Gentleman's Magazine* in the long inscription to Lora, Viscountess Downe, 1812. The window in the northeastern transept, depicting the life and miracles of St William of York, commissioned *c.*1414, is one of the finest in the Minster. Now to the ***Lady Chapel***, dominated by the remarkable great

Great West Window, York Minster

Dowager Lady Ros and pet dog, St William Window, York Minster

east window (1405–08), its main lights consisting of 144 panels depicting the biblical history of the world. More monuments to archbishops; the table tomb on the north side, without an effigy, much restored, is to Archbishop Scrope, beheaded at York in 1405 for his part in a rising against Henry IV, and later venerated as a saint. On the south side in All Saints' Chapel, William Wentworth,

2nd Earl of Strafford, 1695, and his first wife are commemorated by possibly the most spectacular monument in the Minster.

The ***South Choir Aisle***, like that on the north, is packed with memorials, including two by Gibbons to Archbishops Dolben, 1686, semi-recumbent, and Lamplugh, 1691, standing figure. More colourful is the monument to an earlier archbishop, Matthew Hutton, 1606. He also served as President of the Council of the North, of which his son-in-law Sir William Gee, commemorated nearby with his two wives, was Secretary. In the southeastern transept is the tall St Cuthbert window of *c.*1440. The ***Crypt*** is entered from either choir aisle; in the west section are great cylindrical 12th-century pillars and the stone coffin of St William, in the east section the relief of the damned in the cauldron of Hell, being stoked by devils, and the delicate damaged carving of the Virgin and Child, both 12th century. On leaving the Crypt enter the ***Choir***, where the lavish fittings of organ case, screens and stalls, and stone screen behind High Altar, by Sir Robert Smirke, after the fire of 1829, are closely based on what had been destroyed. Exit the Minster via the shop.

St Mary's Abbey and Museum Gardens: The ruins of what was one of the wealthiest and most powerful Benedictine monasteries in England stand picturesquely in the extensive grounds of the Yorkshire Museum (*grounds open daily, free*). St Mary's Abbey was founded in 1088, for monks who had come to York from Lastingham two years earlier, by William II, who granted them land outside the city wall and cut the first turf for the church. Nothing of this Norman church remains above ground. The outline of its east end, consisting of seven graduated apses, is marked out, along with the later church choir. Various remains and a remarkable series of Romanesque figures of *c.*1200 from the Norman church can be seen in the Yorkshire Museum. Totally rebuilt 1270–94, the church was about 360 ft (110 m) in length, longer than Beverley Minster. All of one style, it 'must have been one of the most splendid and consistent examples of the Geometric phase of Gothic architecture' (Pevsner). Only the north wall of the nave, a crossing pier and part of the west front, and the reconstructed part of the earlier 'sumptuous' entrance to the chapter house remain above ground today, but this is enough to demonstrate the building's size and outstanding architecture.

Other than the abbot's lodgings (*King's Manor;* see below), little survives of the other monastic buildings. The so-called Hospitium was most probably a barn. Of two storeys, 14th–15th century, the lower part stone, the upper part timber-framed, the floor supported by two rows of octagonal stone columns. Adjoining the Hospitium is a stretch of wall and a gateway of *c.*1500. The entrance to the abbey grounds was through the late 12th-century gatehouse on Marygate, which pre-dates the adjoining precinct wall, which ends with a circular tower on the bank of the River Ouse. The precinct wall, begun in the 1260s and the most extensive to survive in Britain, is nearly complete along

left: Relief of the damned, York Minster
opposite: St Mary's Abbey, York

Marygate and Bootham. St Olave's church adjoins the gatehouse on Marygate, and its history is closely linked to that of the abbey. Just before St Mary's was founded, the Lastingham monks had been granted the Anglo-Saxon Minster church of St Olaf, and it was considered within the abbey precincts, although also serving the people of Bootham and Marygate. (See below, *Outside the Walls: Bootham Bar to Clifton Green*.)

When St Mary's Abbey was dissolved in November 1536 there were 50 monks resident. Lead was immediately stripped from the roofs, but it was not until the 1630s that most of the monastic buildings were demolished. The ruins became a source of stone for reuse in the city and elsewhere, and the site became gardens and pasture. In 1828 the Yorkshire Philosophical Society, founded six years earlier for the study of natural science, was granted the abbey ruins and 3 acres (1.2 ha) to set up a museum and botanic garden. The ***Yorkshire Museum***, designed by William Wilkins, of nine bays with imposing pedimented Greek Doric portico, opened in 1830.

The following year the museum hosted the inaugural meeting of the British Association for the Advancement of Science, and in 1833 the small astronomical observatory was built in the gardens. The York Philosophical Society still has its offices in the Museum Lodge, 1874, but the Museum and Gardens are run by York Museums Trust. The Yorkshire Museum (*open daily*) holds a remarkable permanent collection of local artefacts of all periods, especially Roman and medieval, with excellent temporary displays.

King's Manor: The King's Manor, a building of great historical and architectural importance, began as the 13th-century abbot's lodgings of St Mary's Abbey. Originally approached from the west, the house was turned back to front in the 1560s with the entrance, as now, away from the abbey and towards the Minster and town. Passing to the Crown at the Dissolution, the abbot's house was handed to the re-formed Council of the North, serving as the official residence of the President and administrative base of the Council from 1561 until its abolition in 1641. From the late 17th century it was leased out for apartments and other uses, and rather neglected. The Yorkshire School for the Blind, founded in memory of Wilberforce in 1833, occupied the building until 1956, making major additions, including the Headmaster's house by Walter Brierley, 1899, in the forecourt. The King's Manor was restored and extended in 1964 for the newly founded University of York, which allows limited public access.

The entrance (east) range and two wings, creating a U-shaped building, is the oldest part and is chiefly a rebuilding in brick of the late 15th century, possibly on the lower stone courses of the original building of *c.* 1270. The Jacobean entrance doorway, with arms of Charles I, leads through the building to the inner courtyard. The upper part of the 15th-century wing on the right, in common with much else here, is Elizabethan, and contains a plaster frieze with the arms of the Earl of Huntingdon, President of the Council 1572–95. The buildings forming the western half of the courtyard, with several elaborate stone doorways, are of the early 17th century. The upper room of the corner range on the left, now reached by a 20th-century external stair, was built as a council chamber and used as an Assembly Room in the 1720s. There is a 17th-century vaulted cellar under the whole length of the University range (1964) on the west side of the second, grassed, courtyard.

York Castle: Until the early 19th century this was the centre for the administration of justice for Yorkshire, and where all the votes for the two Members of Parliament for the county were cast. It was only here that Yorkshire really functioned as a county; other matters were devolved to the ridings. The castle was built on its present site by William the Conqueror after he crushed the rebellion of 1068, and a second castle (its motte now represented by Baile Hill) was built on the opposite side of the river after a second rising, in January 1069. Both were captured and dismantled by the Danes in September 1069 but re-established soon afterwards by William. Now known as ***Clifford's Tower*** (*English Heritage, open daily*), the castle, or tower on the motte, is a rebuilding in stone *c.*1245–72 of a timber structure blown down in a storm in 1228, which in turn replaced that burned down in the horrific anti-Jewish riots of 1190. It is of an unusual four-lobed design, more common in France. The tower is reached by 55 steps up the high motte, and entered through the forebuilding, repaired by Henry Clifford, Earl of Cumberland, during the Civil Wars, and bears his arms and those of Charles I. The interior was destroyed by an explosion in 1684, and it is now a roofless shell, but the inside walls reveal much of its history. On the ground floor was the main guardroom with a well, and two smaller rooms with fireplaces and latrines. The first floor, supported by a central column, contained the main private rooms, used by the king when in York, or by royal clerks and treasury officials. From the walkway at the top of the tower there are spectacular views of the city, and in the distance of the North York Moors and the Wolds.

Below to the southeast, on three sides of a large grassed square, are the splendid 18th-century Assize Courts (***York Crown Court***) and the Debtors' and Female Prisons (***Castle Museum***). The buildings occupy the castle bailey, once surrounded by a high wall, containing barracks, stables, stores, kitchen, chapel, mint and prison. The Debtors' Prison, on the south side, was built as the County Gaol in 1701–05, to designs attributed to William Wakefield, architect of Duncombe Park in North Yorkshire. An innovative Baroque façade influenced by the work of Sir John Vanbrugh and Nicholas Hawksmoor, the centre with clock turret and cupola, and two projecting wings. Of this building Arthur Young commented in 1768 that it was 'perhaps the most airy, healthy and pleasant prison in Europe', although whether prisoners found it pleasant is doubtful. The Assize Courts, on the west side, built 1773–77, were designed by John Carr. Of eleven bays with Carr's favoured arched ground-floor windows and an imposing Ionic portico with pediment topped by a figure of Justice. Two splendid domed courtrooms inside, 'perhaps the finest rooms in York' (Pevsner). The Female Prison, on the east side, was built 1780–83, the end bays 1802, its design echoing externally the Assize Courts. Something of the hardships of prison life is revealed in the excellent Castle Museum, a lively social history museum with re-created Victorian street.

Clifford's Tower, York Castle

Walk 1

The Historic City – Along the City Walls | Free. Open every day 8 am–dusk

The walls of York extend for 2¾ miles (4.4 km), enclosing 263 acres (106 ha), and are the most complete in England and the best maintained. They are the only town walls set on high ramparts, and York retains all five of its medieval bars (gateways) and 34 of its 39 interval towers. The stone walls, built between 1250 and 1380, include a short section of Roman walling in the Museum Gardens. It is possible to walk along the greater part of the surviving walls, in three sections: Bootham Bar to Layerthorpe Tower, Red Tower to Fishergate Postern, and Baile Hill to Barker Tower. The pleasure is as much for the views as the experience of the walls themselves. If only one stretch is to be walked, it should be the

York Minster from the City Walls

first. Small brass studs showing a tower mark the route when not on the walls, and there are information boards at all the key access points.

Bootham Bar to Layerthorpe Tower. Bootham Bar is on the site of one of the principal Roman gateways, and the first stretch of the wall as far as Monk Bar is built on top of the Roman defences. The outer arch of ***Bootham Bar*** is late 11th century, the inner arch 12th century; in the 14th century the bar was heightened and the barbican, or outer defence projecting from the front, added. The barbican was demolished in the 1830s. The walk goes through the room in the bar, and along the wall with Gillygate on the left and the Minster on the right, to ***Robin Hood's Tower***, constructed at the corner in the 1880s when the wall was restored and the walkway built. From the corner there is a good view of the ditch and ramparts along the south side of Lord Mayor's Walk, a tree-lined promenade laid out in 1718. The buildings of ***York St John University*** are on the north side of the Walk, the oldest the original Tudor-style buildings of York Diocesan Training School by G.T. Andrews, 1846. From the wall here there are splendid views southwards of the Minster with the Deanery gardens and Minster Library in the foreground, and then Gray's Court and Treasurer's House. ***Monk Bar***, early 14th-century with late 15th-century top storey, is the tallest and strongest bar, and still has its portcullis with mechanism. It now hosts the Richard III Experience. Almost immediately after the bar, down on the left, is the brick dome of a Georgian ice house cut into the ramparts. On the right-hand side are the excavated remains of a Roman interval tower and section of wall, and soon afterwards the medieval ***Merchant Taylors' Hall*** with timber framing exposed in the gable end.

Then comes the successful 1980s infill housing along Aldwark and finally the quiet public garden behind St Anthony's Hall, before the wall comes to an end at ***Layerthorpe Tower***, rebuilt 1645. Now, for almost ⅓ mile (0.5 km), there is no wall; the River Foss, which here widened into the extensive King's Fishpool, a large, marshy lake, was considered enough of a defence. It was drained following the formation of Foss Navigation Company in 1792.

Bootham Bar, York

Monk Bar, York

Fishergate Bar, York

Walmgate Bar, York, with barbican in foreground

Micklegate Bar, York

Walk along ***Foss Islands Road***; on the left is the very tall incinerator chimney, 1899. If you follow the Foss as it bends away to the right you come to Leetham's flour mill (Rowntree Wharf), 1890s, by Penty & Penty, but continuing along the main road the walls begin again at the Red Tower.

Red Tower to Fishergate Postern. The rectangular ***Red Tower*** (so called because it was built in brick rather than stone), with its charming pyramidal tiled roof, was constructed in 1490. Partly rebuilt and re-roofed in 1857. To the west St Margaret's church can be seen flanked by decent local-authority housing up to ***Walmgate Bar***. This was the main entrance from Beverley and Hull, mid-12th century, the only bar that retains its 14th-century barbican on the east side. The west front has a curious Elizabethan addition, standing on two Tuscan stone columns, with transomed windows flanked by Tuscan and Ionic columns to the first and second storeys and a balustraded balcony on top. Then comes ***Fishergate Bar***, the fifth and last medieval bar to be built, a simple gateway compared to the others. It was first mentioned 1315, burnt by rebels in 1489, then blocked up until 1827. At the next corner is a substantial 14th-century tower overlooking the junction of the Ouse and Foss rivers before the wall ends at ***Fishergate Postern***, with a 14th-century gate and rectangular tower, *c.*1505, with later tiled roof.

After leaving the wall cross Piccadilly, past the 21st-century hotel, its circular entrance tower making a reasonable attempt to fit its location, and cross the Foss by Castle Mills Bridge. To the right is the reconstructed Raindale watermill. Follow the edge of the castle wall, before crossing the road to the Tower Gardens and the low section of the city wall in front of Tower Place, ending with the 14th-century ***Davy Tower***, converted to a Georgian summer house. Then turn left along the River Ouse, up steps and over ***Skeldergate Bridge***. (South of the bridge, after the car park, is the New Walk, laid out as a fashionable place to promenade in the 1730s and soon afterwards extended past Pikeing Well, the stone well house by John Carr, 1752. Further south is the futuristic ***Millennium Bridge***, a footbridge across the Ouse.)

Red Tower, York

Leetham's flour mill, York

Skeldergate Bridge, York

Millennium Bridge, York

Baile Hill to Barker Tower. Once over Skeldergate Bridge, access to the wall is via the steps in the small octagonal Victorian tower on the corner. You are now on the edge of ***Baile Hill***, the motte of the other Norman castle built by William I. The motte is 40 ft (12 m) high and 180 ft (55 m) in diameter. At the next corner is ***Bitchdaughter Tower***, origin of name unknown, then Victoria Bar, a gateway constructed in 1838 to give access to Bishophill. Views across pleasing, modest Victorian housing to the tower of St Mary Bishophill Junior before ***Micklegate Bar*** is reached. First mentioned in the 12th century, this was the main entrance to the city from the south, a place where royal visitors were welcomed and traitors' heads displayed. Now home to the Henry VII Experience. After the next corner tower the wall's later history is linked closely with the coming of the railway. Five arches were cut through the wall, three for the railway 1840–45, when the first station was built inside, and two for roads in the 1870s giving access to the present station outside the wall. From here there are good views of the station, 1871–75, with its great train shed, and the vast contemporary station hotel (Principal), and the classic view of York Minster. The walkway on the wall ends at the medieval ***Barker Tower***, circular with a conical tiled roof, by Lendal Bridge.

Barker Tower, York

Crossing the bridge the line of the wall, with part surviving, can be traced towards Bootham Bar, where the walk began. Starting at ***Lendal Tower***, 14th century, with 17th-century addition when first used as waterworks, the wall runs alongside Museum Gardens, up to the ruins of St Leonard's Hospital. Then go into the gardens, where in the northeast corner the wall incorporates a stretch of the Roman defences, with a stripe of red tiles, ending with the ***Roman Multangular Tower***. The final surviving section of the city wall then runs along the right-hand side of the passage beside King's Manor, leading into ***Exhibition Square***.

Multangular Tower, York

Walk 2

Within the Walls: Northeast – Circular from the Minster

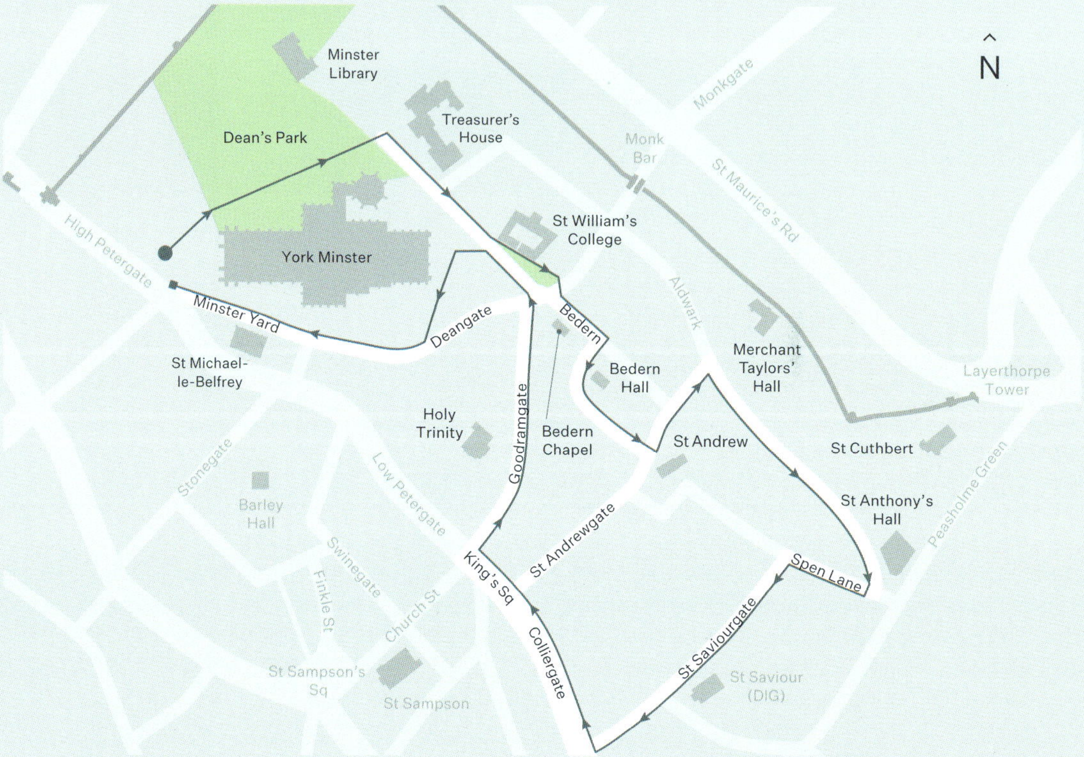

Starting at the west end of the Minster, go through the iron gates into the quiet of ***Dean's Park***, a great place to view the Minster close up. Here stood a palace of the archbishops, used from the 12th to mid-16th century, when Bishopthorpe became their favoured York residence. On the north side of the park is a 12th-century arcade, part of the Great Hall, fronting the grounds of the 1820s Tudor New Residence by R.H. Sharp. The palace chapel, *c.*1230, was restored to serve as the ***Minster Library*** in 1806–11. It houses the largest English Cathedral Library and the archives of the Dean and Chapter. Adjacent is the present Deanery, Neo-Georgian, late 1930s, and then the charming ***Minster Court***, cream-painted houses around three sides of a cobbled square, externally early to late Georgian, but No. 2 contains a 15th-century roof and early 17th-century ceiling. Next is the ***Treasurer's House*** (*National Trust*), entered from Chapter House Street. Medieval origins, rebuilt by Sir George Young in the late 16th century and remodelled by his grandson, who lived there 1628–48. Projecting wings with shaped gables and an entrance flanked by pairs of Roman Doric pillars with Ionic pilasters above. Numerous changes in the 18th century, when it was used as a town house by various Yorkshire gentry families and by Canon Jaques Sterne, uncle of the writer Laurence Sterne. Skilfully restored with internal alterations and additions by Temple Moore for the industrialist

York Minster, Treasurer's House and Gray's Court from the walls

Frank Green in 1897–1906. Moore also restored ***Gray's Court*** at right angles in the courtyard to the rear, which contains what remains of the medieval Cathedral treasurer's house.

After Chapter House Street is No. 4 Minster Yard, set back, late 18th-century front but earlier behind, and then ***College Green***, dominated by the great east end of the Minster. On the north side is the impressive long front of ***St William's College***, built 1465–67 as the College for the Chantry Priests of the Minster. Restored in 1906 by Temple Moore, who added the oriel windows to the jettied timber-framed first floor and retained the Georgian shop fronts to the stone ground floor. The building forms a large courtyard incorporating the earlier house of the Prior of Hexham. A timber-framed gateway leads into ***Goodramgate***. Cross the road and go through the arch into ***Bedern***, the location of the College or 'Bedern' of the Vicars Choral – as many as 36 of them – responsible for the daily services in the Minster. What remains, much altered, is the 14th-century chapel (York Glaziers Trust), immediately on the right, and round the corner on Bartle Garth the ***Bedern Hall***, which retains its original oak scissor-braced roof dated 1370. Restored in 1980, it is now the hall of three York guilds. Bartle Garth continues through into ***St Andrewgate***, and the modest medieval ***St Andrew's church***, closed 1599 and – after many uses, some dubious – once again a place of worship. Along the street on the right can be seen the five-bay pedimented house built for himself by the architect Thomas Atkinson *c.* 1780. Go left to ***Aldwark***, passing the building with Tuscan pilasters, built as the fire-engine house for the Yorkshire Insurance Company. Set back off Aldwark, a gentle curving street running parallel to the city walls, is the medieval ***Merchant Taylors' Hall***, L-shaped, 17th- and 18th-century brick exterior, but timber-framed inside. Main hall with tie-beam roof of *c.* 1400, and the remains of a screens passage. Alongside is the simple single-storey almshouse, 1730.

East end of York Minster and St William's College

Back on Aldwark, ***Oliver Sheldon House*** of *c.*1720, eight bays, hipped roof with deep dentilled cornice and rusticated pedimented doorway, contains fragments of late medieval timber framing. The street has now been redeveloped successfully; the 1980s courtyard housing on the left is behind the brick boundary wall of long-demolished Saltmarshe House, 1693, with a rusticated round-arched doorway and piers for a carriage entrance. Towards the end of the street, just past an intrusive office block, is York's earliest purpose-built ***Methodist chapel***, 1759, brick, rectangular with hipped roof. The buildings opposite, by Demaine & Brierley, 1887, were built for the Bluecoat School, then housed in the adjoining ***St Anthony's Hall***, Peasholme Green. The latter was built for the Guild of St Martin (founded 1446) on the site of a chapel of St Anthony, a substantial building, medieval stone to the ground floor, 17th-century brick above replacing timber framing, large main hall with fine medieval roof. It now houses the ***Quilters' Guild Museum*** (*see website*). Nearby is ***St Cuthbert's church***, mid-15th century with later 15th-century tower, but the east wall, 11th century, is made up of Roman masonry and bricks. The timber-framed ***Black Swan***, opposite, was built as a private house in the 16th century, and extended in the 17th, the date of the staircase. The north wing is *c.*1940. It is a great contrast to the adjacent vast curved, glass-fronted office for Hiscox Insurance, 2015, by Ken Shuttleworth (Make Architects), who sketched the original designs for London's iconic 'Gherkin' building for Foster & Partners. An elegant concrete stairway curves upwards in the four-storey atrium, which has at its centre a decommissioned Russian rocket. Why?

Opposite is ***St Saviour's Place*** with the grand Peasholme House, 1752, attributed to John Carr. Then turn left into ***St Saviourgate***, the first half lined with fine Georgian houses, detached and terraced, dating from the 1720s onwards. One can appreciate the historian Francis Drake's comment that it was 'one of the neatest and best-built Streets in the City'. Set back through pretty cast-iron gates on the north side is the unusual ***Unitarian Chapel*** (originally Presbyterian), built 1693, brick in cruciform shape. Lady Hewley (see Blue Plaque on No. 31), who was a major funder of the chapel, also founded almshouses, which were resited in St Saviourgate in 1840. Tudor, stone, by J.P. Pritchett. They lie at right angles to the street, next to ***St Saviour's church***, largely rebuilt 1845, which now houses ***DIG***, 'a hands-on archaeological adventure', run by York Archaeological Trust. Opposite the giant stone portico of the Centenary Methodist Church, 1840 by James Simpson, looks on to the much-derided concrete Stonebow development, recently refurbished.

At the end of St Saviourgate is the curiously named Whip-Ma-Whop-Ma-Gate. At this point turn right up ***Colliergate***, chiefly Georgian, through King's Square, the site of the medieval Christ Church, before turning right into ***Goodramgate***, a narrow street that curves pleasantly from King's Square to Monk Bar. Wrought-iron gates in a brick archway, a short distance on the left, past the Old White Swan, lead into the peaceful secluded churchyard of ***Holy Trinity*** (Churches Conservation Trust), a modest but most enchanting church of stone patched with brick, with a saddleback tiled roof. Eleventh-century origins, but chiefly of the 14th–15th centuries, including the arcades and tower. Remarkably well-preserved Georgian interior with a great jumble of box pews on an

Holy Trinity, Goodramgate, York

Statue of Constantine, York

Rainwater head, St Saviourgate, York

uneven floor, an early 18th-century reredos and three-sided communion rail with semicircular centre. The east window has very fine late 15th-century stained glass. The church is hidden from the street by ***Lady Row***, Nos 60–72 Goodramgate, built on the churchyard *c.* 1316. Originally eleven single-bay tenements, reduced to seven in the 18th century, it is the earliest dateable example of timber framing in York. Still stuccoed in the original manner, as is the jettied Snickleway Inn (formerly Anglers Arms) further down the street. Either side of the latter the timbers on Nos 41–45 and 49–51, prominent three-storey ranges of the late 15th–early 16th century, have been exposed and painted black, the result of restoration in 1929–30.

At the junction with ***Deangate***, which was disastrously cut through the Minster Precinct in 1903, but since 1989 has been closed to through traffic, cross on to ***College Green*** and the east end of the Minster. Go left into ***Minster Yard***, passing the three-storey, red-painted Old Residence, 1720s, and along the south side of the Minster. Here are a statue of Constantine and a re-erected Roman stone pillar, found nearby. Behind the pillar is a castellated stone Gothic range, designed as an office for the Dean and Chapter by Pritchett, 1837, but used as two private houses. Good Georgian houses flank the entrance to Minster Gates; that on the left has a rainwater head dated 1763. Pritchett was also responsible for the similarly styled No. 12 Minster Yard, the former Consistory Court, adjacent to ***St Michael-le-Belfrey***, the largest of the city churches, somewhat dwarfed by the Minster. First mentioned in 1294, it was entirely rebuilt 1525–36, on the eve of the Reformation. Designed by the master mason of the Minster, the light and spacious interior has excellent stained glass, showing Flemish influence. Superb Corinthian reredos and ornate carved communion rail by William Etty, 1712. Many monuments, the most imposing that to Robert Squire, d. 1709, and his wife, Priscilla, life-size figures standing rather casually with arms resting on flaming urns. Guy Fawkes was baptised here in 1570. The tour ends where it began, at the west end of the Minster.

Walk 3

Circular from the Minster

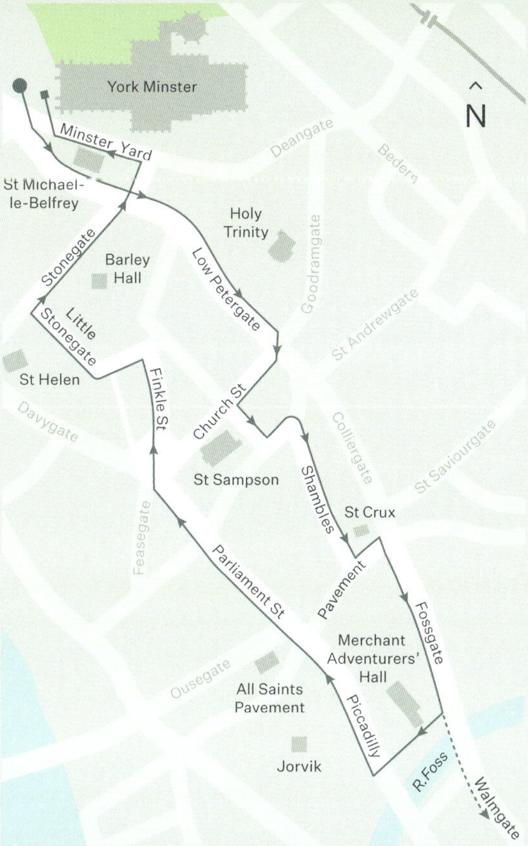

From the west end of the Minster, go south along ***High Petergate*** with St Michael-le-Belfrey church on the left and a fine Georgian terrace on the right. Pass the junction with Stonegate and Minster Gates, with the elegant Regency shop front guarded by a figure of Minerva, goddess of wisdom, with her pile of books, and carry on down ***Low Petergate***. This is another street with York's usual entertaining mixture of late medieval and Georgian/Regency buildings. Much of the early section is of the 18th–early 19th century, beginning on the southwest side with the four-storey block of the late 1820s, curving round from Stonegate, with delightful Victorian shop front. Opposite are Nos 40–50, late 1830s; No. 52, dated 1772 with elephant crest of Dean Fountayne on the rainwater head; a timber-framed range of *c.* 1500; then No. 62, the rather distinctive house built *c.* 1725 for the lawyer John Shaw, who was Diocesan Registrar. It was for many years York College for Girls. It incorporates to the rear the timber-framed former Talbot Inn. Lots of jettied and stuccoed timber-framed buildings, of which the most impressive are Nos 71–81, three storeys, seven gables, late 14th to mid-17th century.

Turn right into ***Church Street***, named after the medieval ***St Sampson's church***. Closed in 1968, it is now a Community Centre for the over sixties. Late 15th-century tower; the rest rebuilt in the 1840s and successfully converted to its present use by George Pace in 1974. At the east end of the church turn down ***Patrick Pool***, with late 16th-century three-storey timber-framed house. At the corner, with medieval stonework, turn left along Newgate, and right into the narrow ***Shambles***, York's most famous street and a honeypot for tourists. Towards the top end, where timber-framed houses jetty out to almost touch across the street, you can get something of the feel of medieval town life, albeit sanitised. Although heavily commercialised with much restoration, some overdone, it is still an authentic street, not a stage set. Originally Flesh Shambles, meaning meat stalls, the street of the butchers. Of the 15th century, Nos 7, 8 and 9 on the east side are the best preserved of the timber-framed houses, rendered as they would have been when built, with shallow canopies. Two have street counters. Nos 10–11 has been identified as the home of St Margaret Clitherow, who was pressed to death for her faith, and not No. 35 as claimed. At the south end is the rebuilt remnant of the medieval ***St Crux church***, Pavement, demolished in the 1880s, now a parish room and open occasionally. Worth visiting to see the monuments, especially the highly coloured one of Sir Robert Watter, d. 1612, and his wife lying side by side below figures of children, under a columned canopy topped by rustic putti. Pavement has the imposing three-storey gabled

The
YORK GHOST
MERCHANTS
Handmade
Artisan
Chocolates
LITTLE SHAMBL

and jettied, timber-framed ***Herbert House***, built *c.*1620 for John Jaques, merchant, although many of the decorative details belong to the drastic 1920s restoration. The 16th-century back wing runs alongside Lady Peckitt's Yard, where there is a good three-storey house of the 1680s with decorative brickwork, casement windows and bold bracketed cornice. The black and white timber façade of Nos 18–22 is of 1893.

Cross the road and go down ***Fossgate***, with the usual mixture of timber-framed and later buildings, past the Doulton-ware façade of the former cinema of 1911 to reach, on the right, the 17th-century gateway to the remarkable ***Merchant Adventurers' Hall***, the greatest and best preserved of York's four medieval guild halls. Built for the Guild of Our Lord Jesus and the Blessed Virgin Mary, licensed 1357, and absorbed in the early 15th century by the Guild of Mercers and Merchants, which became the Company of Merchant Adventurers of the City of York in 1581. A large mid 14th-century building comprising a brick-walled undercroft divided down the centre by substantial timber posts with, on the first floor, a great timber-framed hall similarly divided. The chapel attached to the undercroft is early 15th century.

(For the more active, it is well worth taking a detour from Fossgate across the bridge of 1812 over the River Foss into ***Walmgate***, a rather overlooked part of York, with a range of older buildings, interesting independent shops and cafes, and two medieval churches. ***St Denys*** has mid-12th-century origins with reset Norman doorway, but is mostly mid-14th century with a fine east window to the north aisle. The attraction of the church is its splendid medieval stained glass. In the Percy vault under the church was buried the 3rd Earl of Northumberland, a casualty of the bloody battle of Towton, 1461. The family mansion, the Percy Inn, stood opposite. Much further down the street, flanked by modern housing, a cast-iron gateway on the left proclaims 'To ***St Margaret's Church***'. The church, now the National Centre for Early Music, was largely rebuilt in 1852, with late 17th-century brick tower and an excellent Norman porch, resited here from St Nicholas's Hospital, which was destroyed in the siege of 1644. Much of the area consists of mid–late 20th-century housing, but to the southwest of the street a pleasant, well-kept two-storey terrace from the 1840s survives on George Street. Irish migrants lived in this area, and for them ***St George's Roman Catholic church*** was built here in 1850, designed by York-born J.A. Hansom. The nearby churchyard of the earlier St George's church contains the grave of the 'highwayman' ***Dick Turpin***, who was executed at York in 1739.)

Back to the walk, and from the rear of the Merchant Adventurers' Hall enter ***Piccadilly***, widened in 1912. At the junction with Coppergate stands ***All Saints Pavement***, with its handsome 15th-century tower and splendid openwork lantern. The chancel was demolished in 1782 to make way for a market. There is 14th-century stained glass from St Saviour's in the west window, and good late 19th-century glass by C.E. Kempe elsewhere. Delightful pulpit 1634, 17th-century

Merchant Adventurers' Hall
opposite: The Shambles, York

Lantern tower, All Saints Pavement, York

brass to former Lord Mayor and tablet to Tate Wilkinson, 18th-century theatre manager of York Circuit. (***Jorvik Viking Centre*** is in the Coppergate Centre, immediately south of All Saints.) Continue along the broad Parliament Street, laid out for the market in 1834–36. At the north end is ***St Sampson's Square***, originally Thursday Market. In the north corner is the Roman Bath Museum under the pub. From here go down the narrow Dickensian Nether Hornpot Lane, entered through an archway, or along Finkle Street, to Back Swinegate. Then left and right into ***Little Stonegate***, with the large cream-brick former Ebenezer Primitive Methodist Chapel by J.P. Pritchett, 1851, with heavy rusticated stone basement. This brings you to ***Stonegate***, 'stone-paved street' (as it still is), the show street of the city, rich in medieval and later timber framing, Georgian houses, fine shop fronts and 'outrageous and enjoyable ... Victorian restorations' (Hutchinson and Palliser).

On the north side, starting at the west end on the corner with Blake Street, is an excellent Victorian cast-iron shop front. Then a run of timber-framed houses, all with altered façades, including No. 8, Regency Gothic, and No. 10, jettied but mid-Victorian covered in Maw tiles. Guy Fawkes was probably born in a house on the site of Nos 32–34. The north side ends with one of the best blocks of largely unaltered timber framing in York, Nos 48–60, all still rendered. Behind Nos 48–50 are two walls of a two-storey Norman stone house. Nos 54–60, three storeys, 14th century, the rebuilding of the upper part at the corner helpfully dated 1646. Now the south side, west to east, with the same mixture of timber framing and Georgian/Regency façades and shop fronts. No. 15, on the corner with Little Stonegate, is mid-Georgian, incorporating 15th-century timber framing. It was originally part of a long two-storey range with the splendid Mulberry Hall, Nos 17–19. Nos 21–25 is also of 15th-century origin, with a passageway leading to No. 23, the premises of the York Medical Society, a large complex of buildings from the late 16th century onwards, including a mid-17th-century brick-built wing ending in a three-storey tower. A little further on, down another passageway, is ***Coffee Yard*** with ***Barley Hall***, a skilful reconstruction by York Archaeological Trust in the early 1990s of a medieval timber-framed building formerly on the site, using some original timbers (*open daily, with displays illustrating medieval life*). Back on Stonegate is No. 35, a 15th-century timber-framed building with a remarkable Victorian façade created by the stained-glass artist J.W. Knowles when it was his home and workshop. It has tiled panels dated 1874. Next but one, No. 37, has the best Regency bow-windowed façade in York. The street ends with Georgian houses and good 19th-century shop fronts. From there cross into the narrow ***Minster Gates***, with its great view of the imposing south transept of the Minster, where the walk ends.

Walk 4

The Minster to Ouse Bridge

1 Art Gallery
2 King's Manor
3 De Grey Rooms
4 York Explore (Library)
5 Theatre Royal
6 Assembly Rooms
7 St Helen
8 Mansion House
9 Guildhall
10 St Martin-le-Grand
11 St Michael
12 Cumberland House
13 Jorvik
14 St Mary
15 Fairfax House
16 Clifford's Tower
17 Tower Place
18 Magistrates' Court

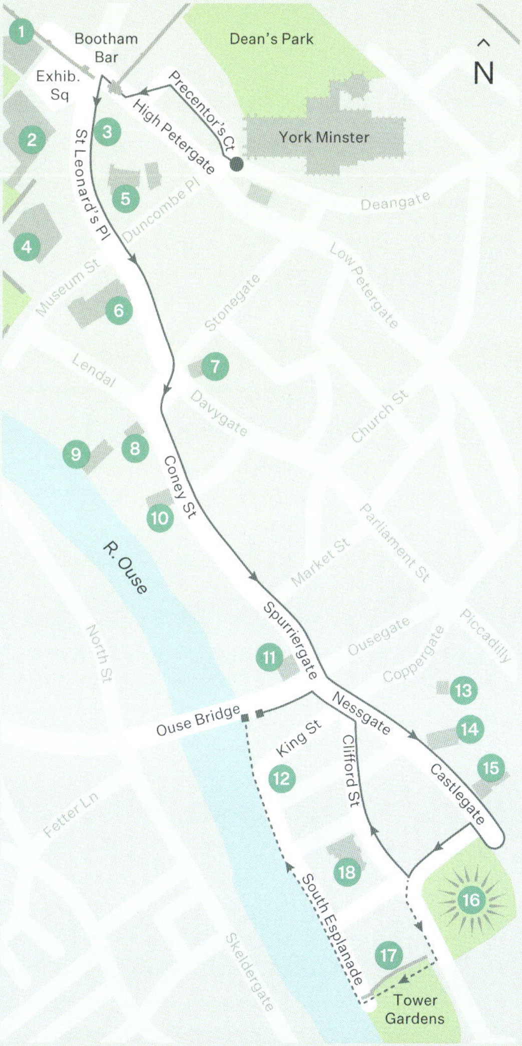

From the usually busy west end of the Minster escape to the peaceful ***Precentor's Court***, the narrow lane that begins between the three-storey brick house directly opposite the west end and the stone gateway to the former Purey Cust Nursing Home. A charming terrace of neat brick houses of *c.*1700, some with original casement windows, shutters and doors, leads to a small square and two handsome early Georgian mansions, both brick with stone quoins, one with an odd brick lantern rising above the hipped roof. From here go down the little passage into ***High Petergate***. Off to the left, the black and white timber-framed range is a skilful replica by Temple Moore, *c.*1905. The jettied buildings opposite, one double-gabled with bay windows to the upper storeys, are timber-framed. Go through ***Bootham Bar*** and cross ***St Leonard's Place*** into ***Exhibition Square***, which was laid out in 1879 when the Art Gallery was built. A rather dour large Italianate building, relieved by a delicate portico and colourful mosaic panels, it houses a splendid collection, particularly of 20th-century ceramics (*open daily*). The statue in front is of local artist William Etty (famous for his nudes), whose paintings are well represented in the gallery. To the south, set back, is ***King's Manor*** (see above). Across St Leonard's Place are the ***De Grey Rooms***, by P.F. Robinson and G.T. Andrews, 1842, stuccoed, of seven bays with long arched and pedimented windows and a pretty cast-iron balcony to the first floor. The rooms, scene of concerts and grand balls, were built initially as a mess to accommodate the officers of the Yorkshire Hussars. There is still a Regency feel, complementing Nos 1–9 St Leonard's Place, the grand stuccoed terrace by John Harper, 1834, the first development along the new street. Harper also designed a new Tudor-style front for the ***Theatre Royal*** opposite, replaced in extravagant Gothic, a cross between a Nonconformist chapel and a town hall, by the City Engineer in 1879. The first theatre on the site, incorporating the vaulted undercroft of the medieval St Leonard's Hospital, was built in 1744. Interior with Art Nouveau feel by Frank Tugwell, 1901–02, and glass foyer and restaurant, entered under plant-like pillared canopies, by Patrick Gwynne and R.A. Sefton, 1968.

Cross over to ***Blake Street*** at the junction with Duncombe Place and Museum Street, passing, on the corner, the Red House, built 1702–04 for Sir William Robinson, MP for York. It was for many years the home of the antiquarian Dr John Burton, the Dr Slop in Laurence Sterne's *Tristram Shandy*. On Blake Street are the splendid ***Assembly Rooms***, built 1732, subscribed for by the gentry of Yorkshire and designed by their most prominent member, the architect and patron of the arts Richard Boyle, 3rd Earl of Burlington (see *Londesborough*). The magnificent Great Assembly Room is surrounded by 44 tall Corinthian columns, lit by clerestory windows by day and many chandeliers by night. Its revolutionary design, based on Vitruvius' 'Egyptian Hall', did not impress the Duchess of Marlborough, who wrote that it exceeded 'all the nonsense and madness that I ever saw of that kind', and complained that the columns stood 'as close as a row of nine pins' and 'nobody with a hoop petticoat can pass through them'. The façade with its large Ionic portico is of 1828, by Watson & Pritchett.

Blake Street ends in ***St Helen's Square***, the civic heart of York. The medieval church after which the square is named was partly rebuilt in the mid-16th century but underwent major Victorian restoration. The west end with octagonal lantern tower is a sympathetic rebuild of 1875. The churchyard was sold to the city and the square laid out in 1745 to provide a suitable setting for the ***Mansion House***, built 1725–30 as the official residence of the Lord Mayor (*open to the public*). A fine open-well staircase leads to the lavish State Room with coved ceiling, Corinthian pilasters and over the fireplaces the Royal and City Arms. Small musicians' gallery on the west wall. A passage to the north leads to the great ***medieval Guildhall***, built *c.*1450, severely damaged in the Second World War and well restored. A massive aisled hall of six bays with tall wooden pillars, and an arched braced roof. Good series of buildings on the north side of St Helen's Square, all of stone, or stone-faced. The former Savings Bank of 1830, Classical, by Watson & Pritchett and the Italianate former Yorkshire

Mansion House, St Helen's Square, York

Insurance Company offices, 1847, by G.T. Andrews flank a dramatic stone Baroque Revival of 1924, with gigantic Corinthian pillars, by Lewis Wade. The nicely finished block opposite, 1930, including Betty's, of brick and stone in a more restrained Baroque, with Ionic pilasters to the upper storeys, has rounded ends and extends down Davygate.

Next turn down ***Coney Street***, one of the principal streets of the medieval city. Its most prominent feature is the large Victorian clock supported by an enormous bracket that juts out from the remnant of the church of ***St Martin-le-Grand***. Rebuilt in the mid-15th century, the church was badly damaged in the Second World War. Only the ornate tower and south aisle were retained in the innovative and colourful 1960s restoration by George Pace. Typical 18th-century York font cover, with scrolls and dove. The east window by Harry Stammers, *c.*1965, depicts the burning of the church, and the 15th-century window opposite the south door records the life of St Martin. Coney Street is architecturally one of the city's most disappointing streets, but many of the shop fronts hide earlier features, such as timber

Font cover, St Martin-le-Grand, Coney Street, York

framing and early 17th-century plaster ceilings. Nos 16–22 south of New Street, three-storey timber-framed and jettied, are late 15th–early 16th-century, two with bays to the first floor. (On New Street is Cumberland Row, 1746, one of the earliest brick terraces in York.) Down a passage after No. 26, ***Judges' Court***, early 18th century, housed the judges for the twice-yearly assizes. Of 20th-century buildings, the best are the Baroque Revival Yorkshire Bank, 1922, and Brierley's NatWest of 1907, and in between them the entertaining half-timbered former Boots (No. 48), also 1907, with painted heads and decorative plasterwork, and the Art Deco former Burtons, 1931. Towards its southern end Coney Street becomes ***Spurriergate***, and at the corner with Low Ousegate is ***St Michael's church***, closed 1984 and now the Spurriergate Centre. On the site of a Saxon church, the present building has late 12th-century arcades. When the tower was added in the 15th century its piers and capitals copied the earlier work. The building was shortened in the 1820s, and the tower lowered during restoration by Pace in the 1960s. Superb early 18th-century reredos and altar rails, which have the semicircular projection found elsewhere in the city.

From the end of Spurriergate go along ***Nessgate*** into ***Castlegate***, the narrow street on the left of the junction with Clifford Street. The spire of ***St Mary Castlegate*** is the tallest in York, 152 ft (46 m). The church is mostly 15th-century, but a dedication stone *c.* 1020 records that it was built by Efard, Grim and Aese. Some pre-Norman walling round the chancel arch. The church is now used for exhibitions by York Museums Trust. The rest of the street is largely Georgian and includes two of the grandest houses in the city. ***Castlegate House*** by John Carr, 1763, was built for Peter Johnson, Recorder of York. ***Fairfax House*** is earlier, possibly before 1745, brick with stone quoins, bands and window surrounds, of five bays, the centre three bays projecting slightly with pediment. After its purchase by Viscount Fairfax in 1759, the interior was completely remodelled by Carr and includes some of the finest plasterwork and woodwork in Yorkshire. After many years in use as part of a dance hall and cinema, it was skilfully restored by Francis Johnson 1982–84, and is now open to the public as a showcase of the lavish lifestyle of an aristocratic family at the height of York's position as the social capital of the North.

Leaving Castlegate go down ***Tower Street***, passing the north side of Clifford's Tower. From here either turn right into ***Clifford Street***, or take a more scenic detour along the riverside (see overleaf). Laid out in 1881, Clifford Street is lined by a series of large, overtly Victorian buildings mostly in a rather ugly, darkish red brick with stone or terracotta detailing. At the south end

FAIRFAX
HOUSE

River Ouse in flood at King's Staith, York | *opposite:* Fairfax House and the spire of St Mary, Castlegate

the remarkably ornate ***Magistrates' Court***, 1890-92, by Huon A. Matear of Liverpool, in a sort of late Gothic, with Perpendicular tracery. Three-storey centre bay, with Romanesque entrance, stone carving of Richard II presenting sword to Mayor in pediment, and above a tall clock tower with cupola. Then the more restrained Romanesque former ***Technical College***, built for the York Institute of Art, Science and Literature, 1884, by W.G. Penty, but even here the entrance bay and the round-arched balustrade are topped by a series of small open cupolas. Least satisfactory is the ***Grand Opera House*** of 1902. Continue along Nessgate and left into Low Ousegate ending at the Ouse Bridge.

Now for the more picturesque route. Instead of turning right into Clifford Street continue left along ***Tower Street***. On the west side gates lead into a small park, Tower Gardens. On the right is ***Tower Place***, an enchanting late Regency terrace, two storeys, with full-height shallow bows. The low stretch of the city wall in front of the houses runs down to a Georgian summer house, built on the base of the medieval ***Davy Tower***, and overlooking the River Ouse. From here turn right onto ***South Esplanade***, with views up and down the river. Go north, past pleasing Victorian terraces, to reach the cobbled ***King's Staith***. When the river floods, the handsome Cumberland House, *c.*1710, and the 17th-century timber-framed King's Arms, are often shown on the TV news. From here it is a short distance to steps which lead up to the elegant triple-arched ***Ouse Bridge***, by Peter Atkinson junior, completed 1821.

Walk 5

Within the Walls: Southwest – Ouse Bridge to the Minster

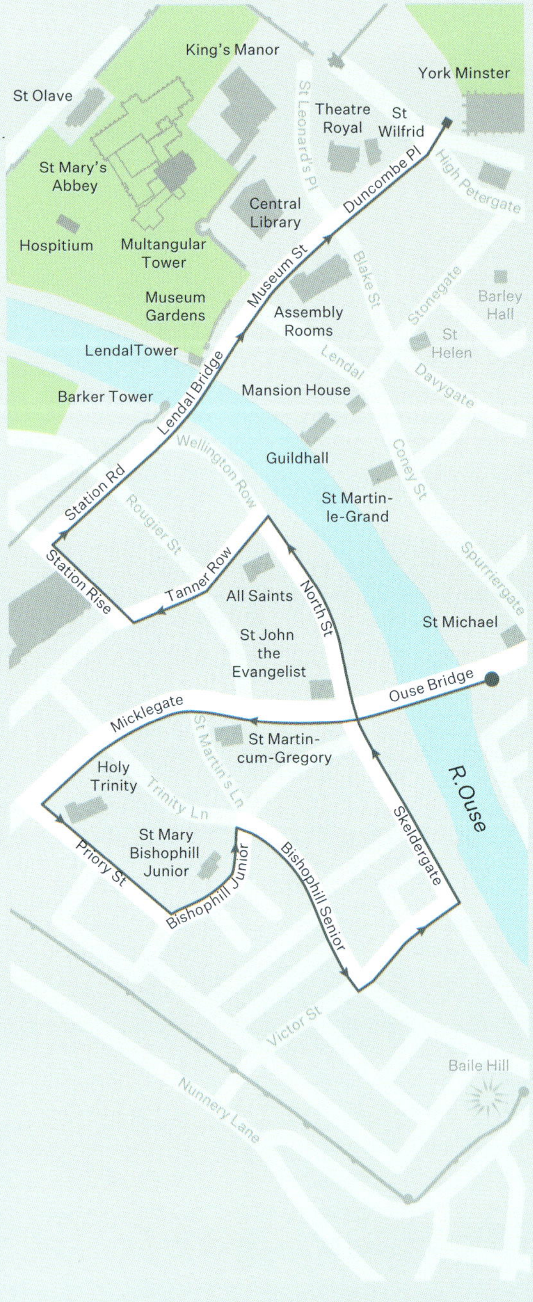

Cross the ***Ouse Bridge***, from the east side, with a view of Woods Mill, a rare survivor of the warehouses and industrial buildings that once lined the west bank of the river. ***Micklegate*** is now reached. On the right is ***St John the Evangelist church***, with some 12th-century features, the north arcade 14th century, the south 15th century. Good early 16th-century aisle roofs and a squat timber and brick tower of 1646. Closed in 1934, the church has had many uses since, including an Arts Centre, and at the time of writing is a cocktail bar!

Further along on the left is ***St Martin-cum-Gregory***, also redundant but put to a more suitable use as a Stained Glass Centre. Existing in 1086, it has reused Roman stones in the tower. Many good furnishings, including 17th-century hexagonal pulpit and font cover, and mid–late 18th-century altar rails, reredos, bread shelves, charity box and poor box. Stained glass, some 14th century, and a window to his daughters by William Peckitt, glass-painter, d. 1795, and one in his memory 'designed and executed' by his 'afflicted widow', Mary. Now for the grand Georgian houses that make Micklegate, in Pevsner's words, 'without any doubt the most architecturally rewarding street in York'. Here, on higher ground, away from the river and the crowded and noisy city centre, the gentry chose to build their town houses. No. 54 was built for the Garforth family of Wiganthorpe, North Yorkshire, almost certainly by John Carr, 1755–57, of brick with stone bands and quoins and pediment with oculus in the centre. Good interior with Rococo plasterwork. Nos 53–55, opposite, of the same date, is also likely to be by Carr, originally one house, divided *c.* 1810. Splendid staircase hall with Rococo ceiling. Nice doorcases on Nos 57–59, with rainwater head dated 1783. More good Georgian houses on both sides of the street, a couple with timber framing behind. Then two more gentry town houses; No. 86, Bathurst House, of *c.* 1720, was heightened to three storeys in the 1820s. Rainwater heads with cherubs and downpipes with Bathurst crest. Nos 88–90, Micklegate House, by Carr, 1753, for the Bourchiers of Beningbrough, is the largest in the street. Seven bays, with Corinthian columns to the doorcase.

Opposite is ***Holy Trinity church***, a remnant of the Benedictine priory established here at the end of the 11th century (*usually open, with exhibition on the priory and local area*). Aisled nave of *c.*1200, tower mid-15th century, Victorian south aisle and chancel, and the west front sympathetically rebuilt in 1902–05 by C. Hodgson Fowler, who also designed the painted reredos. Another good scrolled font cover, 1717, and a 1960s organ case in distinctive George Pace Perpendicular. Gothic wall tablet to the antiquarian Dr John Burton, d.1771, showing his *Monasticon Eboracense*. Nearby in Trinity Lane is ***Jacob's Well***, a small late medieval timber-framed building with elaborate bracketed door canopy,

Georgian houses and doorcases, Micklegate, York

resited from Davygate. More timber-framed buildings on Micklegate west of Holy Trinity: Nos 85–89, three storeys with jetties, *c.* 1500; and Nos 99–103, now rendered and brick-faced, the remains of a long row of seven mid-14th-century tenements with crown-post roofs. The Nag's Head, opposite, has early 16th-century timber framing. Nearer Micklegate Bar is No. 114, birthplace of the architect J.A. Hansom, inventor of the hansom cab, and No. 118, an ideal small town house, built *c.* 1742.

Now turn left into ***Priory Street***, laid out on the former grounds of the Benedictine priory in the mid-1850s, to a plan by G.T. Andrews. A number of pleasing mid-19th-century houses and three large Nonconformist chapels: Baptist, Gothic-style, of stone, 1868, by William Peachey; and two Italianate, the white-brick URC, 1879, by T.B. Thompson, and the former Wesleyan Methodist, 1856, by James Simpson, dark brick with stone dressings, the best of the three. The wide street gives access to ***Bishophill***, a little-visited but intriguing area of York. To the left is the tower of ***St Mary Bishophill Junior***, mid-11th century and as such the oldest standing ecclesiastical structure in York, with reused Roman stone in the lower part and herringbone stonework above. The north arcade of the nave is mid-12th century with round pillars, south arcade and north chapel early 14th century. Chancel largely rebuilt in 1860. Almost opposite are the large former works of Thomas Cooke & Sons, optical instrument makers, by Walter Brierley, 1916, in a restrained Arts and Crafts style, with blue brick to the first storey and truncated gables. The works extend along ***Bishophill Senior***, where on the east side is the early 18th-century Bishophill House and in the distance the trees of the churchyard of St Mary Bishophill Senior, demolished *c.* 1970.

Alongside the churchyard go down the steep, curving ***Carr's Lane***, where at the beginning on the right, hidden behind modern flats, is the Society of Friends' burial ground with graves of the American Quaker and anti-slavery pioneer John Woolman, the American grammarian Lindley Murray, and William Tuke, founder of the Retreat (York's pioneering 18th-century psychiatric hospital), and his family. Emerge into ***Skeldergate***,

Jacob's Well, Trinity Lane, York

St Mary Bishophill Junior, York

where immediately on the right and set back is the charming ***Ann Middleton Hospital*** (now Middleton's Hotel), an almshouse founded in 1659 and rebuilt in 1827–29 by Peter Atkinson junior. A statue of its benefactor in Puritan dress in the niche above the door is presumably from the original building. The handsome Skeldergate House (No. 56) – five bays, three storeys, pedimented with urns and oculus – was built for the merchant Ralph Dodsworth *c.* 1777. It has been attributed to John Carr, whose own house, which stood a little further north, was demolished after the Second World War. Much of Skeldergate, running parallel to the river, has been redeveloped in recent years with apartment blocks, most echoing with varying degrees of success the 19th-century warehouses they replaced.

At the north end of Skeldergate, go across Micklegate to ***North Street***. It is not a promising start, with the view dominated by the appallingly insensitive slab block of the Park Inn, but soon you reach ***All Saints' church***, which has one of the finest collections of medieval stained glass of any parish church in Britain. Starting as a simple rectangle in the late 11th century, it grew wider and longer over the next three centuries with the addition of chancel, aisles and chapels, taking on its present form when it was extended two bays west, with a tall tower and spire, in the early–mid-15th century. Of this date are the wonderful hammer-beam roofs in chancel and chapels, supported by a host of angels 'painted like a funfair roundabout' (Simon Jenkins). Some late medieval stalls, and a hexagonal pulpit, 1675, with painted panels. Unusual anchorite's cell attached at the west end, by architect and antiquarian E. Ridsdale Tate. The best of the glass is that of the 15th century in the north aisle, including the Pricke of Conscience window, depicting the events of the final fifteen days of the world, and the Corporal Acts of Mercy window, with scenes of people undertaking good works.

The charming Church Cottages, next to All Saints, originally a timber-framed row of three, has been dated to 1398 by dendrochronology. Turn left up ***Tanner Row***, with more timber framing, then cross Rougier Street to the upper part of Tanner Row, largely of the late 1840s, including No. 37, nine

15th-century stained glass, All Saints, North Street, York
top and middle: Prick of Conscience window
bottom: Corporal Acts of Mercy window

bays, still Georgian in character, with a delicate cast-iron balcony to the first floor. Opposite, pretty wrought-iron gates lead into Station Rise, and off on the left, facing Tanner Row, is York's first permanent ***railway station*** (now York City Council Offices), 1840, by G.T. Andrews, Italianate, stone, seventeen bays. At the east end on Station Rise is the former Station Hotel, added 1853, also by Andrews, of cream brick, with rounded ends. It is dwarfed by the monumental Grand Hotel opposite, built as the London North Eastern Railway headquarters, 1900–06, by William Bell and Horace Field. An impressive Queen Anne-style building of brick with stone dressings, shaped gables, rows of dormers, tall banded chimney stacks and a grand Baroque entrance. Nearby is the LNER war memorial by Lutyens, 1924, with slender obelisk. (The present railway station, 1877, and Royal

Lendal Bridge, York

Station Hotel (Principal) are beyond the arch cut through the city walls. Leeman Road leads directly to the wonderful ***National Railway Museum***, quite rightly located in York.)

Now turn right on to Station Road, which leads to ***Lendal Bridge***, 1863, of cast iron, by Thomas Page, engineer of London's Westminster Bridge. Little turreted lodges (originally toll houses) at each end. From here there are good views along

the river, the range of castellated Gothic stone buildings on the east bank comprising Council Offices, at the rear of the medieval Guildhall. Of the late 1880s onwards by the City Surveyor, they make a significant contribution to the riverscape. They were clearly the inspiration for the vast limestone-faced building opposite, designed for General Accident (now Aviva) in the early 1990s by the Hurd Rolland Partnership and, despite its scale, not entirely out of place. (Alongside Lendal Tower, on the riverside, at the east end of the bridge, cast-iron steps with pretty Gothic tracery lead down to an enjoyable ***riverside walk***, named after the actor and York native Judi Dench.) From ***Museum Street*** divert on to ***Lendal***, the narrow street opposite the Museum Lodge, to see the ***Judges' Lodgings***, built *c.*1720 for Dr Clifton Wintringham, who may have had a hand in its rather individual Baroque design.

Back on Museum Street, on the left is the ***Central Library*** (now York Explore), 1927, Edwardian Baroque by Brierley & Rutherford. In the foreground are the ruins of St Leonard's Hospital, accessed from Museum Gardens (see *St Mary's Abbey* above), and in the grounds at the rear the ***Multangular Tower*** (west corner of the Roman fortress) and the ***Anglian Tower***, possibly late Roman. At the junction with St Leonard's Place go straight across to ***Duncombe Place***, a new road of the early 1860s, where the tall tower of ***St Wilfrid's Roman Catholic church*** attempts unsuccessfully to upstage the wonderful west front of the Minster. Built 1862–64, designed by locally born George Goldie, St Wilfrid's was originally the pro-cathedral of the short-lived Roman Catholic Diocese of Beverley, and deserves more praise than it usually receives. Not helped by the building materials, it is nevertheless a most competent exercise in early French Gothic, with an impressive entrance porch elaborately carved. Opposite, in a very showy red-brick Gothic, is the multi-gabled and turreted former Dispensary, 1897, by Edmund Kirby of Liverpool. Next door in a cream brick, with Gothic touches, is the more restrained former Probate Registry Office by Henry Tanner, 1885. Then the open green with the Boer War memorial cross by Bodley, and the Minster, where the walk began.

Excursions outside the walls

There is much to see outside the walls. Two excursions are particularly rewarding, going northwest from Bootham Bar to Clifton Green, and southwest from Micklegate Bar to Dringhouses.

Bootham Bar to Clifton Green. Begin at Bootham Bar, said to have narrowly escaped demolition when its barbican and part of the city wall were demolished to give access from St Leonard's Place. On the right is ***Gillygate***, a busy street, chiefly of the late 18th and 19th century, with a welcome array of small independent shops. On the left are a postern gate and square tower, 1497, at the beginning of St Mary's Abbey precinct wall. Visible in Exhibition Square and the Art Gallery gardens, the wall runs behind the buildings on the south side of Bootham and is exposed for a short stretch before the circular 14th-century ***St Mary's Tower***. It then runs along ***Marygate***, a delightful street that slopes down to the river. ***St Olave's***, Marygate, successor to the Anglo-Saxon Minster of St Olaf, was rebuilt in the mid-15th century after the church was given parochial status, and the tower was added *c.*1480–1500. Damage during the Civil Wars, when a gun platform was placed on its roof, and later neglect necessitated a rebuilding using existing and abbey stone in 1720–22. The short chancel was added in 1889. Fifteenth-century stained glass in the east window; the rest mainly early 20th-century by Shrigley & Hunt. Wall tablet to the architect-joiner William Thornton, d.1721, and in the churchyard a table tomb to the artist William Etty, d.1849.

On the north side of Bootham stands ***Wandesford House***, built as an almshouse for 'ten poor maiden gentlewomen' in 1739. Bust of the foundress in a niche in the pediment, and windows set in giant blank arches. Convincingly attributed to gentleman-architect James Moyser, who was responsible for similar buildings at Beverley. From the mid-18th century Bootham was a favoured location for gentry residences, occupied in the winter season, well represented here by Nos 39–61, a handsome run of a dozen three-storey Georgian houses. The earliest, No. 49, has late 17th-century origins with 1730s façade , and the latest and most accomplished, No. 51 (***Bootham School***), is of *c.*1804, by Peter Atkinson senior. No. 47, built 1752, is among the earliest of the architect John Carr's town houses. Also by Carr, and set back some distance from the street, is the former ***Bootham Park Hospital***, built as the County Lunatic Asylum in the 1770s, an impressive eleven-bay building with pediment supported by giant Doric half columns. The York–Scarborough railway line, opened in 1845, runs along the west side of the former hospital grounds, going under Bootham and in deep cuttings on either side. The south side of Bootham, after Marygate, is chiefly early–mid-19th century, including Nos 54–56, two substantial 1840s houses of white brick, the first the birthplace of the poet W.H. Auden. ***Ingram's Hospital***, built by Sir Arthur Ingram of Temple Newsam, Leeds, in 1632, restored after the Civil Wars, is the oldest building on Bootham. A low two-storey brick building with central four-storey tower, resited Norman doorway, and shaped gable to the rear. Opposite stands the Churchill Hotel, No. 65 Bootham, built *c.*1827 with central bow and projecting eaves, a glazed lantern rising above the roof and, rather oddly, a tall chimney at each corner.

Bootham now becomes ***Clifton***, and although there are some good Georgian houses – including the pedimented pair Nos 14–16, possibly a late work by Thomas Atkinson – the township underwent its greatest development after 1836, when much of the De Grey estate was sold. Grange Hotel, originally a semi-detached pair, was one of the first new buildings, as was ***St Peter's School***, built 1838. In a rather lavish Late Gothic by John Harper, it was initially a proprietary school, taken over by the Dean and Chapter in 1844 for St Peter's, the successor to the medieval Minster school. Many later additions. Opposite, ***St Peter's Grove***, laid out *c.*1880, has a pleasing collection of late Victorian middle-class housing, with touches of Tudor, Queen Anne and Art Nouveau, by James Demaine alone

opposite: Tympanum over entrance, St Wilfrid (RC), Duncombe Place, York

St Peter's School, Clifton, York

and with Walter Brierley. The latter was the architect of the rebuilding of the Burton Stone Inn, 1897, with the medieval base of a cross (Burton Stone) set in the boundary wall. (More work by Brierley down Burton Stone Lane: ***St Luke's church***, Gothic, unfinished, 1902; and round the corner the splendid former Shipton Street Schools, 1890, Low Countries influence with stepped and shaped gables and decorative tie plates.)

Back on the main road, next to St Peter's School, are two neat grey-brick villas of 1835–40, followed by the red-brick ***Clifton Methodist Church***, 1909, in an old-fashioned Victorian Gothic, which rather dominates the view with its spiky tower and spire. Opposite is the restrained Art Deco Clifton Cinema (Clifton Bingo), 1937, unexpected in this area. ***The Avenue***, a street that owes much to the architects Penty & Penty (Demaine & Brierley's main local rivals), has some good houses including Nos 2–9, tile-hung with canted bays reminiscent of Norman Shaw's Bedford Park. The Pentys virtually rebuilt The Old Grey Mare at the start of ***Clifton Green***, a triangular 'village' green, with trees and a pretty tiled canopy over a water trough, but rather too much traffic. Of the surrounding houses the more interesting include No. 16, a Gothic estate cottage with corner turret, built *c.*1839; No. 8, a late 17th-century farmhouse refronted in the mid-18th century; and, at the northeast corner, a pair of cottages, originally single-storey with attics, built 1839, one of which retains its Gothic windows.

Mid-19th-century Artisan Mannnerist house, No.66 Clifton

Less village-like in character is the tall white-brick terrace with shaped gables, 1870s, dominating the east side. At the beginning of Shipton Road is ***St Philip and St James' church***, 1867, by G.F. Jones, in Early English style with a 'ponderous' west tower. More successful is the vicarage, tile-hung, gabled with tall chimneys, by J.L. Pearson, 1879, who also designed the former school.

Instead of returning to the city centre via the same route, the more adventurous might choose to ***walk back alongside the River Ouse***. Follow Water End, which runs southwest from the Green, passing on the right the John Burrill Almshouses, Tudor brick and stone, 1931, by Ward & Leckenby. Later comes The Homestead, 1904, a modest house by Fred Rowntree for the social reformer Seebohm Rowntree, who provided the excellent landscaped ***Homestead Park*** (*public access*) next door. Cross to the opposite side of the road and continue as far as the corner of Government House Road, where you will see a sign to the Town Centre via the riverside walk.

Bar Convent and school, Blossom Street, York

Micklegate Bar to Dringhouses. This was the route along which travellers from the south approached York, and along which the condemned travelled in the opposite direction to their fate at the gallows on Knavesmire. At ***Micklegate Bar*** monarchs and other dignitaries were greeted and escorted into the city. The first stretch of the route outside the bar is ***Blossom Street***, where on the corner with Nunnery Lane stands the ***Bar Convent*** (Roman Catholic Convent of the Institute of St Mary), established here in 1686 (*open most days, with excellent museum*). The handsome seven-bay main front, 1786–89, is by Thomas Atkinson, with his distinctive treatment to the central first-floor window and the three-bay pilastered and pedimented Classical schoolroom on the left by G.T. Andrews, 1845. Atkinson was also responsible for the 1760s chapel, with pretty circular sanctuary, its dome supported by eight Ionic columns.

Opposite, the former car showroom, 1930s, and evocative Moderne-style Odeon Cinema (Everyman), 1937 by Harry Weedon, with its angular blocks and rounded corners, are a great contrast. Back on the east side, running off the main road, is the charming ***South Parade***, a terrace of twenty Regency houses with front gardens, with bows to basement and first storey. A little further on comes East Mount Road, a pleasant Victorian terrace that ends with an open area, part of ***Micklegate Stray*** (or common), and to the north Scarcroft Road School, 1896, described by Hutchinson and Palliser as 'Brierley's masterpiece and one of the grandest of York's buildings'.

Past the Holgate Road, Blossom Street becomes ***The Mount***, the name coming from a fortification constructed during the Civil Wars. The street is lined with trees. On the right is a run of modest Regency houses, including No. 104, below which is a Roman vault. Nos 116–132 are of the 1830s–40s in quite a mixture of styles, ranging from simple Georgian brick to ashlar or stuccoed Italianate some with nice ironwork balconies. Then the delightful ***Mount Parade***, 1820s, a row of eighteen two-storey houses, some with bow windows, with

Scarcroft Primary School, York

The Mount, York

front gardens, leading to the equally satisfying ***Mount Terrace***, off Holgate Road. Back on The Mount, another good Regency terrace, before much grander Victorian houses and larger front gardens. On Dalton Terrace is the Mount School, *c.*1856, and the Byzantine 1930s ***English Martyrs Roman Catholic church***.

Set back on the east side of The Mount is a series of detached 1830s villas, Tudor Gothic to begin with, then Classical, stuccoed. Opposite, on the corner of Driffield Terrace, is the ***Elmbank Hotel***, with Italianate tower, built *c.*1870, but with a wonderful Arts and Crafts interior by Penty & Penty and decoration including Art Nouveau stained glass by George Walton, a protégé of Charles Rennie Mackintosh. At the beginning of ***Tadcaster Road*** is St George's Place and more Arts and Crafts houses, of which the best by far is ***Bishopsbarns***, 1905, by Walter Brierley, for himself, with garden by Gertrude Jekyll. It shows a Jacobean influence, of small handmade bricks and flat tiles, with gabled wings and tall chimney stacks. On a triangular plot at the junction of Tadcaster and Knavesmire Roads, the bargeboarded Herdsman's Cottage, cross-shaped, marks the beginning of ***Knavesmire***, the greater part of Micklegate Stray, the largest of York's medieval common pastures. As well as horse racing, public entertainment on the Knavesmire included until 1812 the hangings at Tyburn. The site of the gallows is now a paved area with seats opposite the entrance to Little Hob Moor on Tadcaster Road. Nos 300–306 Tadcaster Road are four neat 1830s villas. ***Dringhouses***, a long village on the Tadcaster Road, expanded between the wars with new streets on the west side. On the east is a good Georgian farmhouse and then the gatehouse to ***Goddards*** (*National Trust*), 1927, one of Brierley's last works. Built for Noel Terry, of the chocolate firm, in a Tudor Vernacular style, with a pleasing light interior. Garden by George Dillistone. The small early Victorian village church, ***St Edward's***, is well designed and well cared for, in Decorated style by Vickers & Hugall of Pontefract, 1849, with contemporary glass by Wailes.

Some other buildings of interest. On every street out of the city there are buildings of note. To the east is the large ***St Lawrence's church***, Lawrence Street, 1880s, with the free-standing tower of its medieval predecessor, and to the southeast, on Cemetery Road, ***York General Cemetery*** with chapel of 1837 by Pritchett. Northeast on Monkgate are

Chapel, York General Cemetery

the *former County Hospital* by J.B. & W. Atkinson, 1849–51, 'one of their best buildings' (Pevsner), and some good Georgian–early Victorian houses. Much further out is ***Heworth***, with ***Holy Trinity*** church, 1869, by G.F. Jones, its tower and spire rivalled by those of the nearby Methodist church, 1890.

Southwest down ***Bishopthorpe Road***, the ***former Terry's Chocolate Factory*** (now apartments) mostly late 1920s, vast Neo-Georgian with tall clock tower. More than a mile (1.5 km) further on, past the racecourse, is ***Middlethorpe Hall*** (Hotel), an impressive seven-bay, three-storey brick house of *c.*1700 built for Thomas Barlow, merchant, of Leeds. It has stone bands and quoins, and the earliest sash windows in York. To the west, on Holgate Road, are ***St Paul's church***, 1851, by the Atkinsons; St Paul's Square, *c.*1855; and Holgate House, *c.*1770. The road divides to become Poppleton Road and Acomb Road. The five-sailed ***Holgate Windmill***, 1780s, stands off Acomb Road, as does the small West Bank Park, the former grounds of the 19th-century Backhouse Nurseries, which contains a statue of Queen Victoria by G.W. Milburn, 1905. For **Acomb**, taken into the City boundary in 1937 but some 2 miles (3.2 km) from the centre, see *City of York Villages*.

City of York Villages

Acaster Malbis On the west side of the Ouse, the prefix suggesting the site of a Roman fort to protect York from attack by river. Northeast of the village is Holy Trinity church, cruciform in shape. Early 14th century, restored *c.*1886, when the neat wooden bell-turret with short broach spire was added. East window with excellent fragments of medieval stained glass attributed to the same workshop as the west window of York Minster. Monument with crossed-legged knight, heart in hand, probably Sir John Malebisse, d.1316. [C1]

Acomb Described in the 1850s as a large parish with 'several good residences ... occupied by families of the first respectability'. It was taken into the City of York in 1937, and initially developed with council housing. By the 1980s a quarter of the city's population lived here. Of the older houses the early 18th-century Acomb House is the grandest. The west end, with a large triangular green, retains the character of a village. On the north side, reached along a passage between the old school and an Italianate villa, both of the 1840s, is St Stephen's church. Transepts, nave and tower of 1831, simple Gothic with lancet windows, by Hansom & Walsh; chancel 1851. Large, atmospheric churchyard, very Victorian, with dark trees and lots of monuments. Also in the parish are two interesting mid-20th-century churches: Our Lady (Roman Catholic), Gale Lane, Byzantine, elaborate interior; and Holy Redeemer (Anglican), Boroughbridge Road, 1964. The latter, 'a masterpiece' (Pevsner) by George Pace, skilfully combines old and new to create a modern church. It incorporates much of the medieval stonework, doorways and windows, and arcade of *c.*1200, from the demolished St Mary Bishophill Senior. [B1]

Askham Bryan A pleasant village with wide grass verges, pond and mellow brick houses including Askham Bryan Hall, an early Victorian villa with oversailing hipped roof. Church of St Nicholas, a pretty little 12th-century building, limestone walls contrasting nicely with the red tiled roof. Porch added in the 19th century incorporating a Norman doorway with three arches, all with chevron design. South of the village is Askham Bryan College (originally the Yorkshire Agricultural Institute), a specialist land-based college that now has a conservation and wildlife park as a visitor attraction. Askham Bog Nature Reserve (*Yorkshire Wildlife Trust*) is a small area of peat bog with boardwalk for visitors. [C1]

Askham Richard Large green and pond providing an attractive setting for the surrounding 18th- and 19th-century brick farmhouses and estate cottages. The simple Norman church, St Mary's, with undivided nave and chancel, and south doorway with Romanesque sculpture, is remarkably similar in design to that at Askham Bryan. Heavily restored in the 1870s. Behind a long wall and best viewed from the churchyard is Askham Grange, 1886, with gables, half-timbering and fancy chimneys, now part of a women's prison. [C1]

Bishopthorpe Seat of the archbishops of York, whose intriguing palace, of many periods, stands close by the River Ouse. The earliest part is a long medieval range that runs north to south, parallel to the river, to which another range was added at right angles to the north end *c.*1480. Further additions on the south side in the mid-17th century with rusticated brickwork, similar to that found at Wilberforce House in Hull. In 1766–69 the palace was given an impressive Gothick west front, and finally a new block was added to the northwest of the north front in 1835. The splendid interior reflects the building's long history, the earliest parts of *c.*1250 including the undercroft to the great hall. Much remodelling in the 1760s by Thomas Atkinson of York, who was also responsible for the west front and the charming stone gateway (*palace open for pre-arranged tours only*).

opposite: Bishopthorpe Palace viewed across the River Ouse

South of the palace is the remnant of old St Andrew's church, rebuilt in Gothick style in 1766 but taken down in 1899, leaving just the west front as a picturesque folly. It stands at the end of Chantry Lane, where there are good houses including the White House with prominent porch and the Chantry, built in 1737 as the vicarage. A large new St Andrew's church was built 1898–1903 on Bishopthorpe Road, in a more traditional style. The main village street has a few older properties among the suburban development, those on the south side set well back. On Sim Balk Lane, with harsh red-brick Methodist church on the corner, is Bishopthorpe Garth. Designed by York-based Arts and Crafts architect Walter Brierley, 1908, with garden laid out by Gertrude Jekyll, it hides behind a contemporary gatehouse formed by a pair of linked cottages with a wide central entrance and long pantiled roof. [C1]

Copmanthorpe Popular commuter village with some older houses, including No. 6 Main Street, *c.*1700 and earlier, the brick moulded detail unfortunately concealed by render. St Giles' church, small with bellcote, 12th century but much altered. The chancel was added in 1889. [C1]

Deighton A few older farmhouses and cottages, including Swan Farmhouse, mid-18th century, facing the A19, but the narrow Main Street is now dominated by modern infill. Away from the village, off Naburn Lane, is Old Hall, a neat five-bay house with hipped roof, early 18th century but with older features inside. [C1]

Dunnington Popular York dormitory village with much building from the 1960s onwards, but with several attractive 18th-century houses in Church Street and York Street. Village cross with ball finial, 1840, on medieval base. The church of St Nicholas is very odd-looking when viewed from the south, with its various parts out of character with each other. Even the clock face is off-centre. The earliest part is the lower section of the tower, early Norman, a contrast to the *c.*1840 'Neo-Norman' nave and Gothic fenestration of the chancel. At the west end a stone-clad extension for meeting room, choir vestry, etc. added in 1987. The interior is more rewarding, with late 12th-century arcades and other features including stone sedilia (seat) and piscina (basin) in the chancel. Base and shaft of 13th-century cross in the churchyard. Large former rectory of the 1820s next door.

At ***Grimston***, 1 mile (1.5 km) southwest, are two large houses either side of the York–Beverley Road. Grimston Hill House, 1830s, painted brick with overhanging hipped slate roof. Opposite is the Jacobean-style Grimston Court, 1903, by Walter Brierley for a York brewer. [B2]

Elvington There are older houses near the splendid village green. Distinctive church (Holy Trinity) by William White, 1877, stone with slate roof and eccentric northwest tower with open timber bell stage with pagoda-style roof. It was built by the rector, as was the long brick terrace in Church Lane, the porches and decorative bargeboards giving an otherwise urban row the appearance of Victorian estate housing. Elvington Hall overlooks the River Derwent, which is crossed by a late 17th-century stone bridge. Airfield west of the village, a former RAF base with 1940s control tower, is home to the Yorkshire Air Museum. [C2]

Fulford An extensive suburban village on the east side of the River Ouse, and separated from it by low-lying ground, Fulford Ings. At the end of the quiet residential St Oswald's Road is old St Oswald's church, 12th century with a late 18th-century brick tower adding to its rustic charm. Converted to a private house in the 1980s. In 1866, when Fulford was expanding, a more imposing church with the same dedication was built in the Decorated style, with aisles, transepts and a tall southwest tower, now missing its spire. It stands on Main Street, part of the busy A19, which has a wealth of 18th- and 19th-century houses of all shapes and sizes. The larger ones include the White House, 1790, and the former Fulford House (York Pavilion Hotel), with three-storey canted bays, rebuilt in the mid-18th century. Sir John

Old St Oswald's church, Fulford

Hunt Memorial Cottage Homes, 1954, is a large group of well-built almshouses, brick with shaped gables. Two more big houses on Fenwicks Lane: Gate Fulford Hall and Delwood Croft, both 1790s for York families. Fulford Hall, 1 mile (1.5 km) south, early to mid-18th century but with an earlier core, has a wonderful setting overlooking the river. To the north on Fulford Road (A19), a medieval cross shaft on a stepped octagonal base stands opposite the remnants of the Victorian infantry barracks. [C1]

Haxby Busy suburban settlement west of the River Foss, with older houses along The Village set back behind broad strips of green. St Mary's church, 1878, extended to the west 1909. [B1]

Heslington Some 2 miles (3.2 km) from the centre of York, Heslington changed dramatically when it was chosen as the site for the city's first university, established in 1960. Imaginatively set around an existing but greatly enlarged lake, the new campus developed rapidly, and the first two colleges, combining residential and teaching facilities, opened in 1965. The Central Hall, jutting out over the lake, is particularly eye-catching. Many of the early buildings, by Robert Matthew Johnson-Marshall & Partners, were steel-framed and clad in concrete, in complete contrast to Heslington Hall, which became the University's administrative centre. Elizabethan in style and origin, the brick mansion dates largely from a major recasting from the 1850s onwards, although some original features survive, notably the 16th-century stucco ceiling of the great hall. The garden has an early 18th-century gazebo and yew topiary.

Heslington village is south of the original campus, or West Campus as it has become known, the University having opened a second site to the east in 2009. Main Street, with its wide verges, trees and well-maintained pinkish brick houses with tastefully painted woodwork, seems a different world, although some of the buildings here belong to the University. Set well back and screened from view is Little Hall, a smart early 18th-century gentry house. Village Farm, almost opposite, is more typical of the area, *c.*1700 with brick stringcourse and cornice so characteristic of the Vale of York. Two sets of almshouses, the earlier the Hesketh Almshouses, 1795, at the south end of the other arm of Main Street. Of the same date is Old School on School Lane, a modest single-storey building that looks across to its handsome replacement of 1856.

St Paul's church with prominent spire is now used by both Anglicans and Methodists. Rebuit 1858 at the expense of the owners of the Heslington Hall estate, hence its traditional estate character. More unusual is the interior following a transformation by R.G. Sims in the early 1970s, when the church

Heslington Hall, University of York
opposite: 'Trio of Swans and Central Hall' (University of York campus, Heslington) © Mark Hearld, 2021

Mark Hearld 2021

was extended by a series of linked octagons on the north side to provide community spaces. Stainless-steel font, 1973, a period piece. [C1]

Hessay Small village with no church until the present one dedicated to St John the Baptist was built in the fields to the north in 1899. Red brick with a high-pitched tiled roof and small bell-turret. [B1]

Holtby Georgian brick church (Holy Trinity) with heavy Victorian Romanesque stone detail. This linear village with plenty of pleasant 18th- and 19th-century houses of local brick has managed to retain at either end the pre-war fingerpost direction signs erected by North Riding County Council. Two boxed public water pumps in use until piped water reached the village in the 1950s. [B2]

Huntington Suburban York, with much new building, although some Georgian brick farmhouses and cottages remain. Former Board School, 1877, with pretty turret and bellcote. Medieval cross stump at the corner of Church Lane, at the end of which stands All Saints' church, largely Victorian but using some early material. Prominent buttressed southwest tower with broach spire. The churchyard overlooks the River Foss. [B1]

Kexby Strung out along the main York to Beverley Road. St Paul's church, 1852, with octagonal bell-turret with spire, was designed by F.C. Penrose, who that year was appointed Surveyor of the Fabric at St Paul's Cathedral. It was paid for by Lord Wenlock of Escrick Park (North Yorkshire), who also commissioned Penrose to design the nearby Tudor-style former rectory. The church, surrounded by a graveyard, is now a private house. Triple-arched bridge across the River Derwent, 1650 with 18th-century repairs, but incorporating medieval stonework including the arms of the Ughtred family, who held the manor in the Middle Ages. [C2]

Murton On Murton Way, overlooking fields, is the tiny Norman church of St James, a simple stone rectangle with bell-turret. Derelict between 1834, when a storm damaged the roof, and 1914, when it was restored, reputedly having served as a pigsty for part of this time. Murton Park is home to the Yorkshire Museum of Farming (*open daily April–October*) and to a short, restored section of the Derwent Valley Light Railway. The eye-catching half-timbered green and cream station building was brought here from Wheldrake and dates from 1912, the year the first part of the line was opened. [B2]

Naburn Ouseside village with some 18th-century houses including pretty cottages with front gardens on Maypole Grove. At the south end is Naburn Hall, 1735, much altered. The medieval chapel of St Nicholas stood in the grounds, but in 1854 a new church was built on a different site. St Matthew's is a sturdy building of stone and slate with a northwest tower with broach spire. A mile (1.5 km) south of Naburn is the handsome Bell Hall (*private*), 1680, exactly right for the date. Five bays, brick with stone quoins and hipped roof. On the River Ouse, separated by an island, are two locks, one made in 1757, the other in 1887. Overlooking them is an unusual and rather austere former Banqueting House built as a meeting place by the Ouse Navigation Trustees, 1825. [C1]

Nether Poppleton Some good Georgian farmhouses in the village, at the east end of which is St Everilda's, an interesting little church with a wide Norman chancel arch. Elaborate 17th-century monuments to the Hutton family, including Sir Thomas Hutton, d.1620, who kneels in prayer on a green and gold cushion. At Manor Farm, next door, is a mid-16th-century timber-aisled tithe barn, encased in brick with rows of ventilation holes (*event venue*). On the opposite side of Church Lane a 5-acre (2-ha) green created as a Millennium project. [B1]

New Earswick In 1901 Joseph Rowntree of York, the Quaker chocolate manufacturer, purchased land 4 miles (6.5 km) north of the city to lay out a garden village, to be administered by a Village Trust. The aim was to provide working-class families with artistic, sanitary and well-built dwellings. Every house was to have a garden, a pair of fruit trees

Chestnut Grove, New Earswick

and space to grow vegetables. Work began in 1902. The first buildings were by Raymond Unwin (architect of Letchworth), with later work by his partner Barry Parker. Built of local brick and often arranged in short terraces, many reached by wide footpaths with vehicular access to the rear, the early houses have a late Arts and Crafts feel. Of particular note is the irregularly shaped Folk Hall, a community meeting space, white-rendered with large sloping pantile roof and low side walls. [B1]

Osbaldwick Typical suburban York, but the core of the village has some nice older houses with green spaces and a stream. The church of St Thomas, 12th century in origin, was restored in 1877, then enlarged and remodelled in 1967. Headstone to Mary Ward, a Catholic nun and founder of a religious order for women, who died in 1645. Her life is celebrated in the Bar Convent Museum, York. [B1]

Rufforth All Saints' church, 1890s by Demaine & Brierley, has a distinctive tower with recessed spire and two simple Norman doorways from its predecessor. 'Perp-style tracery tinged with Art Nouveau' (Pevsner). Opposite the Methodist chapel stands an old village pump and horse trough. [C1]

Skelton Described by Pevsner as 'an amazing building', the mid-13th-century church of St Giles is a superb example of the Early English style of architecture, all of a piece. It was under the patronage of the treasurers of York Minster, and built by the masons working there. Simple plan of nave and chancel with a bellcote in the middle. What is strange is the scale of some of the internal features, perhaps an indication that greater things were planned. Also remarkable is the quality of the restoration by Henry Graham, who was only nineteen when he began work on the church in 1814.

He died in Naples five years later, shortly after the restoration was completed, and was buried at Skelton. His monument mentions how he had been willing to tolerate 'the dissipating and corrupting air of foreign lands' in the furtherance of his profession. Overlooking the small green that adjoins the churchyard is the mid-18th-century Pyramid House (named for the shape of its roof), formerly used as the village school. Skelton Manor, with 16th-century origins, and Skelton Hall, a white-brick Regency house set in large grounds, lie behind the church. [B1]

Stockton-on-the-Forest The name relates to the former Royal Forest of Galtres. A very long village street, stretching for about 1½ miles (2.5 km), with some attractive Georgian houses of warm brick in the characteristic local style. Stockton Hall, late 18th century, is now a hospital. More unusual is Stockton House, where the Methodist owners incorporated a chapel and schoolroom, with Georgian Gothic windows to the right-hand half of the façade. Holy Trinity church was built in 1843 but much altered in the late 19th century, when the porch and northwest tower with very distinctive spire were added. [B2]

Strensall Much modern development, but a few pleasant Georgian houses represent the original settlement. St Mary's church is by the Atkinsons of York, 1865. An army camp (Queen Elizabeth Barracks) lies south of the village. Strensall Common is an area of heathland managed by the Yorkshire Wildlife Trust. Spanning the River Foss on Haxby Moor Road is a brick humpback bridge built by the Foss Navigation Company at the end of the 18th century, and on Sheriff Hutton Road is a fine stone bridge designed by John Carr, 1798. [B1]

Upper Poppleton To the southwest of Nether Poppleton, with modern housing developments linking the historic cores of the two settlements. The older part still feels like a proper village, with its large triangular village green with maypole, other subsidiary greens, and plenty of 18th- and 19th-century houses. All Saints' church was built in 1891 but incorporates 13th-century fragments from the chapel of ease it replaced. Small square tower with spirelet, supported inside by a triple-arched arcade. The village is still served by the railway, which came in 1848. Good station buildings, privately occupied, and a former railway nursery, which supplied plants for the splendid floral displays once found at many stations, now run as a community venture. [B1]

Wheldrake Long village street with a mix of modest cottages, Victorian estate houses, later infill and some of the best examples of vernacular architecture in the Vale of York. Exposed timber framing at Nos 53–55 Main Street, much restored and now called Elizabethan House, although probably not built until the 17th century. Next door, No. 51 also has some timber framing inside, but externally is a typical early to mid-18th-century mellow brick and pantile farmhouse. Distinctive first-floor brick band found on several of the older village houses, a hallmark of the region. St Helen's church, at the east end, has a medieval stone tower, but the rest is pinkish-brown brick with darker brick and stone details and dates from 1779, as recorded on the delightful painted inscription inside, under the tower. The charm is in its simplicity: rectangular nave with polygonal apse, well-lit by round-arched windows with a pretty oval window over the door. Former rectory next door, mid-18th century and later. Wheldrake Ings is a wetland nature reserve on the River Derwent, managed by the Yorkshire Wildlife Trust. [C2]

Wigginton Church, duckpond and much suburban development that makes it difficult to distinguish where Wiggington ends and Haxby to the east begins. St Mary's church with twin bellcote dates from 1860. Late 20th-century hall built on the south side designed by Stephen Parry in a complementary style, using similar stone. [B1]

St Giles, Skelton

Further Reading

Detailed information on buildings can be found in the 'Pevsner' Buildings of England series published by Yale University Press. York and much of East Yorkshire are covered in N. Pevsner and D. Neave, *Yorkshire: York and the East Riding* (1995) and D. and S. Neave, *Hull* (2010). See also P. Leach and N. Pevsner, *Yorkshire West Riding: Leeds, Bradford and the North* (2009) and R. Harman and N. Pevsner, *Yorkshire West Riding: Sheffield and the South* (2017). A revision of Pevsner's *North Riding* (1973), by Jane Grenville, is forthcoming.

Much has been written about York. For an authoritative and readable introduction to the city, see J. Hutchinson and D.M. Palliser, *York* (Bartholomew City Guide, 1980). Many of York's historic buildings are covered by the volumes published by the Royal Commission on the Historical Monuments of England.

Picture Credits

Images © David and Susan Neave except those itemised by page number below
[*t* = top, *m* = middle, *b* = bottom, *l* = left, *r* = right]

We are grateful to the following for permission to reproduce the images:

© 43 Clicks North/unsplash.com: 171
© A G Baxter/Shutterstock.com: 200*tl*
© Agnieszka Mordaunt/unsplash.com: 80
© Aisle/Alamy stock photo: 83
© Alan Curtis/Alamy stock photo: 157
© Alexey Fedorenko – stock.adobe.com: 184
© Alistair Wallace/Shutterstock.com: 203*b*
© Allan Harris/flickr.com: 8
© AlmacUK/Shutterstock.com: 54
© andy/medcalf/EyeEm/stock.adobe.com: 25*t*
© Angela Baker/unsplash.com: 155
© Ann Chapman: 45*b*
© Bernard Sharp/geograph.org.uk: 53*tl & r*
© Billy Wilson: 187*t*, 192–193, 197
© Burton Constable Foundation/R&R: 69*l*, 70–71*t*, 134–5
© calumsmith0308 – stock.adobe.com: 69*l*, 219*t*
© C.B. Newham: 17
© Chapter of York Minster: Reproduced by kind permission: 191, 193*t*
© Chris Cobley: 65
© Chris Hepburn/iStock.com: 88
© Chris Morgan/geography.org.uk: 151*t*
© Corpus of Romanesque Sculpture/ Rita Wood: 22*t*, 22*m*, 55*r*, 141
© Corpus of Romanesque Sculpture/John McElheran: 22*b*, 60
© Danieirao/iStock.com: 202*b*
© Dave- stock.adobe.com: 62–63*t*
© Dave Longhorn: 75
© Dave Pickersgill/geography.org.uk: 174*b*
© David Bigwood/Alamy stock photo: 95
© East Riding of Yorkshire Council: 49
© Electric Egg Ltd – stock.adobe.com: 7
© Gaid Kornsilapa/Shutterstock.com: 200*tr*
© Gordon Ball LRPS/Shutterstock.com: 12*b*
© Gordon Plumb: 36*b*, 38, 97, 130–131, 140, 144*t*, 162, 193*b*, 221
© Grzegorz Lenkiewicz – stock.adobe.com: 81
© Historic England: 160, 164
© Howard Duckworth: 84–5
© Hull and East Riding Museum/flickr.com: 123
© Jack Cousin/Shutterstock.com: 185, 202*b*
© Jaroslav Moravcik – stock.adobe.com: 199

© jax10289/iStock.com: 194
© johnwmiller/iStock.com: 208*t*
© karambol/iStock.com: 19
© Karl Everett/Shutterstock.com: 159*t*
© Karl Moran/Shutterstock.com: 210
© Kit Leong/Shutterstock.com: 203*t*
© Les Gibbon/Alamy stock photo: 17*b*
© LFM Visuals/Shutterstock.com: 102–3
© Loop Images Ltd/Alamy stock photo: 20
© MalcolmC/Shutterstock.com: 6
© Mark Eastham/iStock.com: 22–223
© Margaret Imrie: 46
© Merchant Adventurers' Hall York: 211
© Michael Shannon – stock.adobe. com: 17*t*
© Mike – stock.adobe. com: 200*ml*
© National Railway Museum/Science & Society Picture Library: 96
© Nick Brundle Photography/Shutterstock.com: 206
© northallertonman/Shutterstock.com: 200*br*
© Paul – stock.adobe.com: 68
© Paul Hurst: 45*t*
© Paul Wishart/Shutterstock.com: 173*t*
© Paul Vinten – stock.adobe.com: 27
© Paula Connelly/iStock.com: 66–67
© Phil and Michael Thomas: 106
© Piranhi – stock.adobe.com: 161
© Richard – stock.adobe.com: 10–11
© Sir Tatton Sykes Bt: 23
© S.P. Wright: 31
© Visit Hull & East Yorkshire (VHEY): 159*b*
© Withernsea Lighthouse Museum: 48
© York Archaeological Trust: 186
© Yorkshire Wildlife Trust /David Nichols: 14
© Zhanna Briede/Shutterstock.com: 156

p.64: David Hockney, *Bridlington Rooftops, October, November, December,* 2005, Oil on canvas, 122 × 152.5 cm (48 × 60 in), © David Hockney. Photo Credit: Richard Schmidt

p.100: David Hockney, *Huggate, St. Mary's Church Spire,* August 2005, Oil on canvas, 61 × 91.5 cm (24 × 36 in), © David Hockney Photo Credit: Richard Schmidt

p.235: Mark Hearld, *Three Swans and Central Hall, University of York, Heslington,* Collage, © Mark Hearld 2021

Cover: David Hockney, *The Road to York through Sledmere,* 1997, Oil on canvas, 122 × 152.5 cm (48 × 60 in), © David Hockney. Photo Credit: Richard Schmidt

Back cover: © Agnieszka Mordaunt/unsplash.com: *tl;* © PhilMacDPhoto/Shutterstock.com: *tr;* © David and Susan Neave: *bl;* © Karl Moran/Shutterstock.com: *bm;* © LFM Visuals/Shutterstock.com: *br*

Index of Names

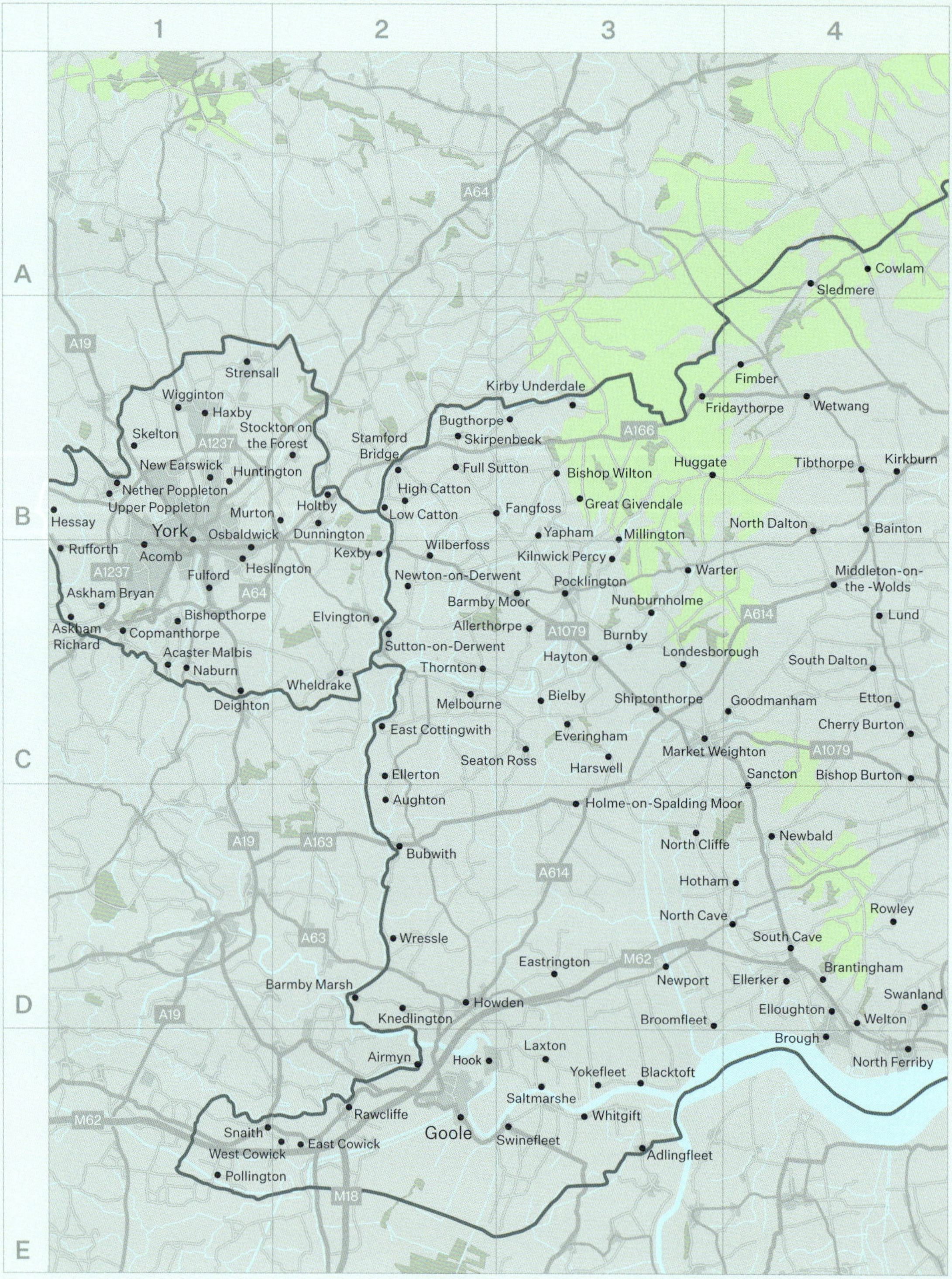

County boundaries

5
6
7
8
A
B
C
D
E
Fordon
Wold Newton
Burton Fleming
Bempton
Grindale
Thwing
Flamborough
Boynton
Sewerby
Rudston
Bridlington
Langtoft
Carnaby
Bessingby
Kilham
Burton Agnes
Ruston Parva
Harpham
Fraisthorpe
Garton-on-the-Wolds
A614
Lowthorpe
Nafferton
Barmston
Lissett
Little Driffield
Great Driffield
Wansford
Foston-on-the-Wolds
Ulrome
North Sea
A164
A165
Skerne
Skipsea
Beeford
Sunderlandwick
Hutton Cranswick
North Frodingham
Dunnington
Nunkeeling
Atwick
Kilnwick
Watton
Bewholme
Beswick
Hornsea
Lockington
Brandesburton
Seaton
Scorborough
Catwick
Sigglesthorne
Leven
Goxhill
Mappleton
Leconfield
Routh
Great Hatfield
Tickton
Long Riston
Rise
Withernwick
Beverley
Skirlaugh
Aldbrough
Walkington
Wawne
Burton Constable
Bentley
Garton-in-Holderness
Swine
Sproatley
Humbleton
Skidby
Sutton-on-Hull
Hilston
Cottingham
Elstronwick
Bilton
Tunstall
Willerby
Kingston upon Hull
Preston
Burton Pidsea
Kirk Ella
Roos
West Ella
Hedon
Rimswell
Anlaby
Burstwick
Halsham
Withernsea
Hessle
Thorngumbald
Paull
Keyingham
Winestead
Hollym
Ottringham
Holmpton
Patrington
Humber Estuary
Welwick
Skeffling
Easington
Sunk Island
Kilnsea and Spurn